D1537253

CHRIST-CENTERED

Exposition

AUTHORS AND SERIES EDITORS
David Platt, Daniel L. Akin, and Tony Merida

CHRIST-CENTERED
Exposition

EXALTING JESUS IN
1 & 2 TIMOTHY AND TITUS

B&H
ACADEMIC
NASHVILLE, TENNESSEE

Christ-Centered Exposition Commentary: 1 & 2 Timothy and Titus
© Copyright 2013 by David Platt, Daniel L. Akin, and Tony Merida
Published by B & H Publishing Group
Nashville, Tennessee
All rights reserved.
ISBN 978-0-8054-9590-4
Dewey Decimal Classification: 220.7
Subject Heading: BIBLE—STUDY AND TEACHING \ BIBLE. N.T.
TIMOTHY—COMMENTARIES \
BIBLE. N.T. TITUS—COMMENTARIES

Printed in the United States of America
3 4 5 6 7 8 • 19 18 17 16 15
SB

TABLE OF CONTENTS

131846

Titus

Commentary by Daniel L. Akin

SERIES INTRODUCTION

Augustine said, "Where Scripture speaks, God speaks." The editors of the Christ-Centered Exposition Commentary series believe that where God speaks, the pastor must speak. God speaks through His written Word. We must speak from that Word. We believe the Bible is God breathed, authoritative, inerrant, sufficient, understandable, necessary, and timeless. We also affirm that the Bible is a Christ-centered book; that is, it contains a unified story of redemptive history of which Jesus is the hero. Because of this Christ-centered trajectory that runs from Genesis 1 through Revelation 22, we believe the Bible has a corresponding global-missions thrust. From beginning to end, we see God's mission as one of making worshipers of Christ from every tribe and tongue worked out through this redemptive drama in Scripture. To that end we must preach the Word.

In addition to these distinct convictions, the Christ-Centered Exposition Commentary series has some distinguishing characteristics. First, this series seeks to display exegetical accuracy. What the Bible says is what we want to say. While not every volume in the series will be a verse-by-verse commentary, we nevertheless desire to handle the text carefully and explain it rightly. Those who teach and preach bear the heavy responsibility of saying what God has said in His Word and declaring what God has done in Christ. We desire to handle God's Word faithfully, knowing that we must give an account for how we have fulfilled this holy calling (Jas 3:1).

Second, the Christ-Centered Exposition Commentary series has pastors in view. While we hope others will read this series, such as parents, teachers, small-group leaders, and student ministers, we desire to provide a commentary busy pastors will use for weekly preparation of biblically faithful and gospel-saturated sermons. This series is not academic in nature. Our aim is to present a readable and pastoral style of commentaries. We believe this aim will serve the church of the Lord Jesus Christ.

Third, we want the Christ-Centered Exposition Commentary series to be known for the inclusion of helpful illustrations and theologically driven applications. Many commentaries offer no help in illustrations, and few offer any kind of help in application. Often those that do offer illustrative material and application unfortunately give little serious attention to the text. While giving ourselves primarily to explanation, we also hope to serve readers by providing inspiring and illuminating illustrations coupled with timely and timeless application.

Finally, as the name suggests, the editors seek to exalt Jesus from every book of the Bible. In saying this, we are not commending wild allegory or fanciful typology. We certainly believe we must be constrained to the meaning intended by the divine Author Himself, the Holy Spirit of God. However, we also believe the Bible has a messianic focus, and our hope is that the individual authors will exalt Christ from particular texts. Luke 24:25-27, 44-47 and John 5:39, 46 inform both our hermeneutics and our homiletics. Not every author will do this the same way or have the same degree of Christ-centered emphasis. That is fine with us. We believe faithful exposition that is Christ centered is not monolithic. We do believe, however, that we must read the whole Bible as Christian Scripture. Therefore, our aim is both to honor the historical particularity of each biblical passage and to highlight its intrinsic connection to the Redeemer.

The editors are indebted to the contributors of each volume. The reader will detect a unique style from each writer, and we celebrate these unique gifts and traits. While distinctive in approach, the authors share a common characteristic in that they are pastoral theologians. They love the church, and they regularly preach and teach God's Word to God's people. Further, many of these contributors are younger voices. We think these new, fresh voices can serve the church well, especially among a rising generation that has the task of proclaiming the Word of Christ and the Christ of the Word to the lost world.

We hope and pray this series will serve the body of Christ well in these ways until our Savior returns in glory. If it does, we will have succeeded in our assignment.

David Platt
Daniel L. Akin
Tony Merida
Series Editors
February 2013

1 Timothy

Authority and Hope for a Pastor and His Church[1]

1 TIMOTHY 1:1-2

Main Idea: The God-inspired letter of 1 Timothy was written by the apostle Paul to Timothy, and the letter was graciously given for the good of all God's people.

I. **A Brief Introduction**
   A. Setting the stage for 1 Timothy
      1. The author, the recipient, and the occasion
      2. The time and the place
      3. The many challenges
      4. The urgent message
II. **A Glorious Greeting (1:1-2)**
   A. First Timothy is authoritative.
      1. It was written by an apostle.
      2. It was breathed out by God.
   B. First Timothy is timely.
      1. It was essential for Timothy.
      2. It is essential for every pastor.
      3. It is essential for every follower of Christ.
   C. First Timothy is filled with hope.
      1. God is our Savior.
      2. Christ Jesus is our hope.
      3. Grace, mercy, and peace are gifts.

---

[1] This section was written by David Burnette.

1

In their book *Health, Wealth and Happiness*, David W. Jones and Russell S. Woodbridge highlight a disturbing trend in the church: "A new gospel is being taught today. This new gospel is perplexing—it omits Jesus and neglects the cross" (*Health, Wealth and Happiness*, 15).

Jones and Woodbridge report that 46 percent of self-proclaimed Christians in the United States agree with the idea that God will grant material riches to all believers who have enough faith (*Health, Wealth and Happiness*, 16). This teaching has become known as "the prosperity gospel." Although it takes many shapes and sizes, the prosperity gospel promises material and physical blessings in *this* life so that central elements of the gospel, such as the finished work of Christ on the cross and the forgiveness of sins, take a backseat. Sadly, professing Christians seem to be taking the bait, and not just here in America. The prosperity gospel is sweeping across large portions of the world. False teachers are alive and well.

The problem of false teachers and false teaching is by no means a new problem for the church. In fact, these battles are quite old—approximately two thousand years old. When Paul was giving his final instructions to the elders in Ephesus in Acts 20:29-30, he warned them that "savage wolves" would enter the church and wreak havoc, luring away disciples. When we turn to 1 Timothy, we see that Paul's predictions were not exaggerated, and they wouldn't require centuries to play out. False teaching was staring the first-century church at Ephesus square in the face.

For a man like Paul, who gave his life to establishing and strengthening churches among the Gentiles, false teaching was more than just an apologetic hurdle. It was a deadly cancer that had to be removed if the church was to remain healthy and continue its mission. As we move through Paul's first letter to Timothy, we'll also consider other important issues the apostle addressed. Like any missionary or church planter, Paul cared deeply about the people to whom he ministered, and he knew that what they needed was not human wisdom. They needed to stand on the truth of God's Word and to fix their hope on the gospel of the Lord Jesus Christ.

A Brief Introduction

We'll begin by **setting the stage for 1 Timothy**, considering both the context and the background of the letter. The letters of 1 Timothy,

2 Timothy, and Titus are often referred to as the Pastoral Epistles. These epistles, or letters, are labeled as "pastoral" because they have so much to say about the responsibilities of pastors in leading and ministering to God's people. While these letters have a number of similarities, each letter has its own unique aspects. Below we'll look at some of the specifics related to 1 Timothy under the following headings:

- The author, the recipient, and the occasion
- The time and the place
- The many challenges
- The urgent message

First, as we think about this powerful letter, we need to consider **the author, the recipient, and the occasion**. First Timothy was written by the apostle Paul to his "true son in the faith," a man named Timothy (1:2). Timothy was younger than Paul, possibly in his thirties (Ryken, *1 Timothy*, 5), and he had assisted Paul in a number of different ministry contexts (see for example, 1 Thess 3; 1 Cor 4:16-17; 16:10-11; and Phil 2:19-24; Towner, *Letters*, 52). Paul, the apostle to the Gentiles and author of 13 letters in the New Testament, had stationed Timothy in Ephesus to do the difficult work of combating false teaching (1 Tim 1:3). Timothy was also told to lead the church to be faithful in a number of different areas, including godly living. Leading God's people is no easy task. However, it is a glorious task worth giving one's life to, and Paul wanted Timothy to be faithful in his calling as a minister of the gospel.

Other factors we need to consider include **the time and place** of the letter. Followers of Christ have always had to face a unique set of challenges related to their ministry context. For example, pastors and churches in our own culture continue to face complex questions related to who we are as humans. Could anyone have imagined, even a generation ago, that Christians would have to think through biblical positions on cloning or gender reassignment? Nevertheless, we would be seriously mistaken to think we are the first generation of Christians to face complex issues. The church at Ephesus is a case in point.

Consider the context for Timothy and the church at Ephesus in the mid 60s of the first century AD (see Carson and Moo, *Introduction*, 571–72). At this time the city of Ephesus was large, diverse, religiously complex, and flourishing commercially (Towner, *Letters*, 38), not unlike a major metropolitan area of the United States today. Since the temple of Artemis was located in Ephesus, the cult of Artemis was especially influential in this Imperial capital. This cult affected commercial activity, and it seems to have engulfed a number of other cult practices such as "the practice of magic, sorcery, and soothsaying" (Towner, *Letters*, 38). Needless to say, Timothy was not ministering in a culture founded on Judeo-Christian values. Ephesus had its own particular brand of sin and rebellion, but this doesn't mean Paul's instructions have no relevance for us today.

The many challenges facing Timothy and the church at Ephesus went beyond their immediate cultural context, as difficult as that context must have been. Consider some of the issues Paul addressed within the church: men and women needed to be instructed about their God-given roles and conduct in the church's gathering, faithful elders and deacons needed to be identified and appointed, widows needed to be cared for properly, and the pursuit of wealth seemed to be a real temptation for some in the congregation. Does any of that sound familiar? Paul's concerns could easily be copied and pasted into a list of issues the church continues to face in the twenty-first century.

As we mentioned earlier, the church at Ephesus was also dealing with the deadly serious problem of false teaching. Paul mentioned Hymenaeus and Alexander as two individuals who had to be excommunicated, or removed, from the church for rejecting "faith and a good conscience" (1:19; see also 2 Tim 2:17). It's not a good sign when two of your elders have to be taught not to blaspheme! We can't be too precise with regard to the content of the false teaching, but Paul did give us some clues throughout the letter. Here is some of what we can piece together about the false teachers:

- They were straying in their doctrine (1:3).
- They were preoccupied with myths, genealogies, and speculation (1:4).
- They misused the law (1:7).
- They were apparently immoral (1:19-20).
- Their consciences were seared (4:2).
- They were forbidding marriage and certain foods (4:3).
- They craved controversy and quarrels (6:4).
- They were using godliness for material gain (6:5).

The false teachers in the Ephesian church may have been influenced by early seeds of a heresy that later became known as Gnosticism.

This heresy came onto the scene in the second century AD after the writing of the New Testament.[2] What seems more certain is that the false teaching in Ephesus had some strong Jewish elements. For example, the apostle mentioned that these teachers wanted to teach the law (1:7) and that they had an unhealthy interest in genealogies (1:4; Fee, *Timothy, Titus,* 41). Many commentators have seen similarities between the false teaching in 1 Timothy and what we see in a book like Colossians. Whatever the precise nature of the false teaching, we know it was dangerous because it diverted people from the truth of God's Word. Paul even referred to such false teaching as demonic (4:1)! The church was not merely dealing with preferences for the style of music—the gospel itself was at stake.

Unfortunately, some Christians have gotten the wrong idea that a book like 1 Timothy is only relevant for the church staff. **The urgent message** it contains is sometimes passed over because the book is referred to as a "leader's manual" for pastors. Now this is definitely a book pastors need to be intimately familiar with, so if you're a pastor, 1 Timothy is certainly in the "must know" column. But that doesn't mean you can ignore this book if you're not in a position of church leadership.

Most people won't say it aloud, but they may be thinking, "I know this book is important, but I'm not a pastor, so I should read something that applies to me." Is that you? If so, let me urge you to rethink your perspective on 1 Timothy. Whether you minister by taking meals to homebound members or by seeking to evangelize unreached people groups, don't ignore this important book. You might be missing more than you think. Consider just a few important questions addressed by Paul:

- How do Old Testament laws apply to Christians today? (chap. 1)
- Can women teach in the church? (chap. 2)
- Who is qualified to be an elder or a deacon? (chap. 3)
- How do I spot false teachers? (chap. 4)
- Which widows should the church support? (chap. 5)
- What should wealthy Christians do with their money? (chap. 6)

---

[2] Gnostics were followers of an extremely diverse set of religious movements which taught that salvation was to be attained through "knowledge" (gnosis) of one's origins. They typically held that the material creation was evil, with some Gnostics advocating a sinful, licentious lifestyle. Other Gnostic groups held to a rigid ascetic lifestyle (Yamauchi, "Gnosis, Gnosticism," 352).

Anyone who professes to be a follower of Christ and who is a member of a local church—those two should always go together—needs to know what God has said about how the church is to function. Consider what Paul said in 1 Timothy 3:15, a verse that is integral to the message of the entire book: "But if I should be delayed, I have written so that you will know how people ought to act in God's household, which is the church of the living God, the pillar and foundation of the truth."

Did you catch that? This letter is all about how God's people conduct themselves in God's household, and Paul was not talking about our personal etiquette in the sanctuary. "God's household" is the church, the gathered people of God. This letter was written so that we would know how to conduct ourselves when we come together as followers of Christ for worship and then when we spread out to serve the Lord throughout the week. This book clearly has relevance beyond church leaders. Its message is for every person and for every context.

As the "pillar and foundation of the truth," the church of Jesus Christ has a weighty calling. But this is an infinitely glorious calling, and God's grace and power are more than sufficient for the task.

A Glorious Greeting
1 TIMOTHY 1:1-2

The church was God's idea. That may sound obvious, but with the number of conferences, books, and magazines offering advice on how to "do church" today, it's easy to forget the church is not ours to run. To be fair, some of the material out there is biblical and much needed; however, too much of the advice being offered today ignores the church's marching orders given by King Jesus Himself. We dare not forget that Jesus Christ is the Head of the church (Col 1:18). Samuel J. Stone's old hymn says it well:

The church's one foundation
Is Jesus Christ her Lord,
She is His new creation
By water and the Word.
From heaven He came and sought her
To be His holy bride;
With His own blood He bought her
And for her life He died.

The church belongs to Jesus Christ. He founded it by His life, death, and resurrection, and since Pentecost He has continued to build it by His Spirit (Acts 2). Therefore, what matters most in the life of the church is not the church's website or the latest statistics on what visitors are looking for in a worship experience. What matters most is what the Lord of the church has said.

The opening words of 1 Timothy demand our attention: "Paul, an apostle." We tend to skim through the greetings of the New Testament as if these were throwaway verses. However, these greetings are so much more than a "Dear Joe" kind of formality. Paul, the author of this letter, was giving us his credentials as an apostle, which means we had better listen to what he said. We're reminded that **1 Timothy is authoritative**.

According to Acts 1:21-22, in order to be one of the original 12 apostles, an individual had to be present during the earthly ministry of Jesus from his baptism by John to his resurrection and ascension. Jesus sent these men, these eyewitnesses of His ministry, to take the gospel message to the ends of the earth, and several of them were even used to pen the Scriptures. In fact, every book of the New Testament is written by an apostle or a close associate of an apostle. So instead of treating the opening of this or any other New Testament letter as trivial, our reaction should be just the opposite. We should pay close attention, for these are words given to us by a special representative of the King of the universe.

Unlike the other apostles Paul did not accompany Jesus during His earthly ministry, nor did he see the resurrected Lord before the ascension. But Paul did have a personal encounter with Jesus, an amazing account of God's sovereign grace recorded in Acts 9. This former persecutor of the church was appointed to the ministry by Jesus Himself (1 Tim 1:12) as the last of the apostles (1 Cor 15:8). Paul would become the greatest missionary in the history of the church and the author of a significant portion of the New Testament. So the first thing that grabs our attention as we start reading through 1 Timothy is that **it was written by an apostle**.

Paul emphatically made his point about being an apostle when he said in verse 1 that his apostleship is "by the command of God our Savior and of Christ Jesus our hope." Paul wasn't elected by men. He was divinely appointed to be an authoritative representative of the risen and ruling Lord. We should not fail to mention that Paul ascribed this command of apostleship to both the Father and the Son. It is clear, then, that Paul assumed the deity of Jesus Christ, for we would be shocked to hear that a command came from God and the apostle John! This exalted view of the Son of God is also evident in verse 2, where we read that "grace, mercy, and peace" are given by "God the Father *and* Christ Jesus our Lord."[3]

Now to be clear, not everything an apostle said or wrote is authoritative. We only need to think of Paul having to confront Peter's hypocrisy in Galatians 2 to make this point (Gal 2:11-14). Authority does not ultimately rest in a group of men, no matter how privileged their position may be. Rather, Scripture carries this authority, for as Paul told Timothy elsewhere, "All Scripture is inspired by God" (2 Tim 3:16). Peter put it this way: "Men spoke from God as they were moved by the Holy Spirit" (2 Pet 1:21). Men are not inerrant; God's Word is. The apostles were fallible men whom God used to pen these inspired words. Therefore, the fundamental reason Timothy, the church at Ephesus, and everyone else since then needs to submit to this letter is because **it was breathed out by God**.

The fact that God's Word is inspired and inerrant is not only a doctrine to be affirmed;[4] it's a firm foundation to stand on in a culture and a world that suppress and oppose the truth of God. When everything around us seems to be caving in, we need to hear God's Word and submit to it, knowing that what God has said is true and good and right. We can imagine that Timothy may have been a little shaken by the issues he was facing in the church at Ephesus. Along with the daily pressures of pastoral ministry, he had to deal with false teachers who were undermining God's Word. In this sense **1 Timothy is timely** in that **it was essential for Timothy** because it dealt with issues he was facing.

Paul called Timothy "my true son in the faith" (1 Tim 1:2). Elsewhere Paul said something similar, demonstrating his affection for Timothy: "But you know his proven character, because he has served with me in the gospel ministry like a son with a father" (Phil 2:22). Timothy traveled with Paul often as a fellow worker in the ministry, so the apostle knew him well. We have, then, a personal letter here from Paul to a younger brother in Christ.

---

[3] The fact that Jesus is called "Lord" is also an indication of His deity since this was the name used for Yahweh in the Greek Old Testament (LXX).

[4] When we say the Bible is inerrant, we mean it contains no errors and is completely truthful in everything it says.

It is also essential to see that Paul's instructions here are meant for a wider audience than Timothy. As we saw in verse 1, Paul spoke as an apostle, and his words as recorded in Scripture bear the authority of God. Therefore, it's not a stretch to say that **it is essential for every pastor** to hear these instructions. The issues that arise in Ephesus are not confined to one time and place, for sin has continued to rear its ugly head ever since the fall in Genesis 3. In fact, we can go even further and say that **1 Timothy is essential for every follower of Christ**. All of us need to know what God has said about how we relate to Him and to one another in the church. The fact that God chose to include this letter in the Bible means it is relevant for every child of God. First Timothy is God's Word to all of us.

We shouldn't bypass this opening greeting without recognizing that **1 Timothy is filled with hope**. Yes, this inspired letter is authoritative and timely as it deals with a number of difficult issues in the church, but it's also full of gospel hope. This is apparent right from the start in verse 1 when Paul referred to "God our Savior." Paul was not sent by some nameless deity. He reminded Timothy and all who hear this letter that the God he serves is the saving God of the Scriptures. So we are reminded at the outset of the letter that **God is our Savior**.

In the next phrase we see more good news. Paul was sent not only by "God our Savior" but by "Christ Jesus our hope." What an encouraging reminder at the beginning of a letter that deals with so many difficult and thorny issues. **Christ Jesus is our hope!** Surely Paul intended for us to think on the hope that is ours based on Christ's death and resurrection. He is, as Paul said later, the "one mediator between God and humanity" (2:5). Paul also talked about the "mystery of godliness" as it relates to Jesus Christ:

> He was manifested in the flesh,
> vindicated in the Spirit,
> seen by angels,
> preached among the nations,
> believed on in the world,
> taken up in glory. (3:16)

While 1 Timothy contains a number of exhortations and commands, we can't forget that Paul gave his instructions in the context of the gospel. This precious gospel should come to mind when we read the close of Paul's greeting: "Grace, mercy, and peace from God the

Father and Christ Jesus our Lord" (1:2). Again, this is one of those portions of the greeting we tend to pass over lightly, but consider what is being said here. God's dealings with His people are full of grace, mercy, and peace. That's good news for those who are still battling sin, which is all of us.

Neither Timothy nor the church at Ephesus was being called to "clean up their act" in order to gain God's favor. For that matter, neither are we as followers of Christ today called to appease a perfectly just and holy God through our obedience. God Himself has decisively dealt with sin in the cross of His dear Son (Rom 8:3), thus securing for us an eternal and unshakable hope. On *this* basis God addresses us. Conducting ourselves rightly in God's household is made possible only by God's grace. Yes, it is imperative that we obey God's Word and conform to His will, for saving faith always produces spiritual fruit. But true, God-honoring obedience is always rendered in the context of a loving relationship made possible by the gospel. The close of Paul's greeting in verse 2 reminds us that **grace, mercy, and peace are gifts**. In the remainder of chapter 1 Paul will continue to reflect on the mercy he has been shown, a mercy that serves as a demonstration of Christ's "extraordinary patience" (1:16; see 1:13).[5]

Reflect and Discuss

1. Which false doctrines seem to be the biggest threat to your church and to Christians you know?
2. Why did Paul call Timothy his "son"? Do you have any children or siblings "in the faith" who seem closer than your blood relatives?
3. What are the greatest cultural changes facing the church today?
4. How do the eight aspects of false teaching on page 4 distract believers from growing in Christ? How do they interfere with evangelism?
5. What leadership roles do you fill in your church or your home? How can studying 1 Timothy guide you in these roles and opportunities?
6. What is the danger when a church identifies more with a dynamic pastor than with the truths of God's Word? How can that mind-set be avoided?

---

[5] Paul's greetings often introduce themes that reappear throughout the body of the letter. Only here and in 2 Timothy does Paul add the term "mercy" to "grace and peace" (Van Neste, notes on 1 Timothy in Dennis et al., *ESV Study Bible*, 2325).

7. What qualified Paul to write Scripture?
8. How does the doctrine of the inerrancy of Scripture form the foundation of all other Christian theology?
9. How can a letter from a mentor to his student find application to all leaders and members of churches through the ages?
10. In what specific ways might you pray for the leader of your church?

The Centrality of the Gospel in the Local Church

1 TIMOTHY 1:3-20

Main Idea: Church leaders must lead God's people to persevere in the gospel in the face of false teaching and other challenges.

I. **We Must Guard the Gospel (1:3-11).**
   A. How not to use God's law
      1. We must not add to the law's demands.
      2. We must not think the law saves.
      3. This produces
         a. arrogance and ignorance among those who teach.
         b. confusion and deception among those who hear.
   B. How to use God's law
      1. To show God's restraint of sin
      2. To show God's condemnation of the sinner
      3. To show God's will for the saved
      4. This produces
         a. responsibility among those who teach.
         b. love among those who hear.

II. **We Must Celebrate the Gospel (1:12-17).**
   A. The gospel of God is
      1. incarnational, yet undeniable.
      2. universal, yet personal.
   B. The grace of God is
      1. unconditional.
      2. purposeful.
         a. It demonstrates God's patience.
         b. It leads to God's praise.
   C. The glory of God is
      1. royal and eternal.
      2. invisible and incomparable.

III. **We Must Fight for the Gospel (1:18-20).**
   A. In our lives
   B. In our churches

The book of 1 Timothy is all about the church. This New Testament letter was written from Paul to Timothy, the young pastor of a struggling church. In it Paul explained to Timothy how the gospel forms who we are and what we do as the church. In 1 Timothy 3:15 Paul said, "I have written so that you will know how people ought to act in God's household, which is the church of the living God." When you ask the question, What is the church supposed to look like? 1 Timothy provides one of the clearest answers in all of the Bible. So let's look at the first chapter and see what is the first consideration—the most important consideration—that Paul would pass on to a young pastor of a struggling church. These words are immensely important, not just for the church at Ephesus two thousand years ago, but also for the church today. In this letter Paul told Timothy that the one thing he must hold on to in the church at all costs is the gospel of Jesus Christ.

We Must Guard the Gospel
1 TIMOTHY 1:3-11

Paul's first instruction to the young pastor Timothy was essentially this: Guard the gospel! This is a fascinating way to open the letter, especially when we consider all the challenges surrounding the church at Ephesus. Ephesus was a city filled with paganism and rampant immorality and idolatry, and because of these cultural pressures, Paul's first concern was to tell Timothy that he must keep people from teaching false doctrine. The summons is clear: Address anything and everything that pulls people away from the gospel.

If we lose the gospel, we lose everything. We may think other things are more urgent or more in need of addressing in the church—things like prayer, leadership, mission, materialism, or caring for one another. Paul would get to all of these things eventually, but he began by telling Timothy to guard the gospel. And we guard the gospel by the way we use God's Word, which in this case concerns His law. In this text Paul shows us **how not to use God's law**—how not to use His Word. We'll consider two ways not to use God's law, and then we'll think about the consequences that come when we use God's law in these unbiblical ways.

First, **we must not add to the law's demands**. In verse 4 Paul talked about the myths and genealogies taught by the false teachers. These false teachers were taking extrabiblical writings that included stories and myths about different Old Testament figures, and they were using these writings to add to God's Word. When we get to chapter 4, we'll see that they were teaching that you shouldn't get married and that you should abstain from various foods (4:3). In essence they were putting rules and regulations on God's people that are not in God's Word.

We can use the law wrongly in a second way, and it is an even worse error than the first. **We must not think the law saves.** These false teachers in Ephesus, along with others in the first century, were teaching that obedience to the law, even some extrabiblical laws, could help someone earn the favor of God. This kind of teaching has been going on since the first century, and it persists into the twenty-first century. Of course, false teachers won't usually come out and say that you need to earn your salvation, and sometimes they may even think they are promoting a more righteous standard for God's people. However, any time we try to add to God's gracious work in the gospel we pervert it. The idea is that by doing certain works—following certain rules or obeying certain laws—you can earn God's favor. This runs counter to the biblical gospel.

When the law is used in the wrong way, the results can be disastrous. Paul said that a wrong use of God's law was producing **arrogance and ignorance among those who teach**. In verse 7 we learn that these teachers were making "confident assertions" (ESV) about things they didn't even understand. Philip Ryken says it well: "There is a dangerous combination here: arrogance and ignorance" (Ryken, *1 Timothy*, 11). Moreover, as a result of their teaching, they were producing **confusion and deception among those who hear**. The "empty speculations" (v. 4) and "fruitless discussion" (v. 6) ultimately lead to deception because people begin to think there are additional rules beyond God's law, and by doing them they can be saved. That's a *serious* deception.

Even if leaders in your particular church are not explicitly teaching that you can't be married or eat certain foods, you still need to be aware that those who teach the Bible are prone to add to the law's demands, implying that doing certain things will lead to salvation. We must be on guard and avoid this kind of teaching at all costs.

So, **how do we use God's law**? After seeing some of the wrong ways to use God's law, we need to see how it *should* be used. The purpose of God's law can be found in many places in Scripture, but remember, we're not talking about things like the dietary laws or regulations for sacrifices. These kinds of laws are no longer binding on Christians because the law given through Moses through the old covenant has been set aside with Christ's coming (Rom 7:6; Gal 3:24-25). There are, however, transcendent moral laws that have an application for God's people in all ages, such as, "Do not murder" (Exod 20:13; see Matt 5:21-22). Let's consider three different uses of God's moral law.[6]

Excursus: The Three Uses of God's Moral Law

The law is intended, on one hand, **to show God's restraint of sin**. God's law helps us recognize the boundaries between good and evil so we might avoid sin. Actually, this is a function of any type of law. For example, think about speed limit signs. Why are they there? They exist because reckless drivers on the road need to be restrained (Stott, *Message*, 48). In this sense the law is written for law-*breakers*. This is why Paul said in verse 9 that the law "is not meant for a righteous person, but for the lawless and rebellious, for the ungodly and sinful." Paul pointed to specific sins in verses 9-10 (murder, sexual immorality, lying, etc.), and these sins seem to correlate with the ways we are prone to break the Ten Commandments (Exod 20:1-17; Deut 5:6-21). The law helps identify and restrain these sins in our lives.

Paul said something similar in Romans 7:7: "I would not have known what it is to covet if the law had not said, Do not covet." The law shows us what is good, and God uses this realization to restrain us from evil. However, because of our sin, the law's restraint is only temporary. Just like my kids, we eventually give in and disobey.

Recently one of my boys found a coin on the ground and proceeded to pick it up and play with it. I said to him, "You can play with it, but don't put it in your mouth." The law was laid down, and sin was restrained . . . for the moment. Two minutes later, and where's the coin? *In his mouth*. The law was broken. And it's the same in all of our lives. The law

---

[6] Paul does not make a clear allusion to the Ten Commandments, but the list of sins in verses 9-10 implies that moral laws are in view here rather than ceremonial laws.

says, "Don't do this," and it may restrain us temporarily, but eventually we sin, all of us. Our predisposition to sinning leads to a second use of the law.

The law is also intended **to show God's condemnation of the sinner**. When we sin, the law becomes a testimony against us, showing us how we have disobeyed. And we have not only disobeyed a dad who said, "Don't put that coin in your mouth"; we've disobeyed the eternal, infinitely holy, just Judge of all sin. The law makes our rebellion apparent, and this realization is an essential part of our salvation.

Before we come to Christ, we stand before the law condemned by God. We have not kept His law; in fact, we *cannot* keep His law (Rom 8:8). The law opens our eyes to the fact that we are guilty before God. But then we look to Christ, who has kept the law of God perfectly, and we see that He is righteous before God. In response we cry out to God, "I need Him!" And that's how we are saved. That's the gospel. Christ, the law-*keeper*, has paid the penalty for law*breakers*. The law doesn't save us; the law leads us to Christ, and *He* saves us. The great Reformer Martin Luther described the law as a "hammer that breaks proud and obstinate hypocrites" (*Galatians*, 166). Luther asks, "What is the purpose of this humbling, bruising, and beating down? It serves to bring us into grace" (*Galatians*, 168). We find this grace in the gospel of Christ.

Finally, there's a third beneficial use of the law: the law functions **to show God's will for the saved**. We want to honor Christ as His followers, so what do we do now that we're saved? God's law instructs us. His moral law—and to some extent the ceremonial law—reveals His character and shows us how to love God and love our neighbor. Now that we are indwelled by His Spirit, we have the desire and the power to obey what God says (cf. Ezek 36:27). As we rest in the righteousness of Christ, possessed by the Spirit of Christ, compelled by the ongoing grace of Christ, we are led from the inside out to walk in God's will. For the Christian, God's law is no longer a crushing hammer but a divine guide.

So, if Paul was telling Timothy to use the law rightly, which of these three uses of the law did he have in mind in this passage? Paul seems to be referring to the restraining function of the law, the first use of the law mentioned above. Instead of the false teachers' wrong application of the law in the lives of Christians, Paul points to the law's role in curbing sin in the lives of unbelievers. This is why he said the law is not for the righteous but for the "lawless and rebellious" (v. 9).

Paul goes on to mention two benefits the right use of the law can give to the church. First, a right use of the law **produces responsibility among those who teach**. Paul referred to "God's plan" in verse 4: those who teach have a responsibility, a stewardship, to guard the gospel. Second, right preaching of the law, which leads lawbreaking sinners to the gospel, **produces love among those who hear**. Verse 5 said it beautifully: "Now the goal of our instruction is love that comes from a pure heart, a good conscience, and a sincere faith." That's what we want. We want to be a people who love God and love others out of the overflow of a pure heart and a good conscience and a sincere faith. Paul tells us that only the gospel produces that kind of response.

At the end of the day, there is no list of rules to follow that I or anyone else can make up that will allow you to earn the favor of God. Whether your background is Muslim, Hindu, Jewish, Baptist, Methodist, Presbyterian, Catholic, or atheistic, the law of God is ingrained on your heart, even if you've never read the Word of God (Rom 2:14-15). You know the difference between good and evil because God has put it within you. Yet you cannot keep God's law perfectly. And you know you can't. The harder you try, the more you realize you fall short; however, there is One who has obeyed the law perfectly.

Christ's perfect obedience to God's will means that He was able to die on the cross to pay the price for your disobedience, and then rising from the grave, he opened the way for you to unite your life with His and be counted righteous before God. If you have never trusted in Jesus, trust Him today to be your righteousness before God. Don't buy into the lie that human achievement can make you right before God.

Ever since the church began two thousand years ago, there has been a tendency to drift away from this wonderful, glorious, gospel truth. So, regardless of who our pastors are and no matter what our programs look like, we must guard this gospel with our lives.

We Must Celebrate the Gospel
1 TIMOTHY 1:12-17

As we guard the gospel in the church, we also celebrate the gospel. In verses 12-17, Paul erupted into his personal testimony, which leads to triumphant praise. In the midst of all this, he gives us one of the most concise, clear, and compelling descriptions of the gospel in all of Scripture. It's a powerful, pregnant sentence that encapsulates the gospel in just nine English words: "Christ Jesus came into the world to save sinners" (v. 15). Here we learn about the gospel, the grace of God, and the glory of God.

Paul tells us that Christ Jesus *came* into the world. So much truth is packed into this one word "came." We learn that **the gospel of God is incarnational and undeniable**.

Christ Jesus, the Son of God, didn't first come into being in Bethlehem. He already existed as the Second Person of the Trinity, the preexistent, eternal Son of God who was there with the Father and the Spirit before the foundation of the world (John 1:1-3). He committed the ultimate act of condescending grace, coming into the world as a baby born in Bethlehem. The One who was with the Father in glory put on a robe of human flesh and came to us. This is the incarnation.

But *why* did Jesus come? Jesus Christ came to live the life we could not live, to die the death we deserved to die, and to rise in victory over the enemies we could not conquer—sin and death. There is no greater wonder in all of history, and yet Paul tells us it's true. This is not like the myths and speculations of the false teachers (v. 4); this is "trustworthy and deserving of full acceptance" (1 Tim 1:15). This is reality. It's undeniable.

The gospel of God is also **universal and personal**. Now that we've established that Jesus came to save sinners, the next question is, Which sinners? Answer: All sinners who would embrace this gospel fully. And Paul said in verse 16 that he was at the top of the list of sinners. That's why we're saying the gospel is both universal *and* personal. It caused Paul to celebrate the grace of God, which he said "overflowed" for him (v. 14).

In verse 13, Paul talked about what he used to be: "a blasphemer, a persecutor, and an arrogant man." The ESV translates this last word as an "insolent opponent." Don't forget, the guy who is writing this letter to the church used to be the church's single greatest threat. He wanted it wiped off the map! Paul oversaw the persecution of Stephen (Acts

8:1), the first Christian martyr, and then he devoted his life to arresting, imprisoning, and killing Christians everywhere he could. In fact, Paul was on his way to Damascus to kill Christians when he met Christ. Amazingly, God caused His grace to overflow to the one person who seemingly deserved it the least.

Paul's example in verse 13 tells us a lot about the nature of God's grace. We learn that the grace of God is **unconditional**, for there was nothing in Paul to draw God to Him. Paul's salvation originated in God and God alone. And the same is true for you and me. We are not saved based on any condition *in us*; we are saved solely on account of sovereign grace *in God*. His grace is unconditional.

God's grace is also **purposeful**. We see this in verse 14, as it produced faith and love in Paul's life. But there are even deeper purposes in God's grace. It **demonstrates God's patience**. Verse 14 is really good news to anyone who has ever thought, "God would not save me. I've hated Him. I've turned against Him. I've fought God at every point in my life." If you think you are beyond the mercy of God, hear this: God chose to take the chief persecutor of the church and make him the chief missionary in the church to show He is patient, He loves, and He beckons sinners to believe in Him for eternal life. No matter who you are or what you've done, these words are worthy of full acceptance: "Christ Jesus came into the world to save sinners" (v. 15).

Not only does God's grace demonstrate His patience; it also **leads to God's praise**. Listen to Paul's response to God's grace in verse 17: "Now to the King eternal, immortal, invisible, the only God, be honor and glory forever and ever. Amen." The apostle was overwhelmed that he would receive mercy from such a King.

Paul's ascription of praise in verse 17 also tells us several things about **the glory of God**. First and foremost, we see that His glory is **royal and eternal**. "Now to the King eternal, immortal." God is King of the ages, now and forevermore. He is immortal. He never grows tired or weary. He never changes. Death and decay cannot and will not ever touch Him. He's royal and eternal. We also see that God's glory is **invisible and incomparable**. He is "invisible, the only God." God is beyond the limits of what we can see or imagine, and no one compares with Him. He is the only God, and He will receive "honor and glory forever and ever. Amen."

Individual believers, local churches, and the church of Christ across the globe will continue to go through difficult times; however, the Head of this church, Christ, our God, Savior, and King, will ever be on His throne. Though opposition and challenges may come, God is the King of the ages, and He will lead, guide, protect, purify, sanctify, and preserve His church.

We Must Fight for the Gospel
1 TIMOTHY 1:18-20

In light of who God is and His gracious purposes, Paul gave Timothy one final exhortation in this chapter: Fight for the gospel. Timothy must "engage in battle" for the sake of the truth. To make his point Paul used Hymenaeus and Alexander, whom we know were among the false teachers at Ephesus and men who had wandered away from the gospel. Many commentators believe these men were elders in the church. This is a great reminder for pastors—and I'm including myself—that no one is immune to the temptation to wander from the gospel. No elder, no deacon, no teacher, no small-group leader, and no member of the church is exempt from this warning. That's why Paul said we must fight for the gospel. This fight is carried out in at least two ways.

We fight for the gospel in our lives. We're in a war, brothers and sisters in Christ, in our lives, in our marriages, and in our families. Whether you're a teenager at school or a businessperson at work, a battle is raging all around you. Spiritual forces of evil in the heavenly realms are active, and they are warring against your soul (Eph 6:12). The Devil and all the minions of hell will entice you with deceptions and incite you with divisions because they do not want the gospel to resound in and through your life, your marriage, your family, or any other area. This battle will look differently in each of our lives, but do not be caught off guard—you are in a war. So fight the good fight. Stand strong amid all the challenges that come from outside and inside the church. Keep "faith and a good conscience" (v. 19).

Finally, **we fight for the gospel in our churches**. Paul talked about Hymenaeus and Alexander being handed over to Satan in verse 20. This is almost certainly referring to excommunication from the church, which we read more about in 1 Corinthians 5:1-5 and Matthew 18:15-20. These two men were cast out of the church to show that they were separated from Christ, with the hope and prayer that they would realize their error and return to Christ. Paul was essentially telling Timothy,

"You and the church must take severe measures at certain times to fight for this gospel. Take them."

Whatever you do, hold on to the gospel. It is the only thing that unites the church, and it is the only thing that will sustain God's people in difficult days. Indeed, this is a gospel worth guarding and defending, and this is a gospel worth celebrating forever.

Reflect and Discuss

1. Is the gospel still under attack today? What pulls people away from the true gospel?
2. What rules and regulations do some current preachers add to the gospel?
3. Why is it a worse error to think that obedience to laws can save a person? How does this teaching sometimes show up as a matter of degrees rather than overt heresy?
4. How do the three uses of God's moral law apply to unbelievers? to believers?
5. How would you state the gospel in one sentence?
6. What is the value in remembering what you were before you were saved? Conversely, what is the danger in not realizing the seriousness of your previous sinful state?
7. What role did God's grace play in your salvation? What role did you play? Do your answers to these two questions correspond to biblical descriptions of salvation?
8. Are you ever stirred or even overwhelmed by thoughts of God's grace in your life? What types of study, meditation, or worship produce the greatest response in you?
9. Do you know personally any church leader who has wandered from the gospel? Which temptations did he give in to? What kinds of temptations are you most vulnerable to?
10. Are we at war with Satan? What happens if we think we are not at war?

Global Prayer for the Local Church

1 TIMOTHY 2:1-7

Main Idea: Pray for and proclaim the gospel to all kinds of people because God desires their salvation and Christ died as ransom for all.

I. **The Initial Exhortation (2:1-2)**
   A. We should pray to God for all people.
   B. The progress of the gospel in the world is dependent on the prayers of God's people in the church.
II. **The Theological Motivation (2:3-6)**
   A. We pray because God desires the salvation of all people.
      1. This does not mean all will be saved.
      2. This does not mean God's will has been thwarted.
      3. This does mean God loves all people.
   B. We pray because God deserves the honor of all people.
      1. Worship is the fuel of world praying.
      2. Worship is the goal of world praying.
   C. We pray because Christ died for the rescue of all people.
      1. Jesus is unique in who He is.
      2. Jesus is unique in what He did.
      3. Jesus is unique in what He does.
III. **The Obvious Implication (2:7)**
   A. As we pray to God for all people, we preach to all people.
      1. We herald the cross of Christ.
      2. We teach the commands of Christ.
IV. **The Coming Conclusion**
   A. We pray with confidence, and we preach with boldness because we know
      1. our mission will prevail.
      2. our Mediator will be praised.

We now live in a culture that is hostile to anyone claiming to know absolute truth. You can live however you please, and you can believe whatever you want—"Obey your thirst," the commercial tells us—just don't impose your beliefs on others. That's the unpardonable sin of our day. This sentiment is especially true when it comes to religious beliefs, which can make it highly uncomfortable for Christians sharing the gospel. After all, our message is, well, pretty much absolute: "There is no other name under heaven given to people, and we must be saved by it" (Acts 4:12).

On the other hand, even though our message is exclusive, our witness should not be. We've been commanded to make disciples of all nations (Matt 28:19). No one is to be left out, regardless of race, nationality, economic status, or any other distinction. The absolute and exclusive claims of the gospel are to be made known universally. The church must not ignore the great spiritual needs all around it, either by becoming exclusively self-focused or by targeting only a certain segment of unbelievers. Paul reminded Timothy in this passage that our hearts must come in line with God's heart. And God desires all people to be saved.

The Initial Exhortation
1 TIMOTHY 2:1-2

Paul provides a foundation—a gospel foundation—in chapter 1 of this letter. He commands Timothy and the church at Ephesus to guard the gospel, to celebrate the gospel, and to fight for the gospel. Now, based on that gospel foundation, Paul begins to give practical exhortations to the church in chapter 2. He starts by talking about public worship. The opening words, "First of all," signal the paramount importance of this initial exhortation. How is it that you guard the gospel, celebrate the gospel, and fight for the gospel? You start, Paul says, by praying.

The church is on a life-saving mission surrounded by people who don't know the salvation of Jesus Christ. These people are destined for an eternal hell if nothing changes. So, as a follower of Christ, what do you do? You pray. It's the easiest thing you can do. You don't have to get out of bed. You don't have to leave your home. You don't have to get dressed up. And you don't even have to talk to people—just to God! Do you want to have influence on the lost people around you and the lost people around the world? Do you want to have influence on presidents, kings, queens, dictators, and rulers? Do you want to be a part of seeing people die and go to heaven instead of hell? Then pray!

Consider in this exhortation from Paul to Timothy **whom we are to pray for**. For emphasis Paul used four different words in verse 1, each having to do with prayer. He urges us to make "petitions, prayers, intercessions, and thanksgivings." All right Paul, we get your point. But *whom* do we pray for?

First, we are to pray for **every kind of person**. This is what Paul meant when he said we are to pray for "everyone" (v. 1). The point is not that every Christian is commanded to pray for each individual person in the world. No, Paul was talking about all *kinds* of people. As a church made up of both Jews and Gentiles, Paul was telling them to pray for one another. As a church where false teachers were limiting salvation to a small group of religious elite, Paul encouraged them not to limit their prayers. Prayer is not an elitist, nationalistic, racist, or selective practice; instead, Paul says there is no category of person you should not pray for. May there be diversity in our praying.

Next Paul says that we are to pray for **leaders in high positions**. Within the broader category of all kinds of people, Paul mentioned specifically that the church at Ephesus was to pray for "kings and all those who are in authority" (v. 2). This exhortation is fascinating when you consider that Paul was writing under the reign of Nero, a Roman emperor who violently persecuted Christians in the first century. At that time there would have been few, if any, Christian rulers in the world. Yet Paul was telling them to pray for these pagan leaders. Pray for the king you suffer under. Pray for the leader you don't agree with. Pray for the ruler you don't approve of. This is God's will.

Paul's instructions also have relevance for those of us who don't experience physical persecution. If you're a Christian in America, pray for the president, regardless of what you think of his politics and policies. Love him and pray for him. And not just for him but also for the vice president, your governor, your senators, and for all your government representatives. We should also pray for leaders of countries like Libya, Israel, Iran, and Afghanistan. The Bible tells us to pray for those in authority. So, are you praying for these men and women? Or are you watching the news and getting frustrated and angry with them? Paul told the Christians in Ephesus to pray, and he wasn't telling them to pray that God would blast Nero into oblivion!

Paul not only tells us whom we pray for but also **what we pray for**. The apostle's specific instructions were to pray for leaders "so that we may lead a tranquil and quiet life in all godliness and dignity" (v. 2). What Paul was saying here is multifaceted. One goal of our praying is **peace amid persecution**. We pray for our leaders in such a way that promotes peace and, consequently, enables the church to flourish. This flourishing is not in opposition to the state but under the protection of the state. Those in authority can provide an umbrella of peace for the church to thrive and proclaim the gospel freely.

In the first century, the time when Paul was writing, there was a period known as the *Pax Romana*, or Roman Peace, which allowed for roads to be built and trade routes to be established. The way was literally "paved" for the gospel to spread across the vast Roman Empire. It's not that the gospel can't spread amid persecution—it can. However, in the context of peace, Christians and churches can freely live out the call of Christ and demonstrate the life of Christ for all to see. In our own day here in America, we have the freedom and privilege of living out the implications of the gospel freely among the people around us. That's a good thing, so pray for it.

We also need to remember to pray for our brothers and sisters in Christ who live in places like Egypt, where peace is in jeopardy, or in places like Saudi Arabia and North Korea, where peace is nonexistent. Pray that peaceful doors would be opened for the proclamation of the gospel. At the same time Paul also seems to be saying that we ought to pray for these leaders so that, even if they persecute us, we will live "a tranquil and quiet life in all godliness and dignity" under their rule. Just imagine the hostility that might grow in your heart toward rulers and leaders who were persecuting you; yet Paul says to pray for them. Through such praying the church will be prepared and equipped to live lives of godliness and dignity amid persecution.

There's also a second goal of our praying. Not only do we pray for peace amid persecution, but we also pray for **salvation for persecutors**. We pray that rulers, leaders, and even persecutors would, to borrow the language of verse 4, "come to the knowledge of the truth." John Chrysostom, one of the early church fathers, pointed out that it is much more difficult to hate someone when you are praying for them (Chrysostom, "Homilies," 13:426). You are less likely to despise and react negatively against them. When you pray for someone, you can actually begin to love that person.

In all of this, Paul is saying first and foremost to the church, "Pray." For all kinds of people and for leaders in high positions. For the spread of the gospel through a peaceful, quiet, godly, and dignified church. This is the picture Paul was painting at the start of 1 Timothy 2, and it leads to this important implication: **The progress of the gospel in the world is dependent on the prayers of God's people in the church.** While salvation ultimately belongs to God, and even our prayers are His work in us, God has chosen to use the prayers of His people to accomplish His will. We desperately need to hear this truth. We are surrounded by people—from our own city to the ends of the earth—who are lost, perishing, and on their way to everlasting suffering. But we want them to know eternal satisfaction in Christ. We're on a life-saving mission, and the Bible is literally urging us here to pray. Richard Baxter, the old English pastor, put it this way:

> Let your heart yearn for your ungodly neighbors. Alas, there is but a step between them and death and hell. Many hundred diseases are waiting, ready to seize on them and if they die unregenerate, they will be lost forever. Have you hearts of rock that cannot pity men in such a case as this? Do you not care who is damned as long as you are saved? If so, you have sufficient cause to pity yourselves, for it is a frame of spirit utterly inconsistent with grace. . . . Do you live close by them? Or, do you meet them in the streets or work with them or travel with them or sit and talk with them and say nothing to them of their souls? If their houses were on fire, you would run and help them. Will you not help them when their souls are almost at the fire of hell? (Di Gangi, *Golden Treasury*, 92–93)

Oh, Christian, see these people! See the faces you work with, the people you live next to. You will stand in a shopping line next to them this coming week. These are souls destined either for eternal suffering or eternal satisfaction—either hell apart from Christ or heaven with Him. Pray and yearn for the advancement of the gospel to all kinds of people in your city and across the world.

A. B. Simpson, the founder of the Christian and Missionary Alliance, was said to wake up in the morning, bow on his knees, clutch a globe, and weep in prayer. May that be a picture of our lives not only as we scatter throughout the week but also as we gather together with other believers. We should take time in our worship gatherings to intercede in prayer for all kinds of people spread across the globe. Next we'll see that there's a theological motivation behind this kind of prayer.

The Theological Motivation
1 TIMOTHY 2:3-6

Paul has told us whom and what to pray for, but what drives us to pray like this? This is where verses 3-6 come in, and they're some of the most beautiful verses in all of Scripture. One writer has said that these words contain "the key, not merely to the New Testament, but to the whole Bible, for they crystallize into a phrase the sum and substance of its message" (Packer, *God's Words*, 109). In short, the motivation behind our praying for the world is God's passion for the world. Paul gives us at least three different aspects of this theological motivation.

First, **we pray because God desires the salvation of all people** (v. 4). When you begin to pray for all kinds of people in the world to be saved—Jews and Gentiles, friends and enemies, Democrats and Republicans, reached and unreached people groups—your heart is coming in line with the heart of God Himself, for He desires their salvation. However, we need to be clear about what this does and does not mean.

This does *not* mean all will be saved. Some people have used this passage to argue for universalism, the belief that all people will be saved. The reasoning runs like this: Because God desires all people to be saved, and God always gets what He desires, then all people will be saved. That's definitely not what this passage, or Scripture as a whole, teaches. Scripture is clear that we are only saved by grace through faith in Christ (Eph 2:8-9), and only those who trust in His salvation will experience eternal life (John 3:36).

In addition, **this does *not* mean God's will has been thwarted**. Some people have made the following argument: If God desires all people to be saved, and not all people are saved, then ultimately God is not in control of everything in the world. This is clearly not true. From beginning to end, Scripture is clear that God is sovereign over all things and that His will cannot be thwarted (Job 42:2). While this topic has long fueled theological discussions, God has both a *decreed* will and a *declared* will. His decreed will involves what He ordains to take place in the world, while His declared will includes what He commands and makes known in His Word.[7] An illustration may be helpful at this point.

Let's assume, for the sake of illustration, that I am going to lie to someone tomorrow. Question: Is my lying to this person in the will of God? Well, no, not in the sense of God's declared will. He has said clearly, "Do not lie" (Lev 19:11 NIV; Col 3:9), so I would be disobeying God's will. At the same time my lie does not catch God by surprise (Ps 139:4). He's not going to say, "Whoa, I didn't see that coming." Everything I do is ultimately under the sovereignty of His decreed will so in that sense my lying is actually in His will. God is sovereign, even over the worst things in this world, though He Himself never sins or does evil.

Putting together our responsibility and God's sovereignty is not easy to understand, but we have to affirm the things Scripture makes clear. God said, "Do not murder" (Exod 20:13; Deut 5:17). That's His declared will. Yet He was sovereign over the murder of His Son on a cross (Isa 53:10; Acts 2:23). God knew it was going to happen, and He ordained it to happen. There's certainly mystery here, but know this: God's decreed will cannot be thwarted (Dan 4:35).

So we've seen that God's desire for all to be saved does *not* lead to universalism, and it does *not* mean He's not in control of all things; however, **this *does* mean God loves all people**. It is clear from 1 Timothy 2:3-4 that God loves all people and He desires their salvation. We find this in other passages as well. Second Peter 3:9 says that the Lord "is patient with you, not wanting any to perish but all to come to repentance." Or listen to God's Word to the prophet Ezekiel:

> *I take no pleasure in the death of the wicked, but rather that the wicked person should turn from his way and live. Repent, repent of your evil ways! Why will you die, house of Israel?* (Ezek 33:11)

Because God desires the salvation of all people, we should pray for the salvation of all people. When you pray for lost family members, friends, neighbors, enemies, and people groups who are hostile to the

---

[7] God's declared will is also referred to as His "revealed" or "moral" will because it refers to what He has revealed for us to do in His Word (Grudem, *Systematic Theology*, 332).

gospel, pray knowing that God loves them and that He desires their salvation.

The second theological motivation behind our prayer is this: **We pray because God deserves the honor of all people**. Paul began verse 5 by saying, "For there is one God." This seems like such a simple statement, but it is full of significance. There is not one god for one group of people, and then another god for a different group of people, so that all kinds of people can worship all kinds of gods. No, one God deserves the praise of all people. John Stott helpfully reminds us that monotheism drives missions (Stott, *Message*, 67). He points to passages like Isaiah 45:21-22:

> There is no other God but Me,
> a righteous God and Savior;
> there is no one except Me.
> Turn to Me and be saved,
> all the ends of the earth.
> For I am God,
> and there is no other.

Ultimately, we live and work and go on life-saving missions all over our city and around the world because we know there is one God and He deserves the praise, honor, and adoration of all people.

It follows that if God deserves the honor of all people, then **worship is the fuel of world praying**. We gather with other believers to declare there is one God. Our God is greater, stronger, and higher than any other. We sing that (Chris Tomlin, "Our God"), we believe that, and we pray like that. This is the heart of the Lord's Prayer: "Our Father in heaven, Your name be honored as holy" (Matt 6:9). However, worship is more than just the fuel of world praying.

Worship is the goal of world praying. We are praying night and day, week after week, for all kinds of people in the world to come to a saving knowledge of God so they might bow down and worship Him. That's what we're after in our praying—worldwide worship. We look forward to the day when all people will worship God's name. Do you see the theological motivation here? We long for God to get the glory He is due.

Finally, there's a third theological motivation behind our prayers: **We pray because Christ died for the rescue of all people**. We read in verse 5 that there is not only one God but also "one mediator between God and humanity, Christ Jesus, Himself human, who gave Himself—a ransom for all" (vv. 5-6). This word "ransom" literally refers to the price that would be paid for the rescue, or release, of a prisoner. This is the gospel in a nutshell. God, the One who is completely holy in all His ways and completely just in all His judgments, stands over against us sinners, who are completely deserving of all His judgments. Therefore, we desperately need a mediator to pay our ransom. Enter Jesus.

Jesus is unique in who He is. He is the perfect mediator because He is uniquely able to identify with both parties. No one else is qualified to represent both God and mankind. **He is fully able to identify with God** because He *is* divine, fully God (Col 2:9). Yet, at the same time, **He is fully able to identify with humanity** since He is "Himself *human*" (emphasis added). Jesus was, and is, fully human, like us in every way "yet without sin" (Heb 4:15). He is uniquely qualified to stand in the middle in order to bring together both God and man.

Not only is He unique in who He is, but **Jesus is also unique in what He did**. He gave Himself as a ransom by dying for us, though He did not deserve death. Jesus had no sin (1 John 3:5). He died even though **mankind alone owed the price**. We are sinners, and we are the ones who deserve to die. But the reality is that we couldn't pay the price that needed to be paid, the infinite wrath of a holy God. **God alone could pay this price** (Anselm, "Why God Became Man," 176). And how did He do that? In Christ! In Christ, God took the full payment of sin upon Himself, and in the process He rescued us from sin and death. The payment was paid and the rescue was made.

Finally, we see that **Jesus is unique in what He does**. Jesus is not just our mediator in the past through what He did on the cross, as glorious as that reality is. **He lives as our mediator** *right now* at the Father's right hand. That's right: today, at this moment, Jesus is interceding for us, standing before God on our behalf. He is the constant, continual means by which we approach the throne of God in worship. Oh, to know that Christ, even now, is our mediator!

Finally, we see that Jesus is unique in that **He leads us on mission**. In the Great Commission, Jesus promises to be with us always, even "to the end of the age" (Matt 28:20). He enables and empowers all that we do. Apart from Him we can do nothing (John 15:5). The Son of God leads His church by His Word and through His Spirit.

The Obvious Implication
1 TIMOTHY 2:7

There is an obvious implication to our prayers and the theological motivations behind them. The implication for Paul is spelled out in verse 7: "For this I was appointed a herald, an apostle (I am telling the truth; I am not lying), and a teacher of the Gentiles in faith and truth." Even though Paul was talking specifically here about his own unique role as an apostle, what he said applies, in large part, to every follower of Christ. **As we pray to God for all people, we preach the gospel to all people**. We know that God desires the salvation of all people (v. 4), that He is worthy of their praise (v. 5), and that Christ has died for their rescue (v. 6), so we should begin to share this gospel with everyone. Consider two different ways in which this plays out in our lives.

First, **we herald the cross of Christ**. Paul referred to himself as "a herald" of the gospel message in verse 7. That word "herald" is not one that we use much today. It was used in ancient times to refer to someone who would make an important announcement, such as an announcer at an athletic event or a political messenger in a royal court. This is a picture of what we do as followers of Christ—we herald the gospel.

You, brother or sister in Christ, are a herald this week. Announce to people who are dying in their sin that there is a Savior. Tell them they don't have to fear death. Tell them Christ the King has conquered death. Tell them about eternal life in Him, that they might be saved from eternal death. This leads us to the second implication.

We teach the commands of Christ. After people trust in the cross of Christ, we teach them the commands of Christ. This too is part of the Great Commission, for Jesus told us to teach everything that He has commanded (Matt 28:20). We make known the truth of God's Word. This is what the church is to be about.

The Coming Conclusion

God's Word leaves no doubt as to the outcome of our mission. Because of God's purposes and the work of Christ on our behalf, **we pray with confidence and we preach with boldness**. Revelation 5:8-10 gives us a glimpse of where our mission is heading, and it has everything to do with what we've just seen in 1 Timothy 2. Revelation 5:8 says of Christ, "When He took the scroll, the four living creatures and the 24 elders fell down before the Lamb. Each one had a harp and gold bowls filled with incense, which are the prayers of the saints." Commentators vary on what exactly the prayers of the saints are here, but most believe they include the prayers of the saints in heaven (see Rev 6:9-11) as well as the prayers of saints on earth who are longing for God's kingdom to come. As those prayers are lifted before the Lord, we read of a new song:

> *You are worthy to take the scroll*
> *and to open its seals,*
> *because You were slaughtered,*
> *and You redeemed people*
> *for God by Your blood*
> *from every tribe and language*
> *and people and nation.*
> *You made them a kingdom*
> *and priests to our God,*
> *and they will reign on the earth.* (5:9-10)

John's vision has everything to do with what our lives are to be about and what the church is to be about. We can pray with confidence for all people to come to a saving knowledge of Christ, and we can preach to them with boldness, all the while knowing that **our mission will prevail** and **our mediator will be praised**. One day individuals from every tribe and language and people and nation will be ransomed. This is what Revelation 5:9 tells us, and it's what God desires according to 1 Timothy 2:4. Therefore, we can be confident in this mission.

Jesus Christ is worthy of the praise of all people. When we take the gospel to our neighbors and to the ends of the earth, we do it for the glory of our King. Make no mistake about it: He *will* be praised!

Reflect and Discuss

1. How do advertisements encourage each person to determine what is good in his or her life? Which particular advertisements promote something as good or desirable when it in fact violates scriptural principles?
2. In what way is praying the easiest thing to do? In what way is it difficult?

3. What different kinds of people are there in your life? In what ways do you pray for them differently? In what ways are their prayer needs the same?

4. What kinds of prayers should you pray for politicians you don't agree with? How might your prayers affect your attitude toward such authorities?

5. What advantages to spreading the gospel are provided by the situation in the country where you live? What are the disadvantages?

6. How does an understanding of the difference between God's decreed will and His declared will help us avoid endorsing universalism on the one hand or compromising God's sovereignty on the other?

7. How would you describe God's sovereignty to a high school class? How would you express a person's responsibility for his own actions in the light of God's sovereignty?

8. What is the connection between what God gets when we pray (worldwide worship) and what people get (eternal life)?

9. Why is it important that Jesus is fully God? Why is it important that Jesus is fully human?

10. How does it encourage you to know that Christ is interceding for you right now?

What About Women, Paul?

1 TIMOTHY 2:8-15

Main Idea: Men and women should glorify God in the church by gladly submitting to the commands and patterns laid out in Scripture.

I. **To Divisive Men in the Church (2:8)**
   A. Pray with purity before God.
   B. Pray with peace before others.

II. **To Distracting Women in the Church (2:9-10)**
   A. Adorn yourself with modest dress.
   B. Adore God through a Christlike demeanor.

III. **On the Distinctive Roles of Men and Women in the Church (2:11-15)**
   A. Two principles
      1. The principle of harmony: We interpret each Scripture in light of all of Scripture.
      2. The principle of history: God has revealed scriptural truth in the context of specific historical and cultural settings.
   B. Two reminders
      1. God created men and women with equal dignity.
      2. God created men and women with complementary roles.
   C. Two prohibitions
      1. Women should not teach as elders/pastors/overseers in the church.
      2. Women should not lead as elders/pastors/overseers in the church.
   D. Two questions
      1. As a woman teaches/leads, is she reflecting God's pattern in Scripture?
      2. As a woman teaches/leads, is she reinforcing God's priorities in the home?
   E. Two reasons
      1. God's design in creation: God gives authority to man.
      2. Satan's distortion of creation: man abdicates authority to woman.

F. Two things we don't know for sure
   1. Is 1 Timothy 2:15 talking about salvation through the off-spring of Eve?
   2. Is 1 Timothy 2:15 talking about the significance of women nurturing children?
G. Two things we do know for sure
   1. Women are sanctified as they glorify God in the distinct roles and responsibilities He has entrusted to them.
   2. Women are saved not through the birth of a child but through the death of Christ, who died to make us the men and women God created us to be.

If you're looking for a passage of Scripture that runs directly counter to the prevailing wisdom of our culture, then 1 Timothy 2:8-15 is a good place to start. Our culture is terribly twisted on issues of gender and sexuality, and the pressure for the church to compromise and conform on these issues is great. Pastor Mark Dever captures the seriousness of these realities:

> The most important revolution of the [last] century has been the sexual revolution. . . . Contraception replaced conception. Pleasure was separated from responsibility. It was as if a license was given out, legitimizing the bending of every part of our lives around serving ourselves. Since that time, divorce, remarriage, abortion, premarital sex, and extramarital sex, as well as homosexuality have been accepted by increasing percentages of the public. Pornography is huge business. This is not just a problem with society out there. Many churches have found their members plagued by failed marriages and illicit affairs, by so-called private sins that turn into public disgraces, some of which are known, some of which are not yet known. (Dever, *Message*, 547–48)

We live in a culture, on a world, and (sadly) amid a church marked by rampant sexual immorality, skyrocketing divorce, the degradation of marriage, and the confusion of gender. The current debate over homosexuality and same-sex marriage is just one example of these disturbing trends. But these issues are much larger than mere politics, and as pastor John Piper has reminded us, the results have been disastrous:

> Confusion over the meaning of [manhood and womanhood] today is epidemic. The consequence of this confusion is not a free and happy harmony among gender-free persons. . . . The consequence rather is more divorce, more homosexuality, more sexual abuse, more promiscuity, more social awkwardness, and more emotional distress and suicide that come with the loss of God-given identity. (Piper, "Vision," 33)

The issue of manhood and womanhood strikes at the core of who we are and who God is, which makes a passage like 1 Timothy 2:8-15 sound laughable to the world. However, this passage is essential to the church. God's Word is not out of line, and it is not out of date; it is true and right and good. May we repent of our unbelief and arrogance and gladly submit to God's good design.

To Divisive Men in the Church
1 TIMOTHY 2:8

When we come to this text, we need to remember that it does not stand alone. It is tied to what comes before it in 1 Timothy and, as we'll see in chapter 3 concerning elders and deacons, what comes after. Paul was calling Timothy and the church at Ephesus to pray and to worship in light of the following realities: God's desire for the salvation of all people (2:4), God's deserving of the worship of all people (2:5), and Christ's death for all people (2:6). So we've already seen in chapter 2 *who* to pray for and *what* to pray for. Now Paul is telling us who we need to *be* as we pray—men and women who bring glory to God in the church.

So this text does not stand alone in 1 Timothy, but neither does it stand alone in history. Paul was clearly addressing situations and problems that were evident in the church at Ephesus in the first century, and these instructions don't just come out of nowhere. They were written to a specific people at a specific time, and though we don't have all of the details, some things are clear from this passage. In verse 8 Paul talked about men who were either not leading in prayer at all, or they were praying in the church while fighting with one another. On the other hand, verses 9-12 talk about women who were wearing some distracting things to church, and they were apparently disrupting the teaching and leadership of the church in some way. Nevertheless, even though these various instructions to men and women come out of a specific historical context, God's Word still applies to *all* people at *all* times. But in order to understand how it applies to all people in all times, we've got to put ourselves in the shoes of the people who were first hearing these words.

Paul mentioned in verse 8 that he wanted men to pray "in every place," which is either a reference to the many homes that the church in Ephesus would meet in, or more broadly, the gatherings of believers across the world. Either way Paul wanted men to pray in all these places, and most importantly he wanted them to **pray with purity before God**. He spoke of "lifting up holy hands," with the emphasis here not so much on posture as on purity. Two examples from the Psalms speak to the kind of purity God desires. The first one comes from Psalm 24:

> *Who may ascend the mountain of the* Lord*?*
> *Who may stand in His holy place?*
> *The one who has clean hands and a pure heart.*
> (Ps 24:3-4)

Psalm 26 says something similar:

> *I wash my hands in innocence*
> *and go around your altar,* Lord. (Ps 26:6)

Both of these passages emphasize the need for God's people to be pure. In Psalm 26:6 the psalmist talks about going around the altar, a reference to the temple worship in the Old Testament. When he speaks of washing his hands, he may be alluding to the pools of water the people washed their hands in before they prayed as a picture of the cleansing of their hearts (Ryken, *1 Timothy*, 78). We see, then, that purity is essential to prayer.

It makes no sense to hold on to sin in your life while approaching a holy God in prayer. Instead, humbly confess your sin, be cleansed by the mercy of God through Christ, and then pray with purity before God. Though Paul was addressing men in verse 8, all followers of Christ need to ask themselves the following question: Is there a deliberate sin that I am holding on to in my life? If so, confess it now. Don't play games with God. Be pure before Him.

Not only does Paul say that we should pray with purity before God, but we must also **pray with peace before others**. This is what it means to pray "without anger or argument." Ask yourself another question: Is there anything in my life right now that is unreconciled with another brother or sister in Christ? Is there anger, quarreling, or conflict? If so, make it right. Peace with God is artificial if there is not peace with others.

Clearly there were false teachers and all kinds of disputes in the Ephesian church, and the situation was apparently contributing to an attitude of anger and conflict among believers (1 Tim 1:4; 6:4-5). To this situation Paul essentially said, "Don't pray before God when you're not right with your brother." We're reminded of Jesus' words in Matthew 5:23-24:

> So if you are offering your gift on the altar, and there you remember that your brother has something against you, leave your gift there in front of the altar. First go and be reconciled with your brother, and then come and offer your gift.

We have a tendency to rush into corporate worship and bypass our need to honestly confess our sin before God. But a right heart attitude is crucial for prayer and for God-honoring worship in the church. By the grace of Christ, let your hearts be clean before God. Worship and pray with purity before God and peace before others.

To Distracting Women in the Church
1 TIMOTHY 2:9-10

After addressing the men, Paul turns his attention to women who had become a distraction in the church. We can infer that this was the case from his instructions in verse 9. So what exactly was Paul talking about here? Do we need to post security officers at the entrance to the church in order to check for braided hair and costly jewelry? This is another situation where it's helpful to understand the culture into which Paul was speaking, a culture that in many ways is parallel with our own.

Like many ancient cities into which Christianity was born, Ephesus was filled with sexual immorality. It was common for women to use ornate fashion to attract attention to themselves, sometimes in seductive ways. But Paul gave the women in the church at Ephesus an altogether different exhortation: **Adorn yourself with modest dress**. And consequently, Christian women today should also have a different motivation in their dress than the surrounding culture.

First, Paul said, **do not draw attention to physical beauty**. Women should not dress in a way that draws other people's attention, particularly men. Their clothing should be "modest," a word that can have sexual overtones (cf. Ryken, *1 Timothy*, 83). Modesty is a huge issue in our own culture, for we are extremely liberal when it comes to what women wear: skin-tight clothes, low necklines, high hemlines, and short shorts are the norm. This kind of clothing falls far short of the biblical ideal of modesty and self-control.

With all due respect to our sisters in Christ, the way some women dress in the church is at best a distraction from honoring God and at worst an attempt to seduce men in the church to sin. Sisters in Christ should not be asking, What makes me look the most attractive? That's the wrong motivation. Instead, the question should be, What can I wear that best demonstrates a humble heart devoted to the worship of God? This biblical and God-centered perspective should affect everything about us, even our clothing.

Along the same lines Paul gave Christian women another exhortation: **Do not draw attention to worldly wealth**. Part of the point of mentioning the "hairstyles, gold, pearls" and the "expensive apparel" is that these things were highlighting the distinction between the wealthy and the poor in the church. This is of the world! Some women were using their dress to assert their social status, and to these women Paul says not to adorn yourself with that which draws attention to you, particularly when you gather with the church for worship. Remember the One you are competing with for attention—God! You want your worship and your life in every way to draw attention to Him.

In addition to modest outer adornment, women should also **adore God through a Christlike demeanor**. Don't miss Paul's point here. He's not saying, "Don't adorn yourself with anything." Instead, he's saying, "Adorn yourself with godliness." This is what matters—the fruit of faith in Christ. Paul calls on Christian women to be adorned "with good works, as is proper for women who affirm that they worship God." When you look in the mirror, look for good works. Jesus' words in Matthew 5:16 come to mind: "Let your light shine before men, so that they may see your good works and give glory to your Father in heaven."

May God raise up women across our churches who refuse to get up any day, especially on Sunday, and think, "What can I wear today that will make me look good to the people around me?" Instead, may our sisters in Christ ask, "How can I dress, and what can I do today that will draw the most attention to the glory of my God?" Women in the church should not distract others but instead live to attract others to God.

On the Distinctive Roles of Men and Women in the Church
1 TIMOTHY 2:11-15

Paul continued addressing women in the rest of chapter 2. Again, he was likely addressing specific things that were going on in the church at Ephesus. We know from chapter 4 that teachers at Ephesus were encouraging men and women not to marry and thereby undercutting the beauty of marriage. And we see in chapter 5 that younger women were not getting married but were instead spending all their time gossiping in the church. When we turn to 2 Timothy, we find out that a group of women were giving in to false teaching and living according to worldly passions (2 Tim 3:6). So what we have in Ephesus is a problem, likely a significant problem, with women undercutting godly doctrine, godly behavior, and godly leadership in the church. Keep in mind, however, that Paul was not just picking on women here. He just spent all of chapter 1 railing against men in the church who were teaching false doctrine. The apostle was addressing a variety of issues in this letter.

First Timothy 2:11-15 represents one of the most controversial passages in the New Testament. As we think about how to understand these verses, we need to begin by considering two principles of interpretation, both for this passage and for any passage of Scripture. The first principle is **the principle of harmony** (Stott, *Message*, 74), which says that we interpret each particular Scripture in light of all Scripture. This fits with what Paul said in 2 Timothy 3:16, that "all Scripture is inspired by God," or as the NIV translates it, "All Scripture is *God-breathed*" (emphasis added). Among other things this verse tells us that Scripture has one author, God. And since we know that He does not contradict Himself, whenever we see two passages that *seem* to contradict each other, we should look at each passage in its context with the conviction that the passages are ultimately unified.

The way we understand the doctrine of the Trinity may provide us with a helpful example of this principle of harmony. In the Lord's Prayer Jesus tells us to pray to the Father, whose name is to "be honored as holy" (Matt 6:9). So the Father is clearly God, fully divine. Then when we get to John 10:29-38, we learn that Jesus is God. Yet, according to Acts 5:3-4, the Holy Spirit is also God. This forces us to ask the following question: How can one God be our Father *and* Jesus the Son *and* the Holy Spirit? We have to understand these truths and these texts in light of one another. There is one God, and He is revealed in three persons: Father, Son, and Holy Spirit. Although we don't have one verse that spells this out completely, the full testimony of Scripture makes the doctrine of the Trinity inescapable. Much more could be said about how we arrive at this conclusion, but the point is this: We put all of Scripture together to understand each individual passage of Scripture. This is the principle of harmony.

We also need to understand **the principle of history**. God has revealed scriptural truth in the context of specific historical and cultural settings. For example, the letter of 1 Timothy was written from Paul to Timothy for the church at Ephesus in the first century, so we have a specific historical and cultural context. This should lead us to ask at least two questions when we approach the text.[8]

First, **what part of the text is cultural expression (which changes)?** Once again, a concrete example will help illustrate the point. Let's consider Paul's exhortation to women about their "elaborate hairstyles" (v. 9). If we were ministering to an African tribe where Christian women had preserved traditional hairstyles with intricate designs, what would we say to them? Is this sinful? Paul was not saying that all elaborate hairstyles were always sinful in all cultures; he was saying that elaborate hairstyles in Ephesus violated modesty, decency, and good sense. So if the women in that African tribe were dressing to elicit lust or envy, then we would address that as a moral issue. But if the intricate braiding is neither a sign of wealth nor an attempt to seduce, then the answer is "no"; we're not dealing with sinful behavior. In African culture elaborate hairstyles are actually modest, decent, and sensible. In that culture, elaborate hairstyles do not express the same meaning as they did in the Ephesian culture. This is why understanding the cultural context matters.

We need to ask a second question as we approach the text, namely, **what part of the text is central revelation (which never changes)?** The specific example Paul gives is "elaborate hairstyles, gold, pearls, or expensive apparel"; the general principle he is commending is "modest

---

[8] John Stott says that we must "discern in Scripture between God's essential revelation (which is changeless) and its cultural expression (which is changeable)" (Stott, *Message*, 78).

clothing . . . decency and good sense." The examples will vary in different cultures, but the principle will remain the same. Clearly God has said to all people of all times in all cultures not to be adorned with things that draw other people's attention for the wrong reasons. That principle always remains true. If something is part of God's central revelation, and not merely a cultural expression, then we submit to His Word.

Let me give one word of caution as we apply this latter principle of interpretation. People have begun irresponsibly to throw all kinds of truths out of the Bible, claiming these truths are just commands about cultural issues. Take the issue of homosexuality as an example. Homosexuality was a problem in the time of the Bible, these people say, because the science wasn't available then to let people know that same-sex desires are natural and thus can't be changed. We know better now, or so we are told. This attitude about Scripture is a dangerous mind-set.

We must be extremely careful not to accommodate our culture by discarding truth that the Bible addresses clearly and repeatedly. Homosexuality, like many other sins, is identified throughout Scripture as part of man's rebellion against God, regardless of one's culture or context (Lev 18:22; Rom 1:26-27). When Paul forbade it, his words were grounded in God's pattern in creation (Gen 1:27-28). This is central revelation, not cultural expression.

Now that we've looked at two general principles for interpreting Scripture, we need to consider how to think about the specific issue of gender. It would take much more space to explain fully the foundation of biblical manhood and womanhood we find in Genesis 1–3, but we should note at least **two reminders** from those important early chapters. First, **God created men and women with equal dignity**. That is, male and female are equally valuable before God.[9] Therefore, to demean men or women is to sin against God. Paul's instructions in 1 Timothy 2 have nothing to do with the *value* of men and women; rather, he was talking about the *roles* of men and women, which leads to the second reminder.

God created men and women with complementary roles. Men and women are different and distinct in their respective roles. Man was created with a role that complements woman, and woman was created with

---

[9] The same thing is taught in 1 Peter 3:7, where husband and wife are called "coheirs of the grace of life."

a role that complements man. And this is all by God's good design. It is even in the nature of God. Once again, the relationships of the Trinity provide us with a helpful analogy.

The Father, as we saw earlier, is fully God. And the Son is also fully God. Yet the Father and the Son have different roles: the Son *submits* to the Father (Phil 2:8), and the Father *directs* the Son (John 14:31). The Son doesn't complain, "Oh, I've *got* to submit to the Father," and the Father isn't domineering over the Son. There are different roles among the persons of the Trinity, though each person has equal value. And all of this is in beautiful harmony. Similarly, God has designed men and women with equal dignity and complementary roles.

God's good design is seen **in the home** as husband and wife relate to each other with specific, complementary roles. In Ephesians 5:22-32 Paul instructed wives to submit to their husbands "as to the Lord" (v. 22), and husbands were commanded to love their wives "just as Christ loved the church and gave Himself for her" (v. 25). In a similar way, 1 Timothy 2:11-15 tells us that there are also complementary roles **in the church**. Men and women have distinct roles to fulfill when God's people gather together. But remember, Paul's instructions in this passage are not new, for they accord with what we see all the way back in Genesis 1–3. Whether in the home or in the church, God has assigned equal value to men and women, yet with roles that complement each other.

So we've considered two principles and two reminders, and this leads us to **two prohibitions** in this text. Paul said in 1 Timothy 2:12, "I do not allow a woman to teach or to have authority over a man." The first prohibition is that women should not *teach* men in the church. We know Paul encouraged women to teach in some settings, since Titus 2:3 makes clear that older women should teach younger women. Paul was not making a blanket statement, as if women like Beth Moore were in sin. But what, then, was Paul saying? To understand the apostle's point, it's helpful to connect these two distinct prohibitions—do not teach and do not exercise authority over a man. This perspective is warranted from the broader context of 1 Timothy.

In chapter 3 Paul talked about elders, or pastors, with authority in the church. And these elders express their authority by doing what? By teaching. In 1 Timothy 3:2 we see that the ability to teach is a qualification for an elder, so that you lead the church through the teaching of God's Word. That's the only authority anyone has to lead in the church. We see the same thing in 1 Timothy 5, where Paul said in verse 17, "The elders who are good leaders should be considered worthy of an ample honorarium, especially those who work hard at preaching and teaching." So the picture in 1 Timothy is clear that elders do two primary things: they lead and they teach. To put it another way, they teach with the authority to lead. Therefore, when Paul said women are not to teach or exercise authority over men (1 Tim 2:12), he was pointing specifically to the two primary responsibilities of elders.

At the very least two things are being prohibited in 1 Timothy 2:11-15. First, based on what we've just discussed above, it is clear that **women should not teach as elders (or pastors or overseers) in the church.**[10] Men who don't have a gift of teaching or who don't meet the qualifications of an elder in 1 Timothy 3:1-7 likewise should not teach as elders in the church. We'll see more about elder qualifications in the next chapter, but Paul was making clear here that even a woman who has a gift of teaching is not intended by God to teach as an elder. Instead, **women listen willingly to the biblical instruction of elders.** When the text says that they should "learn in silence with full submission" (v. 11), it is not saying that once a woman steps into the gathering of the church, she should go mute. We know that because at other points in the New Testament we see women praying or prophesying when Christians gather (1 Cor 11:5). This text is simply saying that a woman should listen attentively with a teachable spirit to the God-ordained leaders in the church when they are teaching the Word.

Paul and other New Testament authors also made clear that **women should teach in various settings of the church in accord with elder instruction.** This means that, outside of elder leadership, there are all sorts of teaching possibilities for women. In addition to the command in Titus 2:3 for older women to teach younger women, Scripture mentions a number of instances where women played a significant teaching role. Consider the following:

- Timothy received instruction from his mother and grandmother (2 Tim 1:5; 3:14).
- Pricilla and her husband Aquila both took Apollos aside and "explained the way of God to him more accurately" (Acts 18:26).

---

[10] The terms "elder," "pastor," and "overseer" ("bishop" in KJV) are synonymous in the New Testament. For example, Paul uses the terms "elder" and "overseer" interchangeably in Titus 1:5-9. (See also Acts 20:17, 28.)

There is also a more general teaching role in the New Testament, applying to both men and women. For example:

- Men and women both make disciples, which involves going, baptizing, and teaching people to obey everything Christ has commanded us (Matt 28:19-20).
- Paul told the whole church—men and women—to be "teaching and admonishing one another" as the word of Christ dwelt in them richly (Col 3:16).
- Paul seemed to allow for women praying and prophesying in public worship, though with proper humility and submission (1 Cor 11).

Women who are gifted at teaching should use their gifts to build up the body of Christ but not in the role of elder. Their teaching should be in accord with, and not contrary to, what the elders of the church teach. Of course, this requirement applies to both men *and* women who are teaching in the church.

After the prohibition for women not to *teach* as elders, Paul gave a second and related prohibition in verse 12: **Women should not lead as elders/pastors/overseers in the church**. Instead of exercising authority, women should "learn quietly with all submissiveness" (v. 11 ESV). By God's grace **women submit gladly to the servant leadership of elders**. I emphasize the term "servant leadership" because it needs to be emphasized, for elders are intended by God to lead by serving, or more specifically, by serving the body with the Word of Christ. An elder or pastor is intended to love, care for, nurture, and serve the body of Christ by diligently and wisely teaching the Word of Christ. And as this happens, Paul said, women (and other men who are not elders) should gladly submit to such servant leadership. They shouldn't rebel against the leadership of qualified, Christlike men in the church.

Does that mean, then, that a woman can never be in any type of leadership position in the church? I don't think that's what Paul was saying at all. Based on the rest of the New Testament, **women should lead in various positions of the church under the authority of elder leadership**. In other words, when they submit to elders, women are free to lead in a variety of different positions. They are intended by God to thrive in various ministries across the church.

When you look throughout the New Testament, you see women teaching, helping, serving, equipping, and spreading the gospel. As

John Piper has said, "The fields of opportunity are endless . . . for the entire church to be mobilized in ministry, male and female. Nobody is to be at home watching soaps and reruns while the world burns. God intends to equip and mobilize [all] the saints [under the leadership of] a company of qualified men who take primary responsibility for leadership and teaching in the church" (Piper, "Freedom to Minister"). Don't tell Lottie Moon or Amy Carmichael or Elisabeth Elliot or Kay Arthur that they are sidelined in the church. These women have embraced exactly what Scripture has outlined, and they have thrived for the glory of God through ministering in the church.

Some might ask, "Apart from an elder, are there any other positions a woman should not lead in? What about a small group? What about teaching theology in a class or at a seminary?" There are so many different scenarios and possibilities, each of which I believe need to be approached by the elders of the church with care and consideration. However, I think there are at least two questions that should guide elders on these issues.

First, **As a woman teaches or leads, is she reflecting God's pattern in Scripture?** We see women doing many different things in the New Testament, and where we see these things happening in healthy ways in the early church, we can be encouraged to see the same things happening in the contemporary church. Just as you see older women commanded to teach younger women in the New Testament church (Titus 2:3-4), so that needs to happen in our churches today. You also see women teaching children, so it is good for us to foster teaching and leadership roles for women among children. (However, please don't forget that our children also need to see prominent men leading them in the church as well!) This leads us to the second question.

As a woman teaches or leads, is she reinforcing God's priorities in the home? We want to be careful not to undercut God's design in the home with the way we lead in the church. Especially in our day, we want to display godly, humble, loving, and sacrificial leadership by men in the church in a way that models that kind of leadership for men in their homes. And we also want to display glad, willing, godly submission of women in the church that models that kind of life for women in their homes. When we gather as God's people, we should point one another toward biblical faithfulness on these issues of gender.

To be clear, I'm not saying these two questions make everything easy or that all of the answers become evident. However, I do believe these questions are helpful in considering what teaching or leadership roles a woman should have. Scripture is clear on the prohibitions against teaching and leading as an elder; beyond this it's not quite as clear. So we need to be clear where Scripture is clear, and we need to be wise where Scripture is not as clear.

Next, I want to consider **two reasons** from Scripture for understanding these verses in 1 Timothy in this way. First, **God's design in creation: God gives authority to man**. As Paul says in verse 13 of our passage, "Adam was created first, then Eve." This statement tells us that what Paul is saying here is not just cultural expression—this is central revelation. The basis for what Paul says goes all the way back to Genesis 1–2 when God created man *before* woman, a reality that undergirds the headship of man. Paul is not basing his view merely on human opinion, which changes, but on divine revelation, which never changes.

After pointing to God's design in creation, he then points to the second reason for his teaching about gender roles: **Satan's distortion of creation: man abdicates authority and woman assumes it**. When Paul said in verse 14 that it was the woman and not the man who was deceived, he was not saying women shouldn't lead because they're more easily duped. No, he was pointing back again to the picture of sin entering the world in Genesis 3, when Satan subverted God's design by approaching Eve instead of Adam, thereby undercutting Adam's responsibility as the leader of his home. In turn Adam sat back and did nothing, and God's design was distorted. In short, sin entered the world when man abdicated his God-given responsibility to lead. Man didn't step up with godly, gracious leadership. Paul used this truth to say to the church that God's design in the home and in the church is good. God's design for qualified men to lead as elders is good, just as God's design for godly men to lead as husbands is good.

All of this leads to one of Paul's most difficult statements in 1 Timothy 2:15: "But she will be saved through childbearing, if she continues in faith, love, and holiness, with good judgment." What does that mean? **Two things we don't know for sure**.

First, **Is 1 Timothy 2:15 talking about salvation through the offspring of Eve?** Some commentators have said that this verse is a deliberate reference to the fact that, even though the woman ate the fruit first and sin entered the world through her, the promise remains that the Savior would enter the world through her. According to Genesis 3:15, a child would be born through Eve's line that would one day trample the serpent. John Stott espouses this view when he writes the following:

> Earlier in this chapter the one mediator between God and men has been identified as the man Christ Jesus, who of course became a human being by being born of a woman. Further, in the context of Paul's references to the creation and fall, recalling Genesis 2 and 3, a further reference to the coming redemption through the woman's seed, recalling Genesis 3:15, would be most apt. The serpent had deceived her; her posterity would defeat him.
>
> So then, even if certain roles are not open to women, and even if they are tempted to resent their position, they and we must never forget what we [all] owe to a woman. If Mary had not given birth to the Christ child, there would have been no salvation for anybody. No greater honor has ever been given to woman than in the calling of Mary to be the mother of the Savior of the world. (Stott, *Message*, 87–88)

Stott gives us one possible interpretation. A second question leads to an alternate interpretation: **Is 1 Timothy 2:15 talking about the significance of women nurturing children?** In light of the ways women's roles in the home, in marriage, and in bearing children were being undercut by false teachers, could it be that Paul was simply emphasizing the one facet that, without question, only women can do—bear children? A culture can do everything possible to minimize the differences between males and females, but this distinction still remains. No guys are giving birth. Paul was possibly saying that God has created women uniquely, and their responsibilities are uniquely good in the church, in marriage, and in bearing children. All of this should be embraced in faith and love and holiness. In other words, women who are truly followers of Christ must and will persevere in obedience to God's will (though never perfectly) as they anticipate full and final salvation. These are the two most plausible interpretations.

This passage does not mean a woman must bear a child in order to be saved. If Paul believed that, he would not encourage some women to stay single, as he did in 1 Corinthians 7. He'd say, "Get married and have a kid . . . *fast.* Your eternity depends on it!" There are a lot of things we know Paul was *not* saying and some difficult questions about what he *was* saying; however, **two things we do know for sure**. First, **women are**

sanctified as they glorify God in the distinct roles and responsibilities He has entrusted to them. There is meaning and significance behind a woman's gender, so sisters in Christ should be working out their salvation, not as generic persons but as women of God with inherent beauty and value as well as distinct giftings and opportunities. Sisters in Christ should thrive in their roles as wives, mothers, and women of God.

Finally, the second thing we know for sure is that **women are saved not through the birth of a child but through the death of Christ**. For that matter, women *and* men are saved through the death of Christ. Sin has disordered this world we live in, and Satan has distorted God's design for our manhood, our womanhood, our marriages, our families, the church, and the culture. But Christ has come, and He has conquered sin and trampled the Devil. In Christ we can all thrive. **He died to make us the men and women God created us to be**. Will you submit to God's good design?

Reflect and Discuss

1. How does the current sexual climate of our culture affect the church's view of men's and women's roles?

2. How does impurity interfere with prayer? How do we become pure in God's eyes?

3. How does interpersonal conflict interfere with prayer?

4. How does learning about the ancient Ephesian culture contribute to understanding this passage? What principles are timeless and universal?

5. How is your sense of fashion influenced by secular culture? Is it hard for you to buck fashion trends in order to follow scriptural principles? Are you dressing for God or for the people in church?

6. What elements of women's fashion imply wealth? How do men draw attention to their wealth?

7. How would you respond to someone who argues that Paul's instructions concerning women as elders only applied to the ancient Ephesian context?

8. Why do some people look for a reason to ignore certain passages in Scripture? Which passages are you tempted to compromise on?

9. How do the complementary roles of the Father and the Son help us understand the roles of men and women?

10. In what roles are women permitted to serve in your church? Is that policy biblical?

11. In what ways can a woman teach in a church while still submitting to the leadership? Have you seen cases of rebellion or insubordination? Was that action merited?

12. How does Paul use Genesis in 1 Timothy 2:13-14 to support his explanation of the roles of men and women? How does that make the principle central rather than cultural?

13. Does the difficulty in understanding the details of some passages disturb your view of Scripture? What clear truths do you cling to when you are tempted to doubt?

The Gospel and Church Leadership

1 TIMOTHY 3:1-13

Main Idea: A biblical model of church leadership is necessary for the church to display the glory of Christ in its worship and in its witness.

I. **Foundations**
   A. The Bible identifies two primary leadership roles in the church:
      1. Elders, who are servant leaders.
      2. Deacons, who are leading servants.
   B. Church leadership is designed by God to be:
      1. A display of His glory.
      2. Dependent on His gospel.

II. **Four Responsibilities of Elders (3:1-7)**
   A. Lead under the authority of Christ.
   B. Care for the body of Christ.
   C. Teach the Word of Christ.
   D. Model the character of Christ.
      1. The Bottom Line: What will happen if the church imitates this leader?
      2. In his personal life?
      3. In his family life?
      4. In his social/business life?
      5. In his spiritual life?

III. **Three Responsibilities of Deacons (3:8-13)**
   A. Meet needs according to the Word.
   B. Support the ministry of the Word.
   C. Unify the body around the Word.

IV. **The Bottom Line**
   A. The church appoints and follows servant leaders who are whole-heartedly committed to accomplishing the mission of Christ.
   B. The church affirms and honors leading servants who use their gifts to build up the body of Christ.
   C. The church is composed of ministers who multiply the gospel throughout the world.

When you encounter a passage of Scripture dealing with church leadership, are you tempted to skip ahead to something more exciting or relevant? If so, you're probably not alone. I would guess many Christians come to 1 Timothy 3 and think, "What does this have to do with my life?" At this point we need to be reminded that church leadership affects every follower of Christ.

Some believers have been encouraged greatly by church leadership, while others have been hurt in their spiritual journey. In some cases the damage done by a church leader has been so deep that those who once professed Christ have even been pushed away from Christianity altogether. This is why looking at church leadership in Scripture, particularly in our own day, is extremely crucial.

If church leaders are casual about God and holiness and mission, then the church will fall short in these areas. And countless numbers of people who have never heard the name of Jesus will continue to be unreached with the gospel. On the other hand, if church leaders are passionate about these biblical truths, then the church will be strengthened, and, we pray, souls around the world will be transformed by the gospel through the church's witness. So no matter who you are or how you serve in the body of Christ, church leadership matters. Consider, therefore, Paul's instructions in 1 Timothy 3:1-13.

Foundations

The Bible identifies two primary leadership roles in the church: elders, who are servant leaders, and deacons, who are leading servants. Both of these roles are identified in 1 Timothy 3. Depending on your denominational background or tradition, different things may come to mind when you hear about elders and deacons. Churches approach leadership differently, sometimes because their beliefs are based more on tradition than on the Word of God. But even among churches that are serious about obeying the Word, there are still a variety of views on church leadership.

While Scripture gives some clear, nonnegotiable truths that should guide our understanding of church leadership, it doesn't always clearly address what these truths look like in practice. This is why different Bible-believing churches can look different when it comes to leadership. The challenge for us is to take an honest look at the nonnegotiable truths in God's Word and then, grounded in these clear truths, consider how they can best be applied in the context of the family of faith, the church. We'll begin our discussion by considering God's design for the church.

First and foremost, we need to understand that **church leadership is designed by God**. It is not man's invention, so we must avoid imposing our own leadership structure on God's design. God has designed the church's leadership **to be a display of His glory**. Think about it this way: the glory of Christ is displayed in the beauty of His bride, and His bride is the church. Therefore, those who lead the church are to be a visible display of God's glory. Sadly, there are countless ways the glory of Christ has been—and continues to be—compromised before the world because church leaders do not display God's glory. This is extremely serious.

Not only is the church's leadership designed by God to display His glory; it's also designed **to be dependent on His gospel**. Nothing Paul tells us in 1 Timothy 3 is possible without the gospel of Jesus Christ. The character qualifications, the roles, and the responsibilities of church leaders are possible only as a result of Christ living in His people. We must keep in mind that Jesus is our leader and that people are qualified to lead only insofar as He is living and working within them.

Paul began his discussion about church leadership by talking about elders. The word *elder* is a fairly common term in Scripture. In the Old Testament, for example, it's used to describe the leadership in Israel that assisted Moses (Exod 4:29). In the New Testament it can refer to someone of a mature age (1 Tim 5:1) or to spiritual leaders in the Jewish community (Matt 26:3). In the context of 1 Timothy 3, it is significant to note that the term "elder" or "elders" is often used in the New Testament to describe a unique leadership role in the church. In fact, nearly every church we know of in the New Testament is specifically said to have elders. Acts 20:17-31 gives us a clear picture of this point, where we read about Paul's address to the Ephesian elders (see also Phil 1; 1 Pet 5:1-2).

The New Testament uses two other words to describe the role of elders: pastors (Eph 4:11) and overseers (Titus 1:7). We know these words are interchangeable because of passages like Titus 1:5-9, where Paul used the term "elders" in verse 5 and "overseer" in verse 7 to refer to the same position of leadership. We see something similar with the elders in Acts 20:28, as Paul said God has made these men "overseers" who are to "shepherd," even though they were previously referred to as "elders" in verse 17 of the same chapter. In Ephesians 4:11 "pastors" translates the Greek word for "shepherds." Therefore, we know that we are talking about the same role within the church regardless of whether the word used is *pastor, elder,* or *overseer.*

We should also note that the term for *elder* almost always occurs in the plural in the New Testament. Throughout Scripture certain individual leaders are highlighted among God's people, but when we see the word *elder,* there's almost always more than one of them in the church. So the picture we have in Scripture is neither a dictatorship nor a democracy; instead, Christ entrusts elders to lead the church.

Four Responsibilities of Elders
1 TIMOTHY 3:1-7

If God has entrusted his church to elders, then we need to consider the responsibilities of such leaders. It may be helpful to look at Paul's address to the Ephesian elders in Acts 20. Here we get a good picture of what's expected of those who lead God's people. We'll look at four different responsibilities from this passage:

> *Be on guard for yourselves and for all the flock that the Holy Spirit has appointed you to as overseers, to shepherd the church of God, which He purchased with His own blood. I know that after my departure savage wolves will come in among you, not sparing the flock. And men will rise up from your own number with deviant doctrines to lure the disciples into following them. Therefore be on the alert, remembering that night and day for three years I did not stop warning each one of you with tears.* (Acts 20:28-31)

The first responsibility of elders is that they are to **lead under the authority of Christ**. That is, elders are entrusted by Christ with the responsibility of overall leadership in the church. Now we can't forget that **elders belong to the church**, so the elders don't have final authority over the church. When we look at Matthew 18:15-20; 1 Corinthians 5:1-13; and 2 Corinthians 2:5-11, we see that the authority of Christ is ultimately invested in the gathered body of the church. The *church* is held accountable in these passages for letting sin persist in its midst. This is why we call elders our *servant* leaders, because even though God has given elders to guide us, they lead as servants of the church.

As those who belong to the church, elders are appointed by the Spirit of God. You don't campaign to get elected to this position. The Spirit sets aside and appoints men as elders. The church is Christ's and

He leads it by His Spirit. So elders belong to the church, and **the church belongs to Christ**. In addition to being appointed by the Spirit of God, elders are accountable to the Son of God. Paul told the Ephesian elders to "shepherd the church of God, which He purchased with His own blood" (Acts 20:28). Did you catch that last phrase "with *His* own blood"? You cannot approach church leadership lightly when you realize the gravity of Acts 20:28. Leading the church was never designed to be a power struggle. Jesus is in control, and He has all power in the church. Therefore, every leader in the church is accountable to Him. This perspective brings the proper humility, even fear, to church leadership.

The second responsibility of elders from Acts 20 is that they **care for the body of Christ**. Acts 20:28 gives us the picture of a shepherd, and we see the same thing in 1 Peter 5:2: "Shepherd God's flock among you." So what does it look like to shepherd or care for the flock? To summarize, it means first of all that **elders protect the flock**. Paul told the elders to "be on guard" against false doctrine and to expect false teachers, individuals whom Paul referred to as "savage wolves" (Acts 20:28-30). Elders have a God-given responsibility to guard their own lives and the life of the church. This is the front line of spiritual warfare.

In addition to protecting the flock, **elders nurture the flock**. Paul committed the Ephesian elders to the Word (Acts 20:32), "which is able to build you up and give you an inheritance among all who are sanctified." The elder's responsibility is not just to *pet* the sheep; caring for the body of Christ involves *feeding* the sheep. This leads us to the third responsibility of elders, that is, to **teach the Word of Christ**. Paul said earlier in this passage that he did not hesitate to proclaim "the whole plan of God" (Acts 20:27) so that they would be equipped to build up the church through the Word. The Word alone has the power to build up the church, which means the elder's leadership is tied to the Word. If the elder knows the Word and obeys the Word, then he is fit to lead in the church. If he wanders from the Word, he is no longer fit to lead in the church. We don't follow elders or pastors simply because they have a position. We follow them because they know the Word, teach the Word, and follow the Word.

The requirement to teach the Word of Christ means that **elders must know the Word extensively**. They study the Word, memorize the Word, and meditate on the Word. They know why they believe what they believe. They know what the Scriptures say about theological issues. These men are equipped by the Word to address hard questions in the church, and they also know what the Word says about practical issues, such as family life, our interaction with the culture, and numerous social issues encroaching upon us.

Clearly, based on what we've seen so far, elders must have a strong, in-depth knowledge of the Scriptures. But they can't just know the Word extensively; it is imperative that **elders communicate the Word effectively**. We see this in 1 Timothy 3:2 where Paul said that an overseer, or elder, must be able to teach the Word (see also 1 Tim 5:17; Titus 1:7, 9). An elder must know the Word and spread the Word throughout the church and from the church throughout the world. He must be able to persuade people with the Word, plead with people from the Word, comfort people with the Word, encourage people from the Word, instruct people in the Word, and lead the church according to the Word. This is nonnegotiable.

So far we've looked at three responsibilities of elders: they lead under the authority of Christ, care for the body of Christ, and teach the Word of Christ. The fourth responsibility of elders is that they are to **model the character of Christ**.

Several passages have lists of qualifications and responsibilities of elders: 1 Timothy 3:1-7; Titus 1:5-9; and 1 Peter 5:1-3. When you put these lists together, most of the emphasis is on character qualifications. Let's consider, then, what is *not* on these lists and what *is* on these lists. First, several things that aren't on these lists:

- Age: older men should not automatically become elders, and young men should not automatically be disqualified.
- Business success: success in the world doesn't necessarily equate with leadership in the church.
- Likeability: this is not simply a group of men everyone likes.

Before moving on to what *is* on these lists, we should also note that women are not mentioned in connection with the role of elder. Scripture gives no indication whatsoever that the position of overall leadership in the church belongs to a female. Remember, this is not an issue of equality or superiority; it's more like the relationship between a husband and a wife. As the husband is the head of the home and leads in this sphere, so elders are to provide leadership in the church. And I'm convinced that the natural reaction of godly women in the church will be to trust and respect godly men who lead us to accomplish the mission of Christ.

Now we want to consider what *is* required of elders. You may be surprised to find that almost everything in the list in 1 Timothy 3:2-7 is expected of every follower of Christ. Other than being able to teach, these qualifications are intended by Christ for every member of the church. We might even say the qualifications for being an elder simply revolve around exemplifying the character of Christ. *Leaders* in the church are to be *models* in the church. This is why Hebrews 13:7 says to "imitate their faith." This truth ought to weigh on anyone who aspires to lead in Christ's church, since a man cannot lead the church somewhere he is not going himself. Here's **the bottom line: What will happen if the church imitates this leader?**

Here are some questions to ask of a leader in the church. These questions have been taken from 1 Timothy 3:1-7; Titus 1:5-9; and 1 Peter 5:1-4, and they are grouped under four different categories.

In His Personal Life

- Is he self-controlled?
- Is he wise?
- Is he peaceable?
- Is he gentle?
- Is he a sacrificial giver?
- Is he humble?
- Is he patient?
- Is he honest?
- Is he disciplined?

In His Family Life

- Is he the elder in his home?
- If he's single, is he self-controlled?
- If he's married, is he completely committed to his wife?
- If he has children, do they honor him?

In His Social/Business Life

- Is he kind?
- Is he hospitable?
- Is he a friend of strangers?
- Does he show favoritism?
- Does he have a blameless reputation (not perfect but above reproach)?

In His Spiritual Life

- Is he making disciples of all nations?
- Does he love the Word?
- Is he a man of prayer?
- Is he holy?
- Is he gracious?

In the end no one will fulfill these qualifications perfectly. Each of us has numerous sins to confess daily. However, elders ought to live lives worth imitating, lives that reflect the character of Christ. They need to know the Word, teach the Word, and obey the Word so that others in the church will be instructed and spurred on to greater faithfulness. Who in your church do these qualifications bring to mind?

Three Responsibilities of Deacons
1 TIMOTHY 3:8-13

In verse 8 Paul turns his attention from elders to deacons. While we do see a list of requirements for being a deacon in 1 Timothy 3:8-13, the responsibilities of deacons are not as clear as that of elders. In fact, in the picture we have of the early church in the book of Acts, we rarely see deacons at all. Even in Acts 6, where we have a form of the word for "deacon," we see the same word used to describe one of the tasks of elders (Acts 6:4). The fact that deacons aren't highlighted in the New Testament may be one reason we've got a variety of opinions about the role of deacons today. However, it should be said that some churches clearly have an unbiblical practice when it comes to deacons. So, if there are some things we *don't* know for sure about deacons, what are the things we *do* know from Scripture?

The word group (both the noun and the verb) for deacon—*diakonos, diakonia, diakoneo*—is used more than one hundred times in the New Testament, almost always referring to some form of ministry or service. It's the same word used in Ephesians 4:12 to refer to "the work of ministry" that is the responsibility of all members of the church. We are all commanded to be servants. At the same time the early church does give us brief glimpses of people who lead out in service, and that's what we see in Acts 6:1-7:

> *In those days, as the number of the disciples was multiplying, there arose a complaint by the Hellenistic Jews against the Hebraic Jews that*

their widows were being overlooked in the daily distribution. Then the Twelve summoned the whole company of the disciples and said, "It would not be right for us to give up preaching about God to handle financial matters. Therefore, brothers, select from among you seven men of good reputation, full of the Spirit and wisdom, whom we can appoint to this duty. But we will devote ourselves to prayer and to the preaching ministry." The proposal pleased the whole company. So they chose Stephen, a man full of faith and the Holy Spirit, and Philip, Prochorus, Nicanor, Timon, Parmenas, and Nicolaus, a proselyte from Antioch. They had them stand before the apostles, who prayed and laid their hands on them. So the preaching about God flourished, the number of the disciples in Jerusalem multiplied greatly, and a large group of priests became obedient to the faith.

A form of the word for *deacons* is used three times in verses 1-4, and in verses 1 and 2 this terminology is applied to those who were responsible for leading others to serve. That's why we're calling deacons "leading servants." Some may respond by saying deacons are simply those who serve in the church. But that's not true because we all serve in the church. Deacons *lead* the church in service. They are leading servants. It's interesting that a form of the word describing how they "handle" financial matters in verse 2 is also used in verse 4 to refer to the apostles' "ministry" of the Word. So even though we don't see this word or the title "deacon" throughout the rest of the book of Acts, we do see two primary leadership roles delineated here in Acts 6. A group of men are responsible primarily for prayer and the ministry of the Word—the elders—and another group rises up to lead out in specific areas of service. This latter group we're referring to as deacons based on the picture we see in 1 Timothy 3.[11]

So the next question we need to ask is this: What do deacons do? Try your best to get the traditional picture of a deacon out of your mind, whatever that may look like according to your background. In the mind of some Christians, deacons are those who meet together, sit in the front of the church, and talk poorly about the pastor. That kind of unbiblical picture of deacons is why we need to take an honest look at what these leading servants did in Acts 6 and the way they are described in

---

[11] Whether the individuals in Acts 6 were actually deacons is debated, but it does seem that these men were at least performing deacon-like responsibilities in this passage. See Bruce, *Acts*, 130.

1 Timothy 3. First, we'll look at Acts 6 and notice three primary responsibilities of deacons.

The first responsibility of deacons is to **meet needs according to the Word**. This is their primary role—spiritual service aimed at meeting specific needs. When you read Acts 6:1-7, you notice that **deacons' ministries arise from specific circumstances**. The church was growing, and as they shared their resources with one another, they needed someone to lead out in the distribution of aid. A specific need necessitated these leading servants. The fact that different needs call for different types of leaders may help explain why we don't see clear responsibilities for deacons spelled out in the New Testament.

In their various responsibilities **deacons are accountable for specific commands**. In the case of Acts 6, Scripture necessitated that the church look after widows. Therefore, in order to carry out God's commands, which reflect His own heart, deacons today must also willingly serve. They meet needs according to the Word. To be clear, some areas of service, such as assisting with parking, may not be specifically mentioned in Scripture, but they fulfill a specific need related to a scriptural mandate. A deacon who leads a parking team enables the church to obey the biblical command to meet together (Heb 10:24-25).

A second responsibility of deacons is to **support the ministry of the Word**. The men in Acts 6 were certainly filling a need, but that's not all they were doing. Because the widows were being overlooked in the distribution of food, the apostles were being taken away from their overall leadership responsibilities, most notably prayer and the proclamation of the Word (Acts 6:4). As a result, the mission of the church began to suffer. The deacons were appointed to free up the apostles' availability for the preaching of the Word. We see, then, the balance that God intends for His church—to be fully devoted to the Word *and* fully devoted to meeting needs in the world. The church needs individuals who are devoted to both of these tasks.

We're beginning to see the vital role deacons, leading servants, play in the church. **Deacons serve elders so they can lead**. Stephen and the others in Acts 6 freed the apostles to devote themselves to prayer and the Word. The deacons were not like a second power block in the church, a body of leaders competing with the elders to provide overall leadership in the church. Unfortunately, that's exactly what many of us have seen in our various traditions when it comes to the role of deacons. Deacons have assumed the role of being supervisors of the staff and the pastor.

This is not biblical. The deacons in Acts 6 are serving fundamentally as supporters and encouragers of the elders in the ministry of the Word.

Deacons not only serve elders so they can lead; **they lead others so they can serve**. Notice that only seven leading servants were chosen in Acts 6, which is certainly not a large enough group to handle the food distribution problem for a church that contained thousands of people by this time. These deacons were surely organizing others to make certain the work was done. Again, though everyone in the church is intended to serve, the deacons are leading servants.

Finally, the third responsibility of deacons is that they **unify the body around the Word**. There were certainly needs to be met in Acts 6, but there were also deeper issues at stake. Physical neglect was causing spiritual disunity, and Christians were beginning to complain against one another. Deacons were appointed to squelch the tension and the rising disunity in the church. Again, this runs directly counter to our typical association of deacons with *dis*unity, gossiping, and complaining. But in Scripture deacons labor to promote unity in the church. They are what we might call the shock absorbers in the church.

Qualifications

Having looked at the responsibilities of deacons, we now turn to their qualifications from Scripture. When we consider 1 Timothy 3:8-13, alongside our discussion of Acts 6 (above), we can see two main qualifications for deacons. First, they must have **a mission mind-set**. The church was growing in the early chapters of Acts at a breathtaking speed, and the church needed leaders who would embrace the mission God had given them and unite others in the same cause. That's why deacons can't be small-minded individuals engrossed in turf wars, maintaining their rights and lobbying for their own causes. Instead, they are to see the mission of the church and work to help others understand that mission. Every facet of their ministry is part of that overarching mission.

The church is on a mission to make the gospel known in all nations, which is exactly why the adversary delights in turning the church of Jesus Christ inward on itself at every opportunity. Satan loves seeing the church embroiled in battles over this or that issue. In such cases deacons may be called in to absorb the shock. Certainly valid complaints and real needs arise, and when they do, deacons should rise to meet those needs so the mission of the church can thrive. Churches can get so engrossed in catering to every complaint that the primary mission gets lost. Therefore, if someone is pulling the church away from its mission, that person is not qualified to be a deacon. This leads to the second qualification.

Deacons must have **a Christlike character**. Scripture doesn't give us a lot of detail regarding what deacons do, but it does make the character of deacons pretty clear. We might say Scripture is more concerned about the sanctity of our lives than the structure of our leadership.

Let's return to 1 Timothy 3:8-13 to look at those character qualifications. What stands out about these qualifications is that they are similar to what is expected of any Christ follower. Deacons are, quite simply, intended to exemplify the character of Christ. Here's a set of questions we might ask to discern whether someone should serve as a deacon:

Questions

- Is this person honorable?
- Is this person genuine?
- Is this person self-controlled?
- Is this person a sacrificial giver?
- Is this person devoted to the Word?
- Is this person faithful? (not perfect, but morally pure)
- Is this person honoring Christ in the home?
- What about women?

This last question, What about women? is the million-dollar question. We've already seen that elders must be men, but what about deacons? There are basically two schools of thought on this question. Bible-believing scholars and pastors that I respect greatly differ on this difficult issue. And depending on what tradition you were raised in, you're probably already inclined to one of these positions. But the reality is that it is not up to our preference on this issue; it's up to the Word. Yet, even while we agree that the Word is the final authority, the Word is not entirely clear or explicit in this instance.

Some believers may look at this passage and think, "This issue *is* clear in Scripture. Can't you read?" After saying that deacons must be "worthy of respect" and that they must have certain character qualifications in 1 Timothy 3:8-10, Paul then went on to say the following in verse 11: "Wives, too, must be worthy of respect, not slanderers, self-controlled, faithful in everything." So both deacons and their wives have to display Christlike character. Doesn't that pretty well settle the issue?

How can women serve as deacons if Paul talked about deacons having wives? This is a valid question, but there's more to consider.

We certainly don't want to succumb to pressures from the culture when we interpret Scripture, and we don't want to come to the text with an agenda; however, based on Scripture, I do believe it's possible for women to serve as deacons in some settings. Let me give four reasons I believe this to be so. First, some English translations of verse 11 address "their wives," but the pronoun "their" is actually not in the Greek, the original language of the New Testament. Some translators think it is implied, but it's certainly not explicit. There's some ambiguity here, though it's very possible that the best translation for verse 8 is not "their wives."

Second, we need to ask this question: Why would Paul talk about deacons' wives and not elders' wives? This is especially curious given that more is said about an elder's responsibility in the home according to 1 Timothy 3:1-7. Despite the fact that elders have stricter qualifications, there is no mention of their wives.

Third, the overall structure of the passage seems to lead to the conclusion that Paul was not referring to the wives of deacons in verse 8. He used the word "likewise" to transition from talking about elders in verse 7 to talking about deacons in verse 8. Paul then used this same word "likewise" in verse 11 (translated "too") to transition into talking about deacons' wives or, as I am trying to argue, deaconesses. It doesn't seem natural for the flow of the passage to run like this: first elders—likewise deacons—likewise deacons' wives. The following seems more likely: first elders—likewise deacons—likewise deaconesses.

A fourth reason for understanding the role of deacon to be open to men and women is the role given to Phoebe in Romans 16. She is referred to as a "servant of the church," and the word used comes from *diakonos*, which would seem to point to a diaconal role. When you couple this with the picture of women who played integral leadership roles in the mission of the church, the case becomes even stronger. Paul specifically mentioned 17 of these women. The issue is not whether women can be leaders but how the Bible describes their role in the context of a local church.

When you consider the responsibilities we have outlined for deacons above—they meet needs according to the Word, they support the ministry of the Word, and they unify the body around the Word—then there is no biblical evidence whatsoever that these responsibilities should only include men. Even with this understanding, however, we need to be careful. The reality is that many churches have deacons that play a significant leadership role over the entire church, and if that's the case, then women should not serve as deacons in those churches because they would basically be serving as elders.

There is much biblical evidence to affirm women who lead in various ways, such as hospitality, children's ministry, and visitation. It may be an adjustment for many people to think of deacons in this way, but I think we're on safe ground in the Word. In fact, I think the Word should lead us to make this adjustment if we want to be obedient in this area. In the end we want everything we do in the church to conform to God's design for the church.

The Bottom Line

Given what we've seen about elders and deacons, what does this look like practically? Two applications stand out. First, **the church appoints and follows servant leaders who are wholeheartedly committed to accomplishing the mission of Christ**. This follows from what we've seen above. How does the Spirit appoint elders? Through the church. So we ask the Spirit of God to show us who these men are in the church. Scripture is obviously not specific about particular names, but we ought to pray for the Spirit's guidance in helping us discern which men are qualified to serve as elders. These are men who, according to Hebrews 13:17, we want to obey. Remember, it's scriptural to obey your leaders.

Second, **the church affirms and honors leading servants who use their gifts to build up the body of Christ**. This includes a variety of ministries within the church carried out by both men and women. Depending on the church, these roles may look a little different. Deacons may be a part of the church's paid staff, they may provide accountability and wisdom in financial matters, they may lead in worship, or they may be a part of a hospitality team. And remember, someone doesn't have to be wearing a deacon's badge to serve as a deacon, nor do they necessarily have to participate in weekly meetings. These men and women are doing what is outlined in Scripture, and they should be honored, prayed for, and relied on to provide unity around Christ and His mission. That's the end goal.

The church is composed of ministers who multiply the gospel throughout the world. Following the appointment of deacons in Acts 6:1-6, we read about the result in verse 7: "So the preaching about God flourished, the number of the disciples in Jerusalem multiplied greatly, and a large group of priests became obedient to the faith." The problems that arose in the church were threatening the growth of the church, but when biblical, Christ-honoring leaders responded, the church reorganized for multiplication. Acts 6:7 is the by-product of a biblical structure of church leadership: elders (servant leaders) gave themselves to prayer and the ministry of the Word, and deacons (leading servants) met needs, supported the ministry of the Word, and unified the body of Christ. And together all members of the church are to minister in order to see the multiplication of the gospel throughout our neighborhoods and among the nations. May it be so in all of our churches.

Reflect and Discuss

1. What church leader has encouraged you the most in your spiritual journey? Have you ever been hurt by a church leader? What processes might have kept that person out of the leadership role?
2. What are the leaders of your church called? How do they function? Which ones fit the description of overseers (elders, pastors), and which ones fit the description of deacons?
3. What evidence does the overseer in your church show that he depends on the gospel?
4. In what ways is the overseer in your church accountable to the church?
5. How does the overseer in your church function as shepherd? Do any of your church's leaders tend to seize power?
6. In what areas is the overseer in your church worthy of imitation? In what areas does he fail as an example?
7. Is someone in your church currently not in a leadership role who seems to fit the qualifications?
8. In what ways do all members of a church "minister" and "serve"? Can this service be made more efficient through the guidance of members who lead other members?
9. What are some unbiblical job descriptions of "deacons" you have seen in churches you have attended?
10. What is the biblical argument against women serving as deacons? What is the biblical argument in favor? Which do you find most compelling? Why? What part does tradition play in your opinion?

The Family of Faith:
Who We Are and What We Do

1 TIMOTHY 3:14–4:16

Main Idea: The church is God's household, and it is charged with living in accord with and upholding the truth of the gospel of Jesus Christ.

I. **Who We Are (3:14-16)**
   A. The significance of the church
      1. We are the expression of God's family.
      2. We are the dwelling place of God's presence.
      3. We are the guardians of God's Word.
      4. The awe-inspiring reality: God dwells among us!
   B. The supremacy of Christ
      1. He reveals the mystery of godliness.
      2. He displays the majesty of God.
         a. Manifested in the flesh
         b. Verified by the Spirit
         c. Praised among the heavens
         d. Proclaimed across the earth
         e. The Savior of all the world
         f. The King over all the universe
      3. The awe-inspiring reality: Christ lives within you!

II. **What We Do (4:1-16)**
   A. We detect error in the church.
      1. The Source
         a. Demonic teachings
         b. Deceptive teachers
      2. The Substance
         a. They deny the goodness of God.
         b. They distort the Word of God.
   B. We declare truth in the church.
      1. Teach with authority.
      2. Live with purity.
      3. Train for eternity.

Despite the importance of the church in the New Testament, and especially in a passage like 1 Timothy 3:14-16, this crucial doctrine is sadly neglected today. In his book *The Church: The Gospel Made Visible*, pastor Mark Dever writes about this disturbing trend:

> For too many Christians today, the doctrine of the church is like a decoration on the front of a building. Maybe it's pretty, maybe it's not, but finally it's unimportant because it bears no weight.
>
> Yet nothing could be further from the truth. The doctrine of the church is of the utmost importance. It is the most visible part of Christian theology, and it is vitally connected with every other part. (Dever, *The Church*, ix)

Unfortunately, Dever's assessment seems all too accurate. The church appears to be irrelevant or optional for many professing Christians today. After all, why bother with the Sunday morning crowds? We can simply download the latest sermon from our favorite pastor or author and—*voila!*—we can have church in the comfort of our own home. But is this really what God intended?

Many professing Christians may be surprised to hear that Scripture gives us a much higher view of the church. Christ founded the church (Matt 16:18-19), He died for the church (Eph 5:25), and He identifies intimately with it (Acts 9:4-5). He even calls the church His own bride (John 3:29) or His body (Eph 5:30). Our current passage, 1 Timothy 3:14-16, also speaks to the high value God places on the church. God has given His people the privilege and responsibility of living in accord with and upholding the truth of the gospel.

Who We Are
1 TIMOTHY 3:14-16

Here near the end of the third chapter, we come to the theme verse that frames the entire letter. Paul tells us explicitly the reason he is writing, and in the process he gives us a purpose statement supporting the significance of the church and a summary of the supremacy of Christ.

First, observe **the significance of the church**. Three descriptions of the church are given in this passage followed by one awe-inspiring reality. The first description of the church is this: **we are the expression of God's family**. We are His household, His family unit, His children.

My own household includes a wife, three sons, and a daughter. And my household operates according to my rules, at least theoretically. Children go to bed at a certain time, they act a certain way at the dinner table, they treat their mother a certain way, they respond to me in a certain way, and on and on. So in verse 15 when Paul tells us we are God's household, he's letting us know we are to operate under God's rules and God's direction. The book of 1 Timothy should encourage us as the children of God to come before our Heavenly Father and say, "How should we behave?" We are, after all, His family.

Second, as the church, **we are the dwelling place of God's presence**. We are, according to verse 15, "the church of the living God." Language like this would have taken first-century Jewish Christians and those familiar with the Scriptures immediately back to Jacob's meeting with God at Bethel (which literally means "house of God"). After encountering God in a dream about a stairway to heaven, Jacob exclaimed, "Surely the LORD is in this place. . . . What an awesome place this is! This is none other than *the house of God.* This is the gate of heaven" (Gen 28:16-17; emphasis added). We hear something similar in God's instructions to Moses concerning the building of the tabernacle: "They are to make a sanctuary for Me so that I may dwell among them" (Exod 25:8). The same thing was also said about the temple built by Solomon (1 Kgs 6:13). God chose to dwell in a particular location.

When we turn to the New Testament, a change takes place. There is no special city, no tabernacle, and no temple (building) where God dwells. Instead, God now dwells with His people. Paul said to the church at Corinth in 2 Corinthians 6:16, "For we are the sanctuary of the living God," and to the church at Ephesus he wrote, "You also are being built together for God's dwelling in the Spirit" (Eph 2:22). Did you catch that? We are the dwelling place for the living God!

The church, the corporate body of Christ followers, is the place where God lives and dwells and manifests His presence. Consider how significant this makes our weekly gatherings: the church gathers and the Lord, the living God, is among us. We are His house, worshiping in His presence, listening to His Word, and partaking of the elements at His table. How awesome is the privilege of being the dwelling place of God's presence!

A third significant aspect of the church emerges in verse 15: **we are the guardians of God's Word**. That's what Paul meant when he said that we are "the pillar and foundation of the truth." When you think of a pillar and a foundation, imagine the temple of Diana in Ephesus, one of the seven wonders of the ancient world. It had a massive, shining, marble roof held high with one hundred strong columns all around it, each measuring over 18 meters high (Stott, *Message*, 105). The church at Ephesus to whom Paul wrote would have easily been able to picture this in their minds.

This rock-solid image should characterize the church's guardianship of the truth of God's Word. Consider two ways in which this should manifest itself. First, the church has the privilege and responsibility of **preserving God's Word: we hold it firm**. From age to age, from generation to generation, we have the responsibility of passing this Word on, holding it fast, and defending it against false teaching that would threaten it, from the first century to the twenty-first century. Our second responsibility is **proclaiming God's Word: we hold it high**. Like the columns of the temple, we lift high the truth of the Word. We want this Word to shine so that the world will see and hear and know the only true God. This truth also means that, as the church, there are some things we don't hold high—man's opinions, man's innovations, man's creativity, man's wisdom, and man's possessions. Instead, we lift up one thing: the Word of God. Let us magnify it, amplify it, spotlight it, and spread it—in the church and all over the world.

So we are the expression of God's family, the dwelling place of God's presence, and the guardians of God's Word. All of this points to **the awe-inspiring reality that God dwells among us!** This is the God who spoke and the world came into being, the God who has absolute authority and sovereign power over all things in creation, the God who calls the stars by name and holds the nations in His hand—the all-powerful, all-knowing, indescribably great, infinitely holy God of the universe. And He considers us, the church, to be His people, His gathering, His household. It's no wonder 1 Corinthians 14 describes the experience of an unbeliever entering a properly functioning assembly of believers as awe inspiring (vv. 23-25). After being convicted of his sin, the unbeliever in that passage cries out, "God is really among you." By the grace of God, may that be the case in all of our churches.

After discussing the significance of the church in verses 14-15, Paul moves on in verse 16 to talk about **the supremacy of Christ**. Paul refers to Christ's supremacy in relation to the "mystery of godliness." The word "godliness" is one of Paul's favorite words in this letter, as it is used nine different times. To have godliness is to have a God-consciousness, a God-centeredness that permeates everything you do. Whether you're awake or asleep, or whether you're thinking, dreaming, desiring, talking, eating, or drinking—whatever you're doing—having godliness means being centered around God. But what is the "*mystery* of godliness"? When Paul talks about a mystery, he is not talking about something unsolved or difficult to figure out. He is talking about something that was hidden for a time but now has been revealed (Ryken, *1 Timothy*, 141).

In verse 16 we learn that the mystery of godliness has everything to do with Christ. Paul's desire to see the Ephesian Christians act the right way in the household of God (3:15) was not simply a call to good behavior. It was a call to act in accordance with the truth of who Christ is and what He has accomplished through His life, death, resurrection, and ascension. Those who have been saved by this gospel will live godly lives. Christ's supremacy is seen first of all, Paul says, in that **He reveals the mystery of godliness**. As verse 16 puts it, "He was manifested in the flesh, vindicated in the Spirit, seen by angels, preached among the nations, believed on in the world, taken up in glory." Christ is the manifestation of God-centeredness, or to put it another way, godliness has been disclosed to us in Christ. But *how* does Jesus reveal the mystery of godliness? Answer: **He displays the majesty of God**. This is the second way in which we see the supremacy of Christ, and it is spelled out in six related truths in this passage.

First, the Son of God was "**manifested in the flesh**" (v. 16). To put it another way, Jesus Christ *is* God in the flesh. Second, He was **verified by the Spirit**. The HCSB says that Jesus was "vindicated" by the Spirit, and in this context it points us to the work of the Spirit in affirming that Christ was God's Son. Jesus' baptism in Matthew 3:16-17 is a good example of this truth, where we see the Spirit descending on Christ, affirming that He was indeed the Son of God. Christ's signs and wonders also bore witness to the Spirit's presence in His ministry. Ultimately, however, the resurrection was the decisive indication of Christ's vindication by the Spirit. Romans 1:4 says that Jesus was "declared to be the powerful Son of God by the resurrection from the dead according to the Spirit of holiness." Romans 8:11 confirms the Spirit's role in the resurrection as well: "And if the Spirit of Him who raised Jesus from the dead lives in you, then He who raised Christ from the dead will also bring your mortal bodies to life through His Spirit who lives in you." This is how we are to understand what it means that Christ was verified, or vindicated, by the Spirit.

Third, Christ was **praised among the heavens**. The Son of God was seen and savored by angels. Angels sang at His birth (Luke 2:13-14), they announced His resurrection (Matt 28:1-7), and they witnessed His ascension (Acts 1:9-11). The angels testify to Christ's glory. Fourth, Christ was **proclaimed across the earth**. As the HCSB puts it, He was "preached among the nations" (1 Tim 3:16). Beginning with the early disciples and continuing until today, Jesus Christ has been proclaimed among the peoples.

Fifth, we see that Christ is **the Savior of all the world**. He was "believed on in the world." Right now, among people in Asia and Africa and Europe and America, people are believing on His name and experiencing salvation from the penalty of their sins. So be encouraged in the morning as you get up to face another day, knowing that God is saving people all over the world and bringing them from death to life. A difficult Monday morning can turn into a *really* good day. Finally, the sixth way in which Jesus displays the majesty of God is by reigning as **the King over all the universe**. Jesus was "taken up in glory" to the Father's right hand. Behold the mystery of godliness!

In telling us these truths in verse 16, Paul was not only proclaiming who Jesus is, but he was also saying to the church, "Realize what this means for you, for godliness in your life and godliness in the church." This is **the awe-inspiring reality that Christ lives within you!** This Christ, the Son of God incarnate, the One who was verified by the Spirit, raised from the dead, praised among angels, proclaimed across the earth, believed on as Savior, and crowned as King over all the universe, lives in you. Let that soak in. The Son of God resides in you, giving you power, strength, and grace. Godliness, or the God-centered life, is nothing more than the overflow of Christ in you.

There is a powerful application here for all of us who follow Christ. Brother or sister in Christ, are you going through a difficult time? Christ lives within you. Are you struggling in weakness? Christ is strength in you. Are you bruised and battered? Christ is healing in you. Are you confused and not sure what to do? Christ is peace in you. Are you wondering if you can overcome the things you are dealing with right now? As 1 John says, "The One who is in you is greater than the one who is in the world" (4:4). He is life. He is strength. He is hope in you. He is "Christ in you, the hope of glory" (Col 1:27). Jesus has conquered sin, death, and the grave, and He now reigns from heaven as the ascended Lord. Because He lives in you, you have nothing to fear.

The God-centered life is the Christ-empowered life. Returning to Paul's words in verses 14-15 concerning our identity as the household of God, we need to realize what these truths mean in the context of the church. These truths about Christ and the gospel should radically change the way we live and the way our churches function. There is nothing like the church in all the world, no other body more significant in all of history, nor will there ever be. Let us, then, pay close attention to God's instructions about the way we live and relate to one another in the body of Christ.

What We Do
1 TIMOTHY 4:1-16

As we move to chapter 4, we're going to look at Paul's instructions. We'll see that these verses have a twofold application. First, these verses are filled with personal instructions to Timothy, the young pastor of the church at Ephesus. At one level Paul's words apply directly to Timothy and the other elders. At the same time, as a second application, Paul is speaking about things that are important to all members of the church concerning what we need to do in these "later times" (1 Tim 4:1). That phrase *later times* is basically the New Testament's description of the period of time between Jesus' ascension into heaven and His second coming from heaven. Being vigilant in these "latter days" is something that should concern every follower of Christ.

The first thing we do, Paul says in verse 1, is **we detect error in the church**. There were apparently people in Ephesus who were questioning the true teaching of the Word and spreading false teaching that did not derive from the Word. Paul told Timothy and the church to watch out for these people. We would do well to consider the source of these errors.

Verse 1 clearly identifies false teachings as **demonic teachings**. Paul refers to people who had apparently paid "attention to deceitful spirits and the teachings of demons." Don't be fooled: false teaching is demonic, straight from hell. And it comes to life through **deceptive teachers**. These teachers are "liars whose consciences are seared" (v. 2). They are men and women who have become numb to the truth and are spreading "irreverent and silly myths" (v. 7). Now don't misunderstand, these are not individuals who rise up in the church and announce, "My conscience is seared, and I'm here to spread lies and silliness." If only it were that simple. That's what makes false teaching deceptive—it often comes from people in the church who claim to be spreading the truth. We're reminded again of Paul's warning to the Ephesian elders in Acts: "Men will rise up from your own number with deviant doctrines to lure the disciples into following them" (Acts 20:30). Remember, Paul was speaking to the *elders*, which implies that some of these false teachers were likely former elders in Ephesus.

False teaching was rampant in the first century, and it is rampant now. The world *and* the church are full of theology that is unbiblical. For example, prosperity theology says that if you trust Jesus, He will give you health and wealth. Cult theology, on the other hand, typically says that Jesus is not who you thought He was. An alternative is offered, which always turns out to be an unbiblical picture of the Son of God. And then there's what we might call popular theology, a theology consisting of ideas about life and possessions and heaven and the afterlife that comes more from best-selling books than from God's Word. Be on guard against such errors.

In light of Paul's warnings about false teachers, **we should not be surprised by them**. When you hear that a church member or a church leader has walked away from Christ and abandoned his or her faith, the Bible says not to be surprised. First John 2:19 talks about some people in the church who seemed to be Christians but who ultimately proved they were not by walking away from the fellowship of believers. Don't let that kind of apostasy throw your own faith into a tailspin. God has told us ahead of time that it will happen.

Even though we shouldn't be shocked by the presence of false teachers, **we should always be saddened by them**. The consequences of false teaching are eternally disastrous, so we should seek to keep more people from being deceived. Paul fully realized the danger of false teaching, for he began this letter by urging Timothy to confront men who were perverting the truth (1:3-4). Timothy needed to wield the Word to wage the good warfare. Likewise, all believers need to be able to detect error in the church. But how do we know when error is being taught?

In order to discern when error is being taught in the church, we need to consider **the substance** of what is being said. The way Paul addresses the specific false teachings in Ephesus applies to the church in all ages, including our own. Addressing the root of the false teaching, the apostle mentions two specific errors: **they deny the goodness of**

God, and **they distort the Word of God**. When we put these two characteristics together, we're reminded of how sin entered the world. The serpent emphasized God's power and greatness, while minimizing His love and goodness. He tempted Eve to doubt that God had her best interests in mind. He asked, "Did God really say, 'You can't eat from any tree in the garden'?" (Gen 3:1). He was leading her to question God's goodness and distort God's Word, and Eve bought into the lie and sinned.

Something similar was happening in Ephesus in Paul's day. If you move forward from Genesis 3 to 1 Timothy 4, you see that some teachers were teaching that certain foods should not be eaten and that people should not get married (1 Tim 4:3). Paul countered these claims by saying marriage and food are both good gifts from God's hand, gifts to be received with gratitude to God in prayer (vv. 4-5). God's people need to watch out for teachers who deny the goodness of God and distort the Word of God, either by adding to it or by taking away from it. We in the church need to be able to detect this kind of error.

Along with detecting error, it is also crucial that **we declare truth to the church**. In verse 6 Paul said to Timothy, "If you point these things out to the brothers, you will be a good servant of Christ Jesus." In other words, put truth before the church. Let it permeate and saturate the church. We do this in several ways.

Paul reiterates three main themes in the last part of chapter 4 related to declaring truth and combating falsehood. First, in order to combat falsehood, we hold to the truth and **teach with authority**. In verse 13 the apostle says, "Until I come, give your attention to public reading, exhortation, and teaching," and in verse 16, "Pay close attention to your life and your teaching." This call to teach with authority is a consistent theme in 1 Timothy. When Paul told Timothy not to let others look down on him because of his youth, the antidote to this was to "be an example to the believers in speech, in conduct, in love, in faith, in purity." Notice the first thing he mentioned—speech. The Word of God should resound from the pastor's lips, and he is to speak with authority. Read the Bible. Explain the Bible. Exhort from the Bible. Teach the Bible. That's the charge. Demonstrate your submission to the authority of Scripture, and you will lead rightly in the church as you declare the truth.

The second way to combat falsehood is to **live with purity**. Purity is not only about doctrine but also about one's life. Defending Christian doctrine is dependent on modeling Christian living. Elders and all

Christians must keep a close watch on their lives. Robert Murray M'Cheyne, a pastor who was used mightily by God in Scotland in the early 1800s, is a great example for us in this regard. M'Cheyne died when he was only 30, and his gravestone reads as follows:

> Died in the 30th year of his age and the 7th year of his ministry, walking closely with God, an example for the believers in word, in conversation, in charity, in spirit, in faith, in purity, he ceased not day and night to labor and watch for souls.

M'Cheyne once said, "My people's greatest need is my personal holiness." These are humbling words, and they ought to lead pastors and all believers to spur one another on with lives of love and holiness. Sadly, however, this is not the testimony of many pastors. Consider the following statistics, which are nothing short of jaw-dropping:

- As many as 50 percent of pastors' marriages will end in divorce.
- Almost 40 percent of pastors admit they have had an extramarital affair since the beginning of their ministry (Krejcer, "Statistics").
- More than 50 percent of pastors say they have visited pornographic sites on the Internet in the last year, and 30 percent admit to doing it in the last month (Rick Warren, pastors.com).

These statistics should cause pastors and all followers of Christ to tremble. We must watch our life and doctrine.

Third, we combat error and uphold truth as we **train for eternity**. Verses 7-8 are the key verses here: "Train yourself in godliness, for the training of the body has a limited benefit, but godliness is beneficial in every way, since it holds promise for the present life and also for the life to come." Scholars believe at this time the people of Ephesus spent a great deal of time and money training athletes for a variety of festivals and athletic contests. This may well have been in Paul's mind as he talked about the "training of the body" (Ryken, *1 Timothy*, 174). Now physical training is certainly valuable, and we need to care for our bodies. After all, our bodies are temples of the Holy Spirit, so we should eat well and exercise well. Nevertheless, that kind of physical training should pale in comparison to your training in godliness. Train in prayer, in the Word, in fasting, in worship, and in sharing the gospel. Spend your time in that kind of training. Your body will only last for a few years, but the gains from godliness will endure forever.

In light of the importance of training in godliness, we can make two final applications. First, **work out your own salvation progressively and persistently**. In verse 16 Paul says, "Persevere in these things," referring to the commands he has already given Timothy earlier in the letter. He wanted Timothy to persist in this kind of godly training in order to save himself, meaning that Timothy's salvation would come to completion as he was molded more and more into the image of Christ. This call for diligence applies to all Christians.

Second, **work hard for others' salvation locally and globally**. Paul told Timothy he would save not only himself but also his hearers. Now obviously Paul is not saying that we, in and of ourselves, can save people. Only Christ saves. That is obvious from Paul's writings and the Bible in general. But Christ has chosen to bring His salvation to people through the church—members and leaders of the body of Christ. Healthy churches mean healthy displays of the gospel to a lost world, which results in men and women coming to Christ.

When the goodness of Christ and the character of Christ and the Word of Christ are evident in the church, people in the world will be drawn to Him. This is why we guard the truth so people will be saved by it. This is why we live with purity so people see the difference Christ makes. This is why we train for godliness so people see in us the majesty of Christ. May everything we do draw people to our great Savior.

Reflect and Discuss

1. How does the church function as the "pillar and foundation of the truth"? Does this mean the church is infallible? Explain.
2. Would an unbeliever visiting your church be convinced that God dwells among you? Why?
3. In what way did the resurrection verify or vindicate the supremacy of Jesus Christ?
4. When do you most sense the power of Christ in you, enabling you to live a God-centered life? When do you most need that power?
5. What false doctrine have you heard on radio, movies, TV, or the Internet? Have you ever noticed any of these errors being expressed by the people in your church? By the leaders?

6. Practically, how do you obey 1 Timothy 4:7 and "train yourself in godliness"?

7. How can false teaching like that mentioned in 4:3 sound very "spiritual"? How does Paul combat these errors?

8. From where does a Christian get the authority to teach or correct people? How do we use that authority rightly, without abusing it?

9. What are the greatest areas of temptation today for Christians? What is the best way for Christians, especially leaders, to avoid falling into sin?

10. Why is it so hard to keep eternity in mind in our day-to-day lives? How would you live differently if you were able to do so? How would it affect the urgency of pursuing a holy life and of telling others about Christ?

The Family of God

1 TIMOTHY 5:1-16

Main Idea: As a family of faith, members of Christ's church should treat one another with love and respect, and this includes wise and compassionate support for widows.

I.   As the Church, We Love One Another like We Are a Family (5:1-2).
II. As the Church, We Care for Those Who Have No Family (5:3-16).
    A.   Honor destitute widows through support.
        1.   They must be devoid of relatives.
            a.   Relatives should support their parents and grandparents.
            b.   This pleases God.
            c.   This demonstrates your faith.
            d.   This relieves the church.
        2.   They must be dependent on God.
        3.   They must be devoted to prayer.
    B.   Enlist older widows for service.
        1.   They must be mature women.
        2.   They must have been faithful wives.
        3.   They must care for children.
        4.   They must be hospitable hosts.
        5.   They must be humble servants.
        6.   They must be unselfish.
        7.   They must be kind.
    C.   Encourage younger widows to marry.
        1.   They must avoid laziness.
        2.   They must abhor gossip.

For many Christians it's fairly easy to walk into a corporate worship service on Sunday, sing a few songs, listen to a sermon, and walk right out the door without any meaningful interaction with fellow believers. We may not even know the people sitting beside us in the pew, and we certainly wouldn't want to interfere with their lives. After all, we should respect people's privacy, right?

The people sitting beside us in the pew each week—if they are genuine followers of Christ—are our spiritual brothers and sisters. They're family—people for whom Christ died (Acts 20:28; Rom 14:15). We ought to be concerned about them. In fact, 1 John tells us that not loving our fellow believers is evidence that we have not passed from death to life (3:14-18). So the way we treat fellow believers is evidently important. It is indicative of our relationship to Christ.

In light of these realities, Paul's instructions in 1 Timothy 5 become all the more significant. After exhorting Timothy to proclaim and live out the truth before the church in chapter 4, Paul hones in at the beginning of chapter five on the way we treat one another in the church.

As the Church, We Love One Another like We Are a Family

1 TIMOTHY 5:1-2

As family, Paul said, we treat one another a certain way: "Do not rebuke an older man, but exhort him as a father, younger men as brothers, older women as mothers, and with all propriety, the younger women as sisters." When Timothy talked to older men or women in the church, he was to talk to them with the respect they were due, even with the affection he might have for his own parents. And when he related to younger men, he was to treat them like brothers. Likewise younger women in the church were to be honored, and their purity was to be protected, just as a brother would for his own sister. This is tender and compassionate wisdom.

Churches are indeed a family, a faith family, and members should relate to one another accordingly. When you see fellow members, love them like brothers and sisters because they are! Jesus said that the world would realize that we are His disciples if we love one another (John 13:35). If we want to bear witness to the world and maintain unity in the church, we will obey this Scripture and treat one another with love and respect.

As the Church, We Care for Those Who Have No Family

1 TIMOTHY 5:3-16

After referring to different groups of people in the church in verses 1-2, Paul focuses on one specific part of the faith family in verses

3-16—widows. We are not only to love one another like a family, but we must also care for one another. Paul gave a great deal of attention to how widows were to be cared for. Along with caring for orphans, God's people are commanded to care for those women in the church who have no one to provide and watch out for them. James 1:27 puts it this way: "Pure and undefiled religion before our God and Father is this: to look after orphans and widows in their distress and to keep oneself unstained by the world." This verse, and others like it, should prompt our churches to ask some tough questions like, What are we doing intentionally to care for the widows God has entrusted to our care? God is not only the Father of the fatherless, He is also the defender of the widow.

Throughout the Old and New Testaments, God shows particular care for widows through His people Israel (Exod 22:22; Isa 1:16-17), through His Son (Mark 12:38-40; Luke 7:11-17), and now through His church (Jas 1:27). He commands us in 1 Timothy 5:3 to "support widows who are genuinely widows." To be sure, this is a sensitive issue for many women who are followers of Christ—godly women, both young and old, who have experienced the loss of a husband. As a pastor, I have preached at some of these funerals and wept with these widows. There are also women in our faith family who have been abandoned by their husbands in divorce. All that to say, we need to be aware of the real pain and hurt among single women and single moms in our congregations as we approach this topic.

We must remember the historical context of 1 Timothy as we consider this passage about widows. There are some significant differences between widows in the first-century setting in Ephesus and the twenty-first-century setting in America. We are, by and large, living in an affluent culture where many people have disability and life insurance, not to mention 401(k)s, nursing homes, and assisted living centers with which to provide for the elderly, and specifically for widows. While these safety nets are certainly not bad, they can lead us as the church to abdicate our responsibility to widows. Our context is very different from Timothy's setting in Ephesus.

We need to think about the specific situation being addressed in Ephesus, for it seems clear from 2 Timothy 3 and 1 Timothy 2 that widows, particularly younger widows, were causing divisions and problems in the church. These issues appear to be in Paul's mind as he was addressing the matter of widows in 1 Timothy 5. This particular context can present somewhat of a challenge as we seek to understand how this text applies to Christians today. So we will examine in a straightforward manner what Paul was saying to Timothy and the church at Ephesus in that setting, and then we'll address what this passage means for us today.

In verse 3 Paul makes clear that we are to **honor destitute widows through support**. The fact that he said to honor those who are "truly widows" meant that some qualifications must be met. Paul didn't simply tell the church to care for every known widow in the world at the time. Instead, he specifically addressed the need to care for widows *in the church*, especially those needing support. Let's look at some of the specific qualifications Paul mentions. First, **they must be devoid of relatives**. Verses 4-5 refer to a widow who is truly alone with no physical family to support her.

Before moving on to other qualifications, we can draw several conclusions from this first one. **Relatives should support their parents and grandparents**. This means a widow's children and grandchildren have the primary responsibility to care for her. The biblical mandate to Christian children of aging parents is clear: support your parents and your grandparents. Verse 4 tells us that "**this pleases God**," and in verse 8 we learn that **this demonstrates your faith**. Paul said that those who did not provide for their own household had "denied the faith." Caring for aging parents is a fundamental display of Christ's love in and through you, so to fail in this area is to deny your faith in Christ. In other words, the Bible is saying that it is impossible for a Christian not to care for the members of his own household. Finally, caring for widows in one's own family is good because **this relieves the church**. The church is not intended to be the first line of defense for widows. Family is to take the lead on this wherever possible, with the church making up the second line of defense. In summary, when relatives care for their aging parents, it pleases God, demonstrates their faith, and relieves the church.

The second qualification for widows who receive support is that **they must depend on God**. Verse 5 says of the "real widow," referring to those who qualify for support from the church, that she has "put her hope in God." And this God-centered hope leads to the third qualification for widows, namely, **they must be devoted to prayer**. She "continues night and day in her petitions and prayers." She is not self-indulgent but Christ centered. This is a wonderful picture of a Christian widow with a unique ministry of prayer. I can't help but think of an 84-year-old widow named Anna in Luke 2:36-38. Luke highlights her devotion: "She did not leave the temple complex, serving God night and day with fasting and prayers." Author Susan Hunt's words are applicable here:

> It seems to me that widows have entered into a dimension of dependence on God that prepares them for the ministry of intercessory prayer. The widow's mite was recognized and commended by Jesus because "she, out of her poverty, put in everything—all she had to live on" (Mark 12:44). Perhaps the widow's "might" is most mighty when these women band together as helper-defenders in intercessory prayer. Older women who do not have the daily responsibilities of jobs are [a powerful] source for intercessory prayer. (Hunt, *Spiritual Mothering*, 103)

Paul was primarily referring to older widows who didn't have the responsibilities of raising children or doing many of the things younger women were responsible for. Older widows were freed up for even greater concentrated time in prayer. Based on Paul's instructions in 1 Timothy 5, widows in the church who are in similar life settings should devote themselves to the ministry of prayer and intercession. This is a deeper level of intimacy with God that is unhindered by their previous responsibilities to husbands and children. Churches should support such widows financially, physically, and in other ways as needed.

Next Paul tells us that we not only support destitute widows, but we must also **enlist older widows for service**. Verse 9 talks about widows who are placed on the "list," and there's some debate about whether he is referring to enrolling widows on a "support list" or referring to how older widows can be enrolled in unique service to the church. While the HCSB translation adopted the former view, the latter is the majority view of biblical scholars, and it seems to be warranted by the context of what Paul is addressing here. He is calling older widows to service in the church, and much like what we saw in chapter 3 concerning elders and deacons, he is putting qualifications on those who might serve in this kind of official capacity.

Concerning women who are to be enrolled as widows, Paul says first that **they must be mature women**. He's referring to their age, since these women had to be "at least 60 years old." This is probably not a hard-and-fast rule but more likely a reference to women who are beyond the ability to work and support themselves. These women are less likely to remarry. Next Paul says that **they must have been faithful wives**, literally a "one-man woman." In addition, **they must care for children** (v. 10).

This doesn't mean a barren widow is disqualified but simply that she has honored God through care for children with the unique gifts God has given her. Other qualifications for widows in verse 10 include the following: **they must be hospitable hosts**, **they must be humble servants**, **they must be unselfish**, and **they must be kind**. Paul was saying that there is a unique and wonderful opportunity for widows who meet these qualifications to serve in the church in significant ways. He was calling widows to maximize their time on earth through service in the church, while at the same time he was calling the church to honor widows by supporting them in this service.

In verse 11 Paul turns his attention to younger widows, where he instructs the church to **encourage younger widows to marry**. We need to remember at this point that Paul was addressing circumstances that were specific to Ephesus. We know this is the case because there are other times, such as 1 Corinthians 7:8-9 (see also 1 Tim 5:14) when Paul encouraged singles to stay single. However, 1 Timothy 4:3 seems to indicate that false teachers were telling the church to avoid marriage, which goes against God's design. As a result, there were women, including younger widows, who were causing problems in the church. Paul gave such women two very pointed exhortations.

First, **they must avoid laziness**. Paul warns that younger widows "learn to be idle" (v. 13), and this easily becomes an occasion for sin. We don't typically think of laziness as a sin, but it is. And it leads to a number of other sins. Second, concerning younger widows, **they must abhor gossip** (v. 13b). Paul is obviously addressing general temptations that all people face, such as laziness and gossiping, but he is pointing out that younger widows are particularly susceptible to these kinds of sins, and they were likely giving in to them in Ephesus at this time. Young widows and all believers must flee such sin and seek to glorify God in whatever situation He has placed them.

Paul's instructions have a number of practical applications. Churches have a clear responsibility to support widows who are devoid of relatives, dependent on God, and devoted to prayer. This is non-negotiable. However, there are differences between younger and older widows; for instance, younger widows are more likely to remarry than older widows. Whether or not younger widows choose to remarry, they must avoid idleness and gossip. For older widows, if they choose not to remarry, they should be devoted to seeking the Lord diligently in prayer and in service to the church with the unique opportunity God has given them. Their time can and should be used for the good of the church and the spread of the gospel.

Is your church intentionally caring for widows? If not, what steps could you take as a body of believers to obey this passage? Are there widows in your own life that you need to reach out to and support? May the gospel of Christ compel us to look out for the most vulnerable among us. May we see our churches not simply as places where individuals gather but as families of faith who take care of one another with particular concern for orphans and widows.

Reflect and Discuss

1. Can you name any specific prayer concerns for at least one member of your church?
2. Do you know any widows in your church? What is your church doing to assure that their needs are being met?
3. Do Paul's commands also apply to widowers? How would their situation be the same? How would it be different?
4. Are there divorced women in your church? Would you say their treatment by the church amounts to coddling, love, shame, or punishment? How should they be treated?
5. If a widow collected life insurance, has a pension plan, and lives in a care facility, what should a church family do for her?
6. What can you do to show Christian love to your parents or grandparents? Do government or church programs relieve children of their responsibilities to care for their parents? Why?
7. Is it difficult to judge whether a widow is dependent on God? What test or criteria might be used?
8. Do you know any widows or retired women who are powerful prayer warriors? What qualities do you admire in them?
9. What roles of service are available for widows in your church? Are there other positions widows would be well qualified to fill?
10. Are young widows today susceptible to the same temptations as in Paul's day—laziness and gossip? Are there other temptations for widows that are specific to modern times?

Caring for Elders, Caring for the Church[12]

1 TIMOTHY 5:17-25

Main Idea: The church should demonstrate its esteem for the ministry of the Word and the glory of God by honoring, protecting, rebuking, and appointing elders.

I. **The Ways We Care (5:17-25)**
   A. Honor faithful elders with generous provision (vv. 17-18).
      1. The command of double honor
         a. Double honor involves respect.
         b. Double honor includes pay.
      2. The Conditions of Double Honor
         a. They must be good leaders in the church.
         b. They must labor diligently in the Word.
   B. Protect all elders from unfounded accusations (v. 19).
      1. We should not be surprised when elders are accused.
      2. We should be cautious when elders are accused.
   C. Rebuke unrepentant elders in the presence of all (vv. 20-21).
      1. We should rebuke as a witness to truth.
      2. We should rebuke as a warning to others.
   D. Appoint each elder with great care (vv. 22-25).
      1. Careful selection is for the benefit of those choosing.
      2. Careful selection is for the protection of the church.
II. **The Keys to Care**
   A. We remind ourselves of the glory of God in the church.
      1. Sense the gravity of casually ignoring God's Word.
      2. See the glory of rightly ordering Christ's church.
   B. We remind ourselves of the kindness of God in the gospel.

Many Christians have become jaded when it comes to sermons about money. There's a perception that the pastor is simply asking for a

---

[12] This section is based on a sermon by Bart Box.

higher salary or that the church is being manipulated into supporting a new building project. To be fair, the church has seen its share of abuses in this area. Nevertheless, such abuses should not keep us from hearing what God has to say in a passage like 1 Timothy 5:17-25. How the church cares for elders, both financially and otherwise, communicates something about its heart.

It may seem as if Paul was randomly dealing with a number of disconnected issues in chapters 4–6, but these themes actually do fit together. The stage was set in 1 Timothy 3:14-16, the verses we identified earlier as providing the framework for the entire letter, so that everything in the remaining chapters flows out of those verses. Paul called the church "God's household, which is the church of the living God, the pillar and foundation of the truth" (3:15). That statement along with the church's confession of the gospel given in verse 16 is unpacked in the rest of the letter. Whether it's identifying church leaders (3:1-13), training for godliness (4:8), showing honor and respect to fellow believers (5:1-2), or supporting widows (5:3), the underlying theme is the same: the gospel should be on display in the church.

Applying those truths to our passage in 1 Timothy 5:17-25, Paul was essentially answering the question, What does leadership look like in the church? In the first part of chapter 5, we see that the church's care for widows sets it apart from the world. Similarly now, in the latter section of the chapter, Paul says that the relationship between church leaders and church members ought to look different as well. In the church the gospel ought to be on full display.

To see this contrast clearly, consider your own experience in the secular workplace. The relationship between a company's leadership and the rest of the employees is usually strained, to say the least. There's gossip, suspicion, favoritism, and harsh leadership, and it all makes for a cutthroat environment. While this may be common in the world at large, it shouldn't be the norm in the church. The household of God ought to look different. In stark contrast to the secular business model, elders should have a genuine concern for the body of Christ, and the body ought to have a loving esteem for its elders. This dynamic is crucial because God intends for unbelievers to look at the church and see the glory of God expressed as the gospel of God impacts the people of God.

The Ways We Care
1 TIMOTHY 5:17-25

We'll group all four instructions we see in this section under an umbrella of care—care for elders and care for the church. Paul was not simply saying that the congregation should care for its elders but also that the elders were responsible and accountable to the congregation. This is a two-way street. After looking at these four instructions, we'll consider two motivations from this passage for carrying out these instructions.

Honor Faithful Elders with Generous Provision

Paul's first instruction is in verse 17. Honoring elders in this way demonstrates the power of the gospel and the glory of God. Verse 17 says that elders are "worthy of an ample honorarium, especially those who work hard at preaching and teaching." Understanding the words "ample honorarium" (literally "double honor") is the key to understanding this verse. Commentators have different opinions about **the command of double honor** and what it means for the church to show this kind of honor to those who rule well in teaching and preaching. Paul never used this expression in any of his other letters, but the wider context of the passage may suggest two ways in which the body of Christ should carry out this command.

First, we need to see that **double honor involves respect**. Normally, when it comes to showing double honor, we think only of financial compensation, which is certainly involved in honoring elders. However, there is also an idea of respect involved here, as Paul noted at the beginning of the next chapter: "All who are under the yoke as slaves must regard their own masters to be *worthy of all respect*" (6:1; emphasis added). Clearly slaves were not intended to pay back their masters financially, since the vast majority of them would not have had the means to do so. Paul had in mind a sense of gratitude and appreciation. Perhaps this principle is best exemplified in Paul's request to the believers in Thessalonica: "Now we ask you, brothers, to give recognition to those who labor among you and lead you in the Lord and admonish you, and to regard them very highly in love because of their work" (1 Thess 5:12-13).

Based on the verses we've just looked at, showing double honor at least includes the idea of showing respect; but there's another aspect to it as well. **Double honor includes pay**, or financial compensation.

Where do we see this? If you look at the beginning of the next verse, you'll notice the word "for." Paul was giving the basis for what he had just said in verse 18 about showing honor to elders. "For the Scripture says: Do not muzzle an ox while it is treading out the grain, and, the worker is worthy of his wages." The apostle was referring to compensation for those men who give themselves either full-time or part-time to the ministry of teaching and preaching. Now to be clear, there were occasions when Paul worked to support his ministry, and there were other occasions when he didn't. Not every context and situation is the same; however, Paul used the Old Testament to remind the church that the laborer is worthy of his wages. In short, elders should be compensated. But what did the apostle mean by *double* honor in terms of pay?

Paul was not being prescriptive in this passage. He wasn't attempting to give us the precise amount we should pay elders. When he referred to an "ample honorarium," I don't think he was referring to extravagant financial compensation; in fact, he is going to warn against materialism and the desire to be rich throughout chapter 6. However, it does seem that the expression "double honor" indicates that God's people should give generously to their elders. Churches that follow the saying, "Lord, You keep him humble, and we will keep him poor," have missed Paul's intention. Worse still, this kind of sentiment is actually antithetical to the church's gospel witness.

It is not uncommon for pastors and their families to be on the short end of financial compensation. Many men labor faithfully in teaching and preaching, yet they do not receive the wages they deserve. This kind of practice violates verse 18, where Paul was calling for a basic sense of fairness when it comes to compensation. Quoting Jesus, Paul said that if a laborer is laboring, he deserves his wages (Luke 10:7; Matt 10:10). Paul also quoted from Deuteronomy 25:4, which says, "Do not muzzle an ox while it treads out grain." An ox is at least allowed to eat as he labors, and the same should be true for pastors. Otherwise, we are treating those who minister the Word worse than a beast!

Failing to adequately compensate a pastor may communicate, even if unintentionally, how much a body of believers values their own money and possessions. This kind of church is not only being unfair to the pastor, but they are also communicating to that congregation and to the outside world how little they think of the ministry of the Word of God. This may seem like a trivial matter, but like all matters of money in the Bible, it really goes beyond dollars and cents—it goes straight to the heart (Matt 6:21). I am grateful to say that I am part of a church that values the Word of God and esteems the ministry of the Word highly. As an expression of their commitment to the Word, these followers of Christ give generously to those who labor in preaching and teaching.

So far we've seen that showing "double honor" involves both respect and financial compensation, but this kind of honor is not automatic. There is no entitlement based on position or background. Paul laid down **the conditions of double honor**, and these two conditions for elders are closely related. First, **they must be good leaders in the church** (v. 17). It's easy to misunderstand this idea of a "good leader" because the word "leader" is sometimes thought of in a heavy-handed way. Paul used this same word three times in chapter 3 (vv. 4-5, 12), and in each of these instances—the first two concerning elders and the third concerning deacons—there is the idea of "managing" a house or a family.

Now certainly there is an administrative side to this kind of management in order to avoid chaos in the home. But this doesn't mean fathers should be heavy-handed. As they lead their homes, they lead by love, care, sacrifice, and the laying down of their lives. So when Paul talked about elders being good leaders, he was not talking about managing the church in a harsh manner, neither was he talking about ruling with efficiency. He was saying elders should shepherd and love the people under their care. This is how they imitate the good shepherd of John 10—they lay down their lives for the sheep.

The question still remains: How do we know when a minister of the gospel is being a good leader? For some people the idea of "good" may bring up certain comparisons in their minds, as though the church needs to find the Christian version of a successful and efficient CEO. But the word "good" here is not used as a measuring stick for their successfulness; rather, it is a word that speaks of goodness or rightness, or of meeting a certain standard. Paul is saying we ought to evaluate elders on the basis of a whether they are faithful. We need to ask, "Is this man doing what he ought to be doing?" And we don't have to go any further than 1 Timothy to answer this question. Recall some of the qualifications for elders Paul gave in chapter 3: an elder must be above reproach, he must manage his household well, he must hold to sound doctrine, he must point out error, and he must be an example to the flock. This is what it takes to be a faithful minister of the gospel. This is what it means to be a good leader.

The second condition for elders to receive double honor is that **they must labor diligently in the Word**. This is certainly not the only responsibility of elders, as if they simply read their Bibles all 168 hours of the week. But an elder should give a large amount of time to the ministry of the Word and prayer. The word "especially" is key to understanding verse 17. After saying that elders were worthy of double honor, Paul then said, "Especially those who work hard at preaching and teaching." That word "especially" might be better translated as "that is," so that the verse might also be translated, "The elders who are good leaders should be considered worthy of double honor, *that is*, those who work hard at preaching and teaching." In other words, good leaders in the church *are* those who labor in preaching and teaching (Knight, *Pastoral Epistles*, 232).

Protect All Elders from Unfounded Accusations

Next we will look at the second main instruction Paul gave in this passage. In verse 19 Paul said, "Don't accept an accusation against an elder unless it is supported by two or three witnesses." In light of this command, **we should not be surprised when elders are accused**. This may sound a little counterintuitive since elders are supposed to be above reproach. It would seem there would be fewer accusations and allegations against such people. Nevertheless, for anyone who has been close to pastoral ministry for any stretch of time, you know this is actually *not* the case. The nature of pastoral work places pastors in numerous sticky and sin-filled situations that demand a firm commitment to the truth in the face of Satanic attack. Consequently, pastors are frequently the target of accusation, even more so than other members of the congregation. The great Reformer John Calvin put it this way: "For none are more liable to slanders and calumnies [a misrepresentation intended for harm] than godly teachers. . . . Although they perform their duty correctly, so as not to commit any error whatever, they never escape a thousand censures" (Calvin, *Timothy, Titus, and Philemon*, 140).

Because of the criticisms that frequently come against elders, **we should be cautious when elders are accused**. The bottom line is that accusations are going to come. We should not be surprised when they do, but we should be cautious. Based on the requirement in verse 19 for two or three witnesses against an elder, we should dismiss charges that don't meet this standard. Of course, we shouldn't ignore serious allegations, but we must take the utmost care and consideration when elders are accused. Someone might ask, "Shouldn't we use that kind of caution with everybody?" After all, why should elders get special treatment? Is this favoritism? The reason Paul said elders deserve this kind of treatment has to do with the public nature of the elder's position. Failure to dismiss false accusations would undermine the trust the congregation had in him. And if a prominent leader were destroyed and later it was found out that the allegations were unfounded, it would be a black stain on the church in the eyes of the world.

In light of what we've seen, then, let us be zealous to do whatever we can to protect the reputation of those who preach and teach in the church, not because they are a special class of Christians but more importantly because the church is the "pillar and foundation of the truth" (3:15). We don't want the display of God's glory diminished in any way, and we don't want the gospel to be hindered in its advance as a result of people in the church or in the community who don't trust the integrity of elders. By God's grace let's be eager to eliminate unfounded accusations. Let's put an end to unhelpful and ungodly criticisms that bring down the reputation of those who labor in the ministry of the Word.

So far Paul has given us two instructions: Honor faithful elders with generous provision, and protect all elders from unfounded accusations.

Rebuke Unrepentant Elders in the Presence of All

When there is credible evidence on the basis of two or three witnesses, Paul gave the following exhortation in verses 20-21: "Publicly rebuke those who sin, so that the rest will also be afraid. I solemnly charge you before God and Christ Jesus and the elect angels to observe these things without prejudice, doing nothing out of favoritism." Such a public rebuke is for the purpose of causing both the elders and the rest of the congregation to fear the consequences of sin. But which sins did Paul have in mind?

I don't think Paul had in mind here every individual sin an elder commits. Yes, all sin is infinitely serious, but not every single sin is worthy of a public rebuke. For example, if two or three witnesses see an elder jaywalking, there is no need for a public rebuke in the presence of all. There should be a certain magnitude to sin that is rebuked publicly, such that the elder can no longer serve as an example to the flock in ways consistent with passages such as 1 Timothy 3:1-7. Since we don't have a prescription as to what deserves public rebuke, congregations should try to make such determinations by praying under the leadership of the Spirit. Those who "continue in sin" (v. 20 NASB) deserve public rebuke, meaning there is a pattern of unrepentant sin. Some leaders in the church refuse to repent of sin that affects their character in the eyes of the congregation.

Does this kind of action seem, well, backwards to you? Does rebuking elders publicly seem inefficient and disruptive? Why not just dismiss the elders quietly and move along? I think Paul gives us two reasons we should rebuke unrepentant elders in the presence of all. First, **we should rebuke as a witness to the truth**. I take this from verse 21. There were false teachers in the church at Ephesus, and Paul was calling for their public rebuke. Do you feel the magnitude of what Paul was saying here? Timothy likely had a personal relationship with these men, but he was nonetheless given a charge to rebuke them, regardless of how painful it would be. Timothy was not to show prejudice or favoritism. The same holds true as we evaluate elders today.

The church witnesses to the truth through rebuking sin because it is the "pillar and foundation of the truth" (3:15). We must align ourselves with the judgment of God, a judgment that is sure to come, either now or on the last day. Paul did not want the church to deny its identity by failing to uphold the truth of God. We must be faithful to the Word no matter how difficult or painful it might be.

The second reason we do these things publicly is that **we should rebuke as a warning to others**. Often the Bible motivates us to obedience by pointing us to God's grace. Galatians 5:1 is just one example: "Christ has liberated us to be free. Stand firm then and don't submit again to a yoke of slavery." But grace is not the only way the Bible motivates. Sometimes God motivates us by fear, and our passage is one of those cases. Paul called for public rebuke "so that the rest will also be afraid" (1 Tim 5:20). Paul wanted other people—and other elders in particular—to look on public rebuke and say, "May it never be so with me. I don't want that." It's like a boy who tries to steer clear of trouble because he has seen his older brothers disciplined for their misbehavior.

Though God is motivating us here by fear, He is still, in a sense, motivating us by grace. Our natural instinct is to think we will never get caught and we will not have to give an account for our sin (Ps 10:13). However, God graciously warns elders that their day of reckoning may come sooner than they think, and this day of reckoning won't be in the privacy of their own home. Even before the final judgment, sin some-times has public consequences. God forbid that such steps would be necessary, but if they are, may God give us the courage to believe His Word and obey it. He has infinitely more wisdom than we do. We may think we have a better or more creative way to uphold the truth, but our way will short-circuit God's intention for the church to be a pillar and foundation of the truth.

Appoint Each Elder with Great Care

So far we've seen that the church is to honor, protect, and rebuke elders, which brings us to Paul's fourth and final overarching instruction. Verses 22-25 make this point. Verse 22 says, "Don't be too quick to appoint anyone as an elder, and don't share in the sins of others. Keep yourself pure." There seems to be a connection between the laying on of hands and sharing in the sins of others, such that being too quick to appoint someone as an elder may result in one's own guilt, a point we will return to below.

Verse 23 continues to draw the attention of many Christians. Paul gave Timothy the following instruction: "Don't continue drinking only water, but use a little wine because of your stomach and your frequent illnesses." It's not exactly clear why Paul made this statement at this point in the letter. This may be a parenthetical remark following up on his command at the end of verse 22 to "keep yourself pure." This is the kind of thing we do sometimes when sending an e-mail. As we are writing about one thing, we may think of another point we want to make, so we put it in parentheses in order to remember it later. This could be what Paul was doing here. In light of the false teaching Paul mentioned at the beginning of chapter 4, Timothy may have given himself to an ascetic lifestyle, including total abstinence from alcohol. Paul was telling Timothy that for the sake of his health he ought to consider drinking a little wine. The best thing Timothy could do in this situation is to use wine as a medicine. In light of the command for purity in verse 22, Paul may have been saying in verse 23, "Don't think the need for purity prohibits you from drinking some wine for your health."

Verse 24 picks up the thought of verse 22 and the need for purity. Paul had warned Timothy in verse 22 not to lay hands on anyone—that is, appoint them as an elder—too quickly. Keep in mind that there is nothing spiritual about the physical act of the laying on of hands, in and of itself, other than the fact it symbolized the recognition of someone as a called-out minister in the church. After this call for caution, Paul added the following in verse 24: "Some people's sins are obvious, going before them to judgment, but the sins of others surface later." Some brothers should not be recognized as elders in the congregation because their sins are immediately apparent, while the sins of other believers will be less obvious, showing up only later. Yes, churches will make mistakes. The main point here is that we need to take all the time, care, and due diligence necessary to make sure a man is qualified to the best of our knowledge. It is not always immediately obvious who should be an elder.

In the matter of appointing elders, Paul presents two ways obedience to God's Word profits the body of Christ. First, **careful selection is for the benefit of those choosing**. Paul's warning to Timothy not to hastily lay hands on anyone is a reminder that responsibility is attached to this high privilege. We don't want to have a part in the sins of others. Second, **careful selection is for the protection of the church**. This point should be fairly obvious. There's always a need for more elders to be raised up in the church; however, the last thing we need is haste in making this kind of massively important decision. To be sure, sometimes we are going to deny brothers we shouldn't deny, and sometimes we are going to appoint brothers we shouldn't appoint. That's just part of our fallen and finite nature. But we need to make sure we are doing everything we can to minimize those mistakes. We need to obey the Word in appointing godly men for the protection of the church.

The Keys to Care

One of the biggest dangers we have related to the issue of appointing elders is indifference. Other issues seem more pressing, such as difficulties in our marriage or stress over our job. With so many other concerns, how can we avoid apathy on this issue? Let me suggest two ways. First, **we remind ourselves of the glory of God in the church**. Even though these matters seem trivial in our eyes, they are not trivial in God's eyes. Acts 20:28 says Jesus has bought the church with His own blood. Take heed: the church of God is precious to God. As we think again about 1 Timothy 3:14-16, we're reminded that God wants to display His glory in the church. So how do we stir ourselves up to realize the glory of God in the church? **We sense the gravity of casually ignoring God's Word**. There are many commands in 1 Timothy 5:17-25, and they are not suggestions. God says to appoint certain men, and He means what He says. Therefore, whatever He says, we are called to obey.

In addition to seeing the gravity of casually ignoring God's Word, **we see the glory of rightly ordering Christ's church**. Many believers have had negative experiences with the church, and in light of all the negative baggage, they just can't see how the church can display the glory of God. We need to be reminded that this is not the way things have to be. It's certainly not God's intention. God's intention is not for shepherds to exploit the sheep or for sheep to abuse the shepherd. God's intention is for pastors to lay their lives down for the flock, living among them and loving them with the love of Christ. In response, the congregation—the sheep—love and follow their shepherds, giving to them generously and willingly as the Word of God is faithfully taught. This is the context in which the gospel flourishes.

We will undermine our efforts to see the advance of the gospel if we don't pay attention to God's design for the church. The end goal of this passage is not that we would have well-paid pastors or public rebukes but that the church would display the glory of God and uphold the truth. The ultimate purpose is that the gospel would go forward from the church. This is why we need to sense the gravity of disobeying God's Word on this issue. God's glory is seen when we order the church according to what He has said.

Finally, in order not to be indifferent to these truths, **we remind ourselves of the kindness of God in the gospel**. How do we avoid the pitfalls of gossip and allegations and suspicions? How do we foster an environment of love and forgiveness and unity among those who are leading and those who are led? There is only one way, and that is through the gospel. As a pastor, I need the gospel to deliver me from self-centeredness, from the desire for shameful gain, laziness, a sense of entitlement, and a host of other sins. At the same time the congregation needs the gospel in order to be delivered from criticism, a spirit of disunity, gossip, and discontentment. In short, all of us need the gospel. Only by the grace of God can elders and the church be cared for properly.

Reflect and Discuss

1. Have you ever worked in a company where labor and management were antagonistic to each other? How does that compare to the atmosphere in your church?

2. In what ways can you show and express respect for your pastor? How can you respect the other leaders in your church?

3. How might the pastor's salary be a reflection on the church's view of God's Word?

4. Have you ever been tempted to criticize your leaders publicly? How does this passage speak to that temptation?

5. What process does your church follow when a leader is accused?

6. How can a congregation avoid prejudice and favoritism when determining whether a leader deserves to be rebuked in public?

7. When done well, what can the public rebuke of a church leader communicate to people outside the church?

8. What processes does your church follow in appointing various leadership and service roles? Would you say your church functions biblically or unbiblically in this area?

9. What is the danger according to 5:22 of thoughtlessly appointing leaders? How might the church be affected when unqualified leaders are appointed?

10. How can a proper relationship between the leaders and the congregation bring glory to God? How does an appreciation of the gospel make this more likely?

What About Slavery, Paul?

1 TIMOTHY 6:1-2

Main Idea: Although slavery is a product of sin, slaves should live for the glory of God and the advancement of the gospel.

I. **Slavery in History**
   A. World history is filled with various types of slavery.
      1. Hebrew servanthood
      2. Roman slavery
      3. Indentured servitude
      4. African slave trade
   B. Biblical history is filled with various perspectives on slavery.
      1. Slavery is not a part of creation; it is a product of sin.
      2. Specific situations in a sinful world warrant specific instructions to a sinful world.
      3. Biblical instructions concerning slavery do not imply biblical approval of slavery.

II. **Slavery in Scripture (6:1-2)**
   A. The Bible condemns slavery.
      1. Slavery undermines God's creation.
      2. Slavery violates God's Word.
   B. The Bible regulates slavery.
      1. God mandates physical protection for slaves.
      2. God requires financial provision for slaves.
      3. God ensures caring supervision of slaves.
      4. God promotes (and in some ways guarantees) eventual freedom from slavery.
   C. The Bible encourages slaves.
      1. Honor unbelieving masters.
      2. Respect believing masters.
   D. The Bible redeems slavery.
      1. The beauty of Christ: Our Master has become our servant.
      2. The essence of Christianity: We gladly become His slave.

Four score and seven years ago our fathers brought forth,
upon on this continent, a new nation, conceived in liberty, and
dedicated to the proposition that all men are created equal.

Thus began one of the most famous speeches in all of American history, the Gettysburg Address, delivered by President Abraham Lincoln on November 19, 1863. Lincoln's call for equality was a direct affront to the practice of slavery that dominated the Confederate South, what some would even call the "Christian South." Pastors and church members across communities in the South were buying, selling, trading, using, and even abusing predominantly African slaves. This was, without question, one of the darkest periods of American Christian history. This dark period of our history makes a passage of Scripture like 1 Timothy 6:1-2 all the more sensitive. The most important perspective on this issue is not man's opinion but God's Word. Here in our passage Paul briefly addressed the issue of slavery.

As soon as they come across Paul's reference to slaves in verses 1-2, many Christians begin to wonder whether the apostle Paul was promoting slavery. Other passages in the New Testament that deal with slavery, like Colossians 3:22–4:1, may leave us wondering the same thing. And when we turn to see how slavery was dealt with in the Old Testament, the issue may be further confused in our minds. Maybe you're wondering even now, "Does God support slavery?"

Slavery in History

The question of slavery is one of the most significant questions posed to Christianity, particularly in light of the kinds of slavery practiced by Christians in Europe and America in previous centuries. That's why we need to understand what the Bible has to say on this issue and, more specifically, why Paul would write what he did in 1 Timothy 6. Although we'll begin by looking at the practice of slavery in history, we need to understand that this issue is relevant for us now in the twenty-first century.

It will be helpful to provide some background and context to our discussion of slavery so that we can better define our terms. **World history is filled with various types of slavery**, which means we should be careful when we talk about this subject. When you hear the word *slavery*, it's likely that certain images immediately pop up in your mind, images that represent abuses and injustices. While many of these images may be historically accurate in certain contexts, not all forms of slavery have looked the same in their respective era or location. Consider below four different ways in which slavery has been practiced in history.

First, we have the model of **Hebrew servanthood**. When we look at God's laws for His people in the Old Testament, we see a system of Hebrew servanthood that was set up for impoverished Israelites to become servants. This servanthood was designed to provide for poorer Israelites and their families. Even though Deuteronomy 15:1-18 tells us that God desires that none of His people are poor, He nevertheless makes provision for those in poverty, since poverty is a reality in a sinful and imperfect world. Leviticus 25:35-43 helps us understand more about God's perspective on slavery:

> *If your brother becomes destitute and cannot sustain himself among you, you are to support him as a foreigner or temporary resident, so that he can continue to live among you. Do not profit or take interest from him, but fear your God and let your brother live among you. You are not to lend him your silver with interest or sell him your food for profit. I am Yahweh your God, who brought you out of the land of Egypt to give you the land of Canaan and to be your God.*
>
> *If your brother among you becomes destitute and sells himself to you, you must not force him to do slave labor. Let him stay with you as a hired hand or temporary resident; he may work for you until the Year of Jubilee. Then he and his children are to be released from you, and he may return to his clan and his ancestral property. They are not to be sold as slaves, because they are My slaves that I brought out of the land of Egypt. You are not to rule over them harshly but fear your God.*

This passage describes a system of servanthood in Israel whereby someone could sell himself into slavery in order to escape poverty. Such an individual was to be treated not as a slave but as a hired servant, a worker. The individual would basically enter into a contractual agreement with an employer, working until he could establish himself as a free and full citizen again. Now there were certainly unjust and abusive slaveholders among God's people. Israel's sin was, after all, apparent throughout its history. However, cruelty was not God's intention for slavery in Israel, for the slavery He chose to regulate was extremely different from the pre-Civil War slavery in the southern United States. In His mercy God even provided a reprieve for slaves by instituting sabbatical years when they had to be released (Exod 21:2-4).

Second, we'll consider **Roman slavery**. Slavery was deeply ingrained into the Roman Empire and its economy. Some scholars estimate that over one-third of the people in the Roman Empire were slaves—that's approximately 50 or 60 million individuals!

Out of those 50–60 million slaves, there were a variety of different practices of slavery in this era of history. Some slaves were simply employees who did a variety of different kinds of work: teachers, craftsmen, managers, cooks, and even government officials. Many slaves owned slaves themselves. It's also important to recognize that Roman slavery was not fundamentally based on ethnicity or skin color but on economic and social status. In order to gain Roman citizenship and thus enter into Roman society, many people would sell themselves into slavery. In many cases slavery was beneficial for poorer individuals, providing security and stability for slaves in a variety of different venues. There were also opportunities beyond slavery, for many slaves were released by the time they were 30 years of age, as they had become capable of providing for themselves at that point.

Despite the more humane practices of slavery in some cases, we don't want to paint an idealistic picture of slavery. After all, a slave was still a slave—marginalized, powerless, and often prone to disgrace or insult. While some slaves were indeed salaried employees with great responsibilities, others were subjected to grueling labor and harsh treatment, including sexual abuse. Slavery could be and sometimes was extremely degrading and destructive. Yet we shouldn't make the mistake of thinking that all slavery in the Greco-Roman world was inhumane. This system, which was so ingrained into the economy of the Roman Empire, was in many ways different from the slavery of the antebellum South.

A third form of slavery we need to consider is **indentured servitude**. This form of slavery was more common in colonial America, as many could not afford to come to the new country on their own. They would contract themselves out as indentured servants and agree to work in certain households in apprentice-type roles until they could earn enough money to pay off their debt. Historians estimate that over one-half to two-thirds of European white immigrants who came to America came as indentured servants. This picture of slavery is much closer to Hebrew servanthood than anything else.

Fourth and finally, there is the picture of slavery connected to the **African slave trade**. This last example of slavery was promoted across the eighteenth and nineteenth centuries, such that millions upon millions of Africans were traded and sold across Europe. They were transported in cruel, grueling conditions that would leave many of them dead before arriving at their destination. Upon being sold into slavery, these slaves were subjected to harsh working conditions as well as physical abuse, sexual abuse, and torture. Frederick Douglass, a leader of the abolitionist movement in the 1800s, wrote the following about his first slave-master, Captain Anthony:

> He was a cruel man, hardened by a long life of slave-holding. He would at times seem to take great pleasure in whipping a slave. I have often been awakened at the dawn of day by the most heart-rending shrieks of an own aunt of mine, whom he used to tie up to a joist, and whip . . . till she was literally covered with blood. No words, no tears, no prayer, from his gory victim, seemed to move his iron heart from its bloody purpose. (Douglass, *Narrative*, 3–4)

Though I hesitate to share such an awful account, I cite this for two reasons. First, this account reminds us of the horror of what took place in slavery in our own country not that long ago. And second, we need to be reminded that this is not the kind of slavery Paul was addressing in 1 Timothy 6. While some slaves had unbelieving and sometimes cruel masters, this passage will be confusing to you if the only picture of slavery you have is the African slave trade. Some of the slaves the apostle was addressing were likely sitting in the church amid Christian brothers and sisters who loved them, cared for them, and were commanded to provide for them as fellow members of the body of Christ. Though Paul was not ignorant of the evils of slavery in his day, he was by no means condoning the mistreatment of slaves.

Now that we've looked at world history, we also need to consider biblical history. **Biblical history is filled with various perspectives on slavery**, from Hebrew servanthood in the Old Testament to Greco-Roman slavery in the New Testament. **Slavery is not a part of creation** (that is, God's original created order); **it is a product of sin**. Genesis 1–2 speaks of the distinction between male and female, but there is no distinction between slave and free persons, since slavery was not a part of God's creation. And if you move forward to the new creation in Revelation 21–22, you see once again that there is no distinction between slave and free in the new heaven and new earth. Heaven will have no poverty that leads to indentured servanthood and no class warfare that leads to a Greco-Roman type of slavery. And certainly there will not be any abuse and mistreatment like what took place during the African slave trade. Sin and slavery will be no more.

The fact that slavery is ultimately connected to sin in Scripture means **specific situations in a sinful world warrant specific instructions to a sinful world**. The instructions in the Old Testament and in 1 Timothy that speak of slaves are addressing specific circumstances surrounding slavery at a specific time. When we understand this context, we see that **biblical instructions concerning slavery do not imply biblical approval of slavery**. Slavery is not God's ultimate design. It is a product of sin. When Paul addressed slavery, he was not endorsing it; he was helping shepherd people who were trapped in a sin-tainted economic and social system that produced the need for slavery.

Consider how Scripture deals similarly with other issues. Was divorce a part of God's original creation? No, absolutely not. Divorce is clearly a result of sin entering the world; yet Scripture addresses divorce by giving us guidelines and regulations for this less-than-ideal reality (Deut 24:1-4; Matt 19:3-9). We see something similar with slavery. Even though slavery was a product of sin, God addressed it at different times and in different ways throughout Scripture.

Slavery in Scripture
1 TIMOTHY 6:1-2

The most important question we need to answer is this: What does Scripture say about slavery? To begin with, there are some clear ways in which **the Bible condemns slavery**. Specifically, the Bible condemns **slavery that undermines God's creation**. Genesis 1:27 should shape our thinking here: "So God created man in His own image; He created him in the image of God; He created them male and female." Based on this truth **we have equal dignity before God**, but slavery undermines this dignity by functionally denying it. Remember, it wasn't President Lincoln who came up with the idea that all men are created with equal dignity; God did. Job implies this when he talks about why he refuses to mistreat his servants. He asks, "Did not the One who made me in the womb also make them? Did not the same God form us both in the womb?" (Job 31:15).

We see this same perspective in the New Testament. Our equal dignity before God can be seen in Galatians 3:28: "There is no Jew or

Greek, slave or free, male or female; for you are all one in Christ Jesus." In other words, even though we have differences, we all have equal dignity before God, and as believers we have an equal position in Christ. This equal dignity is also the basis James uses for arguing against favoritism in the church (Jas 2:1). In these and other examples, the Bible is not expressly prohibiting all forms of slavery, but it is definitely ripping apart the core foundations behind many forms of slavery. As we think about these biblical texts, we need to be reminded that the first-century Roman slavery of the New Testament period was not based on ethnicity or skin color like the African slave trade. The New Testament vehemently opposes any form of ethnic or racial superiority.

Just as all individuals have equal dignity before God, as believers, **we are equally submissive to God**. When Paul addresses slaves or their masters, he says that everything they do ought to be done in submission to Christ and in reverence for Him. In Colossians 3:22 Paul gives the following exhortation: "Slaves, obey your human masters in everything. Don't work only while being watched, in order to please men, but work wholeheartedly, *fearing the Lord*" (emphasis added; see also Eph 6:5; Col 4:1). One reason we are to submit equally to God is that **we will receive equal justice from God**. In Colossians 3:25 Paul tells us that God is impartial, and in Ephesians 6:9 we hear the following warning: "And masters, treat your slaves the same way, without threatening them, because you know that both their Master and yours is in heaven, and there is no favoritism with Him." In other words, earthly masters have a Master in heaven who will act with perfect justice in response to how slaves are treated. As for Christian slaves, even though they may endure temporary injustice, eternal justice awaits.

So we've seen that the Bible condemns slavery that undermines God's creation; next we see that the Bible likewise condemns **slavery that violates God's Word**. In clear, unequivocal language the Bible speaks against slavery in two specific ways. First, **the Bible denounces physical abuse**. This prohibition would apply to many forms of physical abuse but particularly when this abuse is associated with the institution of slavery. In Exodus 21:26-27 God made clear that physical abuse is intolerable, for if the master of a slave caused the slave to lose an eye or a tooth, the slave was to be set free. In verse 20 of the same chapter, we read that if a slave died as a result of physical abuse, then the owner was to be punished. In short, physical abuse of any kind by masters of slaves was directly condemned by God.

Second, we know slavery is condemned because **the Bible denounces human trafficking**. Exodus 21:16 says, "Whoever kidnaps a person must be put to death, whether he sells him or the person is found in his possession." Kidnapping a slave is punishable by death, and that death penalty applies to the one selling the slave and the one buying the slave. We're reminded at this point about what Paul said earlier in 1 Timothy concerning the need for the law to restrain evil. Paul explicitly mentions—alongside murder, sexual immorality, and homosexuality—the sin of kidnapping (1:10). The word "kidnappers" in the original means a "man-stealer" or a "slave-dealer" (BDAG, 76). Anyone who kidnaps people in order to sell them as slaves is "lawless and rebellious . . . ungodly and sinful . . . unholy and irreverent" (1:9).

I have emphasized the evil of human trafficking for two reasons. First, if these truths had been embraced and obeyed by Christians in the eighteenth and nineteenth centuries, slavery never would have existed as it did in the South. The Bible is not at all silent on this issue, and it in no way tolerates the kind of slavery that took place in this country. Pastors and church members who used God's Word to justify the practice of slavery were living in sin. Paul clearly considered the kind of practices promoted in the African slave trade as abominable, a violation of God's Word, and a denial of God's gospel.

Second, the issue of human trafficking is important to think about because it is so prevalent around the world today. There are an estimated twenty-seven million slaves in the world today, which is more than any other time in history. Human trafficking, which includes buying, selling, trading, and exploiting people for forced labor or for sex, is the second largest and fastest growing industry in the world today. The statistics are staggering (from Random Facts):

- Approximately 80 percent of trafficking victims are women and girls, and half are minors.
- According to UNICEF, 30 million children over the past 30 years have been sexually exploited through human trafficking.
- Over 10,000 Nepali girls as young as nine have been sold into India's red-light district over the last decade.
- Over 10,000 children between the ages of six and fourteen are currently in brothels in Sri Lanka.

Human trafficking is one of the fastest growing criminal enterprises because it is relatively low risk with high profit potential. Criminal organizations are increasingly attracted to human trafficking because, unlike drugs, humans can be sold repeatedly. According to the U.S. State Department, human trafficking is one of the greatest human rights challenges of this century, both in the United States and around the world. As followers of Christ, we cannot ignore these horrific tragedies. We need to see that this is a reality in the world today and that the Bible condemns it. We are called to stand up against these evils (Eph 5:11).

We've seen that the Bible condemns human trafficking and other forms of oppression. Next we need to understand that **the Bible regulates slavery**. As we saw in Exodus 21 earlier, **God mandates physical protection for slaves**. Slaves abused by their masters were immediately to be set free and compensated for their injuries (Exod 21:16, 26-27). In addition, **God requires financial provision for slaves**. Leviticus 25:39-40 talks about impoverished Hebrew servants who sold themselves to a master, and it says the master must provide ample provision for the servant. Likewise, 2 Samuel 9:9-10 talks about the economic rights of slaves, including the right of slaves to have other slaves. Many of these passages communicate a similar idea, namely, **God ensures caring supervision of slaves**. Leviticus 25 prohibits masters from ruling ruthlessly over their slaves, even giving slaves the right to enjoy the Sabbath. The Old Testament also gives us examples of close, caring relationships between slaves or servants and their masters, such as the relationship between Gehazi and Elisha (2 Kgs 4–8).

Finally, we see that **God promotes (and in some ways guarantees) eventual freedom from slavery**. Several passages in the Old Testament prohibit masters from keeping slaves for more than six years, unless the slave consented to it (Lev 25; Exod 21; Deut 15). All the slaves in Israel would be released in the seventh year of each seven-year cycle so that slavery would not be a perpetual state for anyone. God provided other ways to keep people out of slavery:

- He commanded the poor to be provided for during harvest times (Lev 19:9-10; 23:22; Deut 24:20-21).
- He commanded Israelites to lend generously to the poor without interest (Deut 15:7-8; Exod 22:25; Lev 25:36-37).
- He instructed that all of a person's debts be canceled in the seventh year in order to guard against poverty (Deut 15:4).

God's promotion of freedom for slaves is a foretaste of the coming heavenly reality when, in the new creation, slavery and the poverty that fuels slavery will be no more. For that reason Paul encouraged slaves in 1 Corinthians 7:21 who could become free to avail themselves of the opportunity.

Our survey of the Bible on the topic of slavery has not been exhaustive, but it has provided a needed context for understanding our passage in 1 Timothy 6. When Paul addresses Timothy in verses 1-2, he is writing to the pastor of a church where there is likely tension between slaves and masters. **The Bible encourages slaves** who are forced to live in this imperfect situation in several ways. They are to **honor unbelieving masters**. That Paul is referring to non-Christian masters in verse 1 is clear from the fact that he made a contrast between unbelieving masters and Christian masters in verse 2. Slaves should treat their unbelieving masters as "worthy of all respect"; after all, they too are created in the image of God. The word "respect" here might also be translated "honor," and it comes from the same root as the command in 5:3, where Paul said to "*honor* widows" (NASB; emphasis added).

Paul wanted slaves to honor their masters. Slaves were to honor unbelieving masters "so that God's name and His teaching will not be blasphemed" (6:1). Let's break this purpose clause down into two parts. First, slaves act this way **for the glory of God**. This is the motivation that drove Paul, and it drives all of Scripture (1 Cor 10:31). In 1 Timothy we've already seen this in several forms. For example, we pray for all people, and we honor widows because this pleases God (2:3; 5:4). Elders must have a good reputation so that God's name is not brought to disrepute (3:7). Paul's deepest concern in addressing the conduct of slaves was for the glory of God to be made known, particularly before unbelieving masters. These unbelieving masters should see the grace of God in the lives of slaves who had become followers of Christ.

There's a sense in which Paul's words apply to all followers of Christ who have unbelieving employers. If you profess to follow Christ, you should honor your employer so that they might see the glory of God in you. Everything you do at work is a representation of your God, so work hard and work well. Even when it's not easy, we are to obey, for Peter said elsewhere,

> *Household slaves, submit with all fear to your masters, not only to the good and gentle but also to the cruel. For it brings favor if, mindful of God's will, someone endures grief from suffering unjustly. For what credit is there if you sin and are punished, and you endure it? But*

when you do what is good and suffer, if you endure it, this brings favor with God. (1 Pet 2:18-20)

Whether you're a student or an employee, remember that every time you turn in a project, hand in an assignment, make a decision, or take an action, you are to reflect the glory of God.

There is another related goal in the way slaves honor masters: **for the advancement of the gospel**. In Titus 2:9-10 Paul said,

Slaves are to be submissive to their masters in everything, and to be well-pleasing, not talking back or stealing, but demonstrating utter faithfulness, so that they may adorn the teaching of God our Savior in everything.

This is a beautiful way to describe the goal of obedience—so that we may "adorn" the gospel. Paul's exhortation has a missionary motivation. Unbelieving masters should see the hard work of believers and be drawn to the glory of God and the fruit of the gospel. Christians should view their jobs as serving this great purpose.

These greater purposes that Paul speaks of remind us that **Christianity is not primarily aimed at social reform**. If the purpose of Christianity was to change societal structures, then we would not expect Paul to speak like he has been in this letter or his other writings. Instead, we would expect him to exhort the Ephesian church to work against the system of slavery, but Paul told slaves to live for the salvation of their masters. That's because **Christianity is primarily aimed at personal redemption**. So that, as people are redeemed, societal structures begin to be transformed. The key is the heart of the people. *That* is the primary way the Bible addresses slavery—by aiming for personal redemption and personal transformation. Redeemed individuals are formed into a community of believers who are one in Christ, who love and support one another regardless of whether they are Jews, Gentiles, slaves, or freemen. When the gospel begins to transform people like this, slavery is seen in a much different light. As one writer put it, the gospel lays "the explosive charge . . . that ultimately—although sadly, belatedly—leads to detonation, and the destruction of slavery" altogether (Harris, *Slave of Christ*, 68).

If slaves are to adorn the gospel in the way they treat their unbelieving masters, how should they treat a master who is a believer? It seems that some slaves were taking advantage of their Christian masters, thinking that they no longer had an obligation to keep their agreements to serve. But Paul says that having a believing master is all the more reason to serve him with joy and hard work. In verse 2 the apostle says that instead of being disrespectful to believing masters, slaves "should serve them better, since those who benefit from their service are believers and dearly loved." Slaves are to **work wholeheartedly** in such situations and avoid slacking off. The same holds true for Christian employees in our own day. They should not take advantage of brothers and sisters in Christ who have authority over them in the workplace. Instead, they are to **serve selflessly**. This kind of selfless service is a fruit of gospel transformation. Does this characterize your life and work?

Ultimately, given everything we've seen so far, **the Bible redeems slavery**. By that I mean that God's Word takes slavery, a product of sin, and turns it into a powerful image of God's goodness. Consider **the beauty of Christ** and the gospel reality that **our Master has become our servant**. As Paul said in Philippians 2:7, the same Jesus who was fully divine "emptied Himself by assuming *the form of a slave*, taking on the likeness of men" (emphasis added). The word "slave" in Philippians 2 comes from the same word we see in 1 Timothy 6:1—*doulos*. Christ took the form of a slave. Jesus took this posture in John 13:4-5 when He wrapped a garment around His waist and washed His disciples' feet. And Mark 10:45 says something similar with regard to the purpose for Jesus' coming: "For even the Son of Man did not come to be served, but to serve, and to give His life—a ransom for many." That's the gospel in a nutshell. That's good news!

The essence of Christianity is that our Master has become our servant and so, in turn, **we gladly become His slave**. The word Paul often uses to describe himself at the beginning of his letters is this same word—*doulos*—translated as "servant" or "slave."[13] A slave is one who belongs to another and is under the authority of another. That was the way Paul wanted to be identified, and it's the way every follower of Christ should want to be identified. We are slaves of the Lord Jesus Christ, and unlike the sinful pictures of slavery we see in the world, slavery and service to the Lord Jesus is glorious freedom! It is glad service rendered to a gracious Master. At the end of the day, the question is not whether we are slaves but whose slaves we are. Either we will serve sin and Satan (John 8:34; Rom 6:11), or we will serve the King of kings.

---

[13] We're reminded that Moses, Joshua, and David were also referred to as "the servant of the LORD" (Deut 34:5; Judg 2:8; Ps 18).

Reflect and Discuss

1. What is Paul's main motivation in instructing slaves according to verse 1, and why is this crucial for this important and sensitive issue?

2. Do you tend to treat Christian employers better or worse than non-Christian employers? If worse, how might verse 2 change your mindset in this area?

3. In light of the emotions attached to the issue of slavery, what kind of attitude should characterize our conversations about this issue?

4. Have you heard anyone criticize the Bible for what it says about slavery? What concerns have you had when you read what the Bible says about slavery?

5. How have Christian societies in the past used the Bible to justify slavery?

6. How was the American slave trade different from the slavery in Old Testament Israel or in New Testament Rome?

7. What is the difference between regulating a less-than-ideal situation, such as slavery or divorce, and condoning it?

8. How do the various forms of slavery violate the principle that all people have equal dignity before God?

9. In what specific ways can you honor your employer this week? How might that glorify God and advance the gospel?

10. How does our understanding of slavery help us appreciate what Jesus did for us? How does it help us understand our proper response?

The Gospel and Materialism

1 TIMOTHY 6:3-10

Main Idea: For the sake of urgent physical and spiritual need around the world, and for the sake of your own soul, be satisfied in God instead of material things.

I. **Open Your Eyes.**
   A. See the urgent spiritual need in the world.
   B. See the urgent physical need in the world.
   C. Realize the extravagant kingdom opportunity in the church.

II. **Watch Your Hearts (6:3-10).**
   A. Don't crave spiritual division, but be content in the gospel!
   B. Don't crave material possession, but be content in God!

III. **Give Your Lives.**
   A. Proclaim the gospel as good!
   B. Live like God is gain!

It's a startling feeling. You're driving along in the right lane, and like any safe, responsible driver, you check your rearview mirror. The left lane looks wide open, so you put on your blinker and begin easing over. But unbeknownst to you, there is a car right next to you. When you begin moving over to the left, the other car lays on its horn. Initially frightened, you swerve back over into your own lane and attempt to catch your breath. Immediately you begin to wonder, "Where did that car come from?" You failed to account for your blind spot.

In our discussion of 1 Timothy 6:1-2, we considered one of the most glaring blind spots for Christians in American history—slavery. Christians in the South gathered on Sundays, singing and studying God's Word, all the while mistreating men, women, and children as slaves. That's scary. It's scary to think that good intentions, regular worship, and even weekly study of the Bible don't altogether prevent this type of "blindness." Part of our sinful nature instinctively chooses to see what we want to see, and to ignore what we want to ignore, until it's too late and the damage is done.

The example of American slavery beckons us to ask the question in our own lives, Where do I have blind spots? Are there areas where we, as individuals or as churches, are blind to our own sin—even blatant sin? In my opinion, 1 Timothy 6:3-10 shines a light on one of the glaring sins of many Christians and churches in America today—materialism.

Open Your Eyes

Materialism has blinded many of us from seeing the things God would have us see. In our culture, in our churches, and in our own lives we have failed to take notice of some pressing needs all around us. We must awaken from our wealth-induced sleep and **see the urgent spiritual need in the world**. Out of the seven billion people in the world, only one-third claim to be Christian. That leaves us with 4.7 billion people in the world today who are on a road that leads to an eternal hell. And two billion of those 4.7 billion unbelievers have no access to the gospel. That's a sobering reality. To put that in perspective, think of one particular region in northern India. Given that the death rate in this region is about five thousand people per day, and the number of evangelicals is estimated at less than .01 percent, about 9,999 people plunge into hell every two days. That is *urgent* spiritual need.

We also need to **see the urgent physical need in the world**. Today over one billion people live and die in desperate poverty on less than one dollar per day. Close to a billion others live on less than two dollars per day. That means nearly half of the world is struggling to find food, shelter, and medical care for the same amount of money you and I can spend on a fountain drink for lunch! Consider that more than 20,000 children will die this very day due to starvation or preventable disease. In the country of Somalia, for example, more than 750,000 people are on the verge of starvation at this moment, and most of them are without Christ. These individuals are poor and powerless, and they are dying quietly in relative obscurity while we comfortably ignore them in our affluence. We live as if they don't even exist. We must open our eyes to the urgent spiritual and physical needs in the world.

Seeing the urgent spiritual and physical needs in the world should lead us to **realize the extravagant kingdom opportunity in the church**. In short, we in America and much of Western Europe are rich. If you make $25,000 per year, you are in the top 10 percent of the world's wealthiest people. Food, water, clothes—God has given us so much.

But what are we doing with these great blessings? Christians give an average of 2.5 percent to their churches, and churches in North America give an average of 2 percent of their funds to overseas missions. Based on these averages, this means that for every one hundred dollars a North American Christian makes, he gives five cents to the rest of the world. Five cents! I wonder if followers of Christ one hundred years from now (if Christ hasn't returned) will look back at Christians in America today and wonder how we could live with such affluence while millions were dying of starvation, many of whom had never heard of Christ? Will they wonder, "How could they prioritize more things, more programs, more comforts for their own kids, while brothers and sisters on the other side of the world were suffering with malnourished bodies and deformed brains?" That's a sobering question our churches need to wrestle with.

What would happen if we truly recognized all that God has given us? And what could we be a part of if we would truly, wholeheartedly, unashamedly, and counterculturally give our lives, our families, and our possessions for the spread of the gospel and the glory of God in a world of urgent spiritual and physical need? That's where I want to be—leading my family and my church to take advantage of the extravagant kingdom opportunity God has given to us for His glory in the world, no matter the cost. I want to see this happen for two reasons.

First, I am convinced by God's Word that when we give extravagantly of our lives and our possessions, we will not only lead others to spiritual and physical life, but we will personally discover where true and lasting joy is found. Second, I am convinced by God's Word that if we don't give in this extravagant way, then not only will other people continue to die spiritually and physically, but *we* may personally find ourselves on a road of ruin and destruction. If that sounds too strong, then consider with me what God says through the apostle Paul in 1 Timothy 6:3-10.

Watch Your Hearts
1 TIMOTHY 6:3-10

Beginning in verse 3, Paul once again addresses the false teachers in Ephesus, referring to two of their destructive "cravings." First, in verse 4 he says that the one who teaches false doctrine has "an unhealthy *craving* for controversy and for quarrels about words, which produce envy, dissension, slander, evil suspicions" (ESV; emphasis added). In verse 10 Paul talks about the love of money and says that "by craving it, some have wandered away from the faith and pierced themselves with many pains." So, based on these two unhealthy desires Paul addresses—the craving for controversy and the craving for money—I want to encourage us to keep a watch on our own hearts in two ways.

The first warning is this: **Don't crave spiritual division**. Paul is addressing those who were teaching "other doctrine," by which he means a teaching that is contrary to the truth, and he says this kind of false teaching leads to division in the church. The caution is illuminating, for Paul tells us that **false teachers are fueled by ignorance and arrogance**. Verse 4 says that they are "conceited, understanding nothing." Being ignorant and arrogant is a bad combination. We also read that **false teaching results in controversy and strife**. Teaching unbiblical doctrine leads to controversy in the church and strife among Christians. Paul listed five different effects of these false teachers on the church: "envy, quarreling, slander, evil suspicions, and constant disagreement" (vv. 4-5). This is what flourishes among those who are "depraved and deprived of the truth, who imagine that godliness is a way to material gain" (v. 5). We need to hear Paul's caution.

Along with Paul's warning, we need to hear **the exhortation: Be content in the gospel**. This is essentially what Paul is getting at in verse 3 when he says to hold fast to the "sound teaching of our Lord Jesus Christ and . . . the teaching that promotes godliness." There is no need to graduate on to something beyond the gospel. As believers, we are to remain in the truth and spend our lives there. We need to be saturated in the gospel of Jesus Christ, His life, His death, His resurrection, His commands, His teachings, and His Word. If we hold fast to this gospel, then it will produce godly minds and godly lives. There is no need to crave anything else. Be content in the gospel.

There's a connection to make here between what the false teachers were teaching and how they were living. These individuals thought godliness was a means of "material gain" (v. 5), meaning financial profit. They were using God to get what they wanted, and this leads to Paul's second warning: **Don't crave material possessions**. We need to be clear on this subject, since Paul states near the end of this same chapter that God "richly provides us with all things to enjoy" (v. 17). Things or possessions are not inherently bad, nor is money intrinsically evil. Remember, it's not money that is the root of all kinds of evil but "the love of money"

(v. 10). As believers, we should take this as a warning to be on guard against a craving for money and possessions that leads us to desire the next gadget, a nicer house, or better clothes. This kind of craving is a real temptation for Christians in our culture.

The caution Paul gave about material possessions is similar to the caution Jesus gave in Matthew 6:19-21:

> *Don't collect for yourselves treasures on earth, where moth and rust destroy and where thieves break in and steal. But collect for yourselves treasures in heaven, where neither moth nor rust destroys, and where thieves don't break in and steal. For where your treasure is, there your heart will be also.*

Did you catch that last statement? Where your money is, there your heart will be also. In other words, your money is an indicator of your heart. Your checkbook reflects your true priorities. That's a scary reality in our culture. Consider how much of our money is invested in our *stuff*. The thing that makes the Matthew passage quoted above, as well as our passage in 1 Timothy 6, so strange is that we are programmed to think of money as a blessing. Of course, it is a blessing in many, many good ways. But Scripture also teaches us that money can be a barrier to God and eternal life. Paul knew this, so he gave us three serious cautions when it comes to materialism.

First, **materialism is deceptive**. Verse 9 talks about those who "fall into temptation, a trap" due to their pursuit of wealth. Money and possessions may look appealing, but Paul tells us they're a trap. Materialism is like drinking seawater. Seawater has a high concentration of salt, so the more you drink, the thirstier you get. In fact, drinking seawater will actually cause you to become dehydrated more quickly. If you continue drinking it, you'll eventually go unconscious and die. Money and possessions can have the same effect on us. Some "things" may look desirable, but if we indulge in them in an unhealthy way, they will kill our souls.

Second, **materialism is dangerous**. It leads people into many senseless and harmful desires. The love of money and things will send you down a path that is fraught with danger. Here are some of its deadly fruits: selfishness, cheating, fraud, perjury, robbery, envy, quarreling, hatred, violence, and murder. Or think of some other effects of materialism, which may immediately come to mind: pornography, blackmail, exploitation of the weak, oppression of the poor, immorality, and injustice. In short, materialism is a breeding ground for thousands of other sins. Are you, Christian, foolish enough to think you are immune to these things?

Consider some warnings from Scripture: Achan and his family were put to death because of Achan's desire for a few forbidden possessions (Josh 7). Solomon, despite his great wisdom, was tempted by the love of money and possessions (1 Kgs 4:26; 6:38–7:1; 10:26–11:1). The New Testament is also full of such warnings. Jesus says to His disciples, "I assure you: It will be hard for a rich person to enter the kingdom of heaven!" (Matt 19:23). Or consider Luke 6:24-25: "But woe to you who are rich, for you have received your comfort. Woe to you who are now full, for you will be hungry." James writes something similar:

> *Come now, you rich people! Weep and wail over the miseries that are coming on you. Your wealth is ruined and your clothes are moth-eaten. Your silver and gold are corroded, and their corrosion will be a witness against you and will eat your flesh like fire. You stored up treasure in the last days!* (Jas 5:1-3)

The Bible is full of these exhortations. Needless to say, then, materialism is dangerous.

Third, **materialism is damning**. If that sounds too extreme, then consider what Paul says in this passage. According to verse 9, materialistic desires "plunge people into ruin and destruction." That word "plunge" has the idea of sinking, and it's the same word used by Luke to describe the fishing boats that were sinking due to an abundance of fish. A love for money and possessions will drown you eternally. Paul is clearly warning us of eternal ruin and the final judgment here, and not just a loss of reward, for a number of reasons. For example, in verse 7 the apostle talks about what cannot be taken out of this world, which is clearly a reference to eternal realities. Similarly, verse 12 talks about fighting the good fight of faith in order to lay hold on *eternal* life. Finally, in verse 19 Paul addresses storing up treasure "for the age to come." The point is clear: heaven and hell are at stake in how we view our possessions. When this life is over, it won't matter how much stuff you have owned. The late Steve Jobs, CEO of Apple, even with all his billions, was not able to take a penny of it to eternity. Possessions will always let you down at the most important point of your life—when death is at hand.

We've seen so far that materialism is deceptive, dangerous, and damning. Based on that, I want to call you to run—run *from* the love of money and run *to* the love of God! This is **the exhortation** from Paul as he tells us to **be content in God**. As opposed to the false teachers who were trying to use godliness as a way to get material gain, Paul said in verse 6, "Godliness with contentment is a great gain." Notice Paul didn't say, "Stop living for gain." Instead, he said to live for great gain, that is, eternal, infinite gain. There's Someone who is better than money. Don't settle for the love of money; be satisfied in the love of God. That's what it means to have "godliness with contentment." When you have God, you don't have to crave more stuff in this world. Paul says something similar in Philippians 4:12-13:

> *I know both how to have a little, and I know how to have a lot. In any and all circumstances I have learned the secret of being content— whether well fed or hungry, whether in abundance or in need. I am able to do all things through Him who strengthens me.*

Whether he had much or little, it didn't matter to Paul. He had Christ, and that was enough.

So how do we fight against the constant desire for more in this culture? We fight an increasing desire for things with an increasing delight in Christ. As Paul goes on to say a few verses later in Philippians 4, "And my God will supply all your needs according to His riches in glory in Christ Jesus" (v. 19). If you are in Christ, why do you need to live for riches here and now, when you have riches in glory?

When you realize that God is gain, then you will begin to live differently from the world. We'll consider several ways in which this plays out. First, you will **live simply**, which is what Paul said in verse 8: "But if we have food and clothing, we will be content with these." Did you catch that? Food and clothing. That's all Paul needed. Christians can and should be content with the simple necessities of life. In a culture of accumulation that is built on having more and more, always consuming, always looking for the next deal, we as believers need to have a counter-cultural perspective. Quite simply, we don't need more. Does God love you? Does He desire your good? Then hear Him saying, "You don't need more stuff. Live simply. And in the process, trust Me to satisfy you far better than more stuff ever will."

Let's believe God in this area of our lives. Let's go against the grain. Let's live simply. Believing in the authority of God's Word, we should live differently from our materialistic culture by being content with the necessities of life and forsaking luxuries. And we do all this because we are content in God. One of the best statements on this issue is from the

Evangelical Commitment to Simple Lifestyle produced by the Lausanne Committee for World Evangelization over 30 years ago:

> Yet we resolve to renounce waste and oppose extravagance in personal living, clothing and housing, travel and church buildings. We also accept the distinction between necessities and luxuries, creative hobbies and empty status symbols, modesty and vanity, occasional celebrations and normal routine, and between the service of God and slavery to fashion. Where to draw the line requires conscientious thought and decision by us, together with members of our family.[14]

A second way in which contentment in God should play out in our lives is that we should **give sacrificially**. This point will come out more clearly toward the end of the chapter, where Paul told Timothy to exhort the rich believers "to do what is good, to be rich in good works, to be generous, willing to share, storing up for themselves a good reserve for the age to come, so that they may take hold of life that is real" (vv. 18-19). The rich, which includes most Americans, should live simply and then take everything else and leverage it all for the glory of Christ in a world of urgent physical and spiritual need. This is a practical takeaway from 1 Timothy 6, both for individuals and for churches. Let's limit our budgets and grow in contentment in order to free up as much of our resources as possible for the purpose of making disciples in all nations. Just to be clear, lest we fall into the trap of legalism, there's not one set figure we can establish for every family or every individual. Rather, we want to resolve to be content with a certain lifestyle and then fight against the desire to live above that lifestyle. Whatever else God entrusts to us, we give away freely to Him. There is deep joy in this kind of living and giving.

As believers we live simply, give sacrificially, and finally, we **thrive eternally**. As we saw earlier in verses 18-19, by being generous and sharing our resources, we are storing up treasures for the future and laying hold of true, eternal life. This principle is illustrated in the life of John Wesley, the Methodist pastor and missionary who lived from 1703 to

---

[14] The full statement can be found here: http://www.lausanne.org/en/documents /lops/77-lop-20.html#3. The section cited above is taken from section 5 titled "Personal Life-style."

1791. In 1731 Wesley began to limit his expenses so he would have more money to give to the poor. One year his income was 30 pounds, and his living expenses were 28 pounds, thus leaving him with two pounds to give away. The next year his income doubled, but he still lived on 28 pounds, which allowed him to give away the remaining 32 pounds. For the next two years his income continued to increase so that in the fourth year he was able to give away 92 pounds to the poor. To put this into present-day figures, Wesley was making about $160,000 a year, but he lived like he was making $20,000 a year.

Wesley believed a Christian's increase in income should result not in an increased standard of *living* but in an increased standard of *giving*. He taught that Christians should not merely tithe but give away all extra income after the family and creditors were taken care of. Wesley continued this practice throughout his life, and even when his income rose slightly over 1,400 pounds, he gave away all but 30 pounds. He was afraid of laying up treasure on earth, so money went out to charity as quickly as it came in. When he died in 1791, the only money mentioned in his will was the miscellaneous coins found in his pockets and dresser drawers. Most of the 30,000 pounds he had earned in his lifetime had been given away.

If we took this same attitude toward money today, the kind of attitude Paul exhorts us to take in 1 Timothy 6:3-10, then we would see Christians and churches breaking free from the deadly danger of possessions. Instead, they would be using their resources to inundate the lost and the poor for the glory of Christ. Some people might call this extreme, or even being irresponsible toward our own families, but I don't think many Christians in our culture are in any danger of giving away *too* much. In all seriousness, do we really believe we're going to stand before Christ one day and hear Him say, "I have this against you—you gave too much away"? Jesus never called someone a fool for giving too much and keeping too little; He did just the opposite (see Luke 12:13-34). Not being rich toward God is the foolish option. May we be those who give lavishly and willingly because we treasure God above our money.

Give Your Lives

When we prize God above our possessions, we will naturally be **proclaiming the gospel as good**. The gospel is, after all, good news. Paul says in 2 Corinthians 8:9, "For you know the grace of our Lord Jesus Christ:

Though He was rich, for your sake He became poor, so that by His poverty you might become rich." The Bible describes the incarnation in the language of riches and poverty. Christ became poor, taking our sin upon Himself, so that we might have His righteousness (2 Cor 5:21). We can tell every person and every people group on the planet that God has become poor so that they might become rich if they will repent of their sins and trust in Jesus Christ. That's infinitely good news!

A materialistic world will not be won by a materialistic church for two reasons. First, we will not show the world that Christ is all satisfying as long as we are on the path of materialism. How will we lead people to abandon the things of this world if we in the church are attached to the same things? We will be communicating that Christ plus our stuff equals satisfaction, but that is not the gospel. Even our church services can evidence a lack of satisfaction in Christ. Brothers and sisters in Christ who live in difficult places around the world gather together not because they like the worship band or the sound system or smooth transitions in the service; they gather because they want to hear the Word of God. Is that enough for us?

The second reason a materialistic world will not be reached by a materialistic church is that the resources needed to win the world to Christ will be kept in our second homes and in our nicer possessions. We'll continue to give our pennies to the Great Commission. Ralph Winter has said, "Obedience to the Great Commission has more consistently been poisoned by affluence than by anything else." Those who love their money do not give it away.

Finally, we not only proclaim the gospel, but we must be **living like God is gain**. Let's live simply and give sacrificially, knowing that this will be for our eternal good. It will also be good for brothers and sisters around the world who are struggling to survive and for the lost around the world who need to know that God is better than everything this world offers.

Reflect and Discuss

1. How does Satan use materialism to blind Christians to the needs of the world?
2. What is holding you back from giving radically of your money, time, and family to God's work?

3. Do false teachers always actively promote division, or does it happen as a side effect of their teaching? Can you think of examples of both?
4. In what way is the gospel simple? In what way is it inexhaustibly rich and deep? Is it possible to spend one's whole life meditating on the gospel? Explain your answer.
5. What steps do you take to maintain a proper attitude toward material things while living in this culture?
6. Where does a person get the idea that he or she is immune to the deception and danger of materialism?
7. Why do people have a tendency to look to materialism for satisfaction rather than to God? How do we fight against this tendency?
8. How might a church unintentionally show preference to wealthier members and visitors? How might this be corrected?
9. Do you know anyone who has been on a short-term mission trip? What opportunities do you have for short-term missions?
10. How much does your church give to world missions? What percentage is that of the total budget? What programs could be reduced in order to increase mission giving?

The Church at War

1 TIMOTHY 6:11-21

Main Idea: In view of the majesty of our great God, we fight the good fight of faith, using our material resources for eternal gain.

I. Recognize the Global Reality
  A. We are involved in a spiritual war.
  B. The enemy in this spiritual war is formidable.
  C. The scope of this spiritual war is universal.
  D. Involvement in this spiritual war is inevitable.
  E. The stakes in this spiritual war are eternal.

II. Fight the Good Fight
  A. Flee evil that pulls you from God.
  B. Pursue goodness that draws you to God.
  C. Experience the life you have been given.
  D. Give for eternal gain.
  E. Guard all spiritual truth.

We turn now to Paul's final words in this letter to Timothy and the church at Ephesus. Consider some of the subjects covered by the apostle thus far: false teaching, the importance of prayer, the role of women in the church, the qualifications for church leaders, instructions about widows and slaves, and the dangers of materialism. You may wonder what is *utmost* in Paul's mind as he brings this letter to a close. This passage contains his final exhortations.

I believe the statement that best sums up Paul's final word to Timothy is found in verse 12: "Fight the good fight for the faith." This is similar to the language Paul used in chapter 1 when he told Timothy to "strongly engage in battle" (1:18). So at the beginning and end of this letter, Paul was reminding Timothy of the battle and the struggle involved in the Christian's life. Timothy needed to realize that he was in a battle for his faith and for *the* faith—the gospel. As followers of Christ, this is precisely the realization we need to come to today.

Recognize the Global Reality

If we profess to follow Christ, then **we are involved in a spiritual war**, whether we realize it or not. The Bible is clear on this: we are in wartime, not peacetime. This truth can be found all over Scripture: Hebrews 12:4 says that we are at war against sin; 1 Peter 2:11 talks about war taking place within our souls; Jude 3 speaks of the struggle for our faith; 2 Timothy 2:3 refers to Timothy as a soldier for the gospel; 2 Corinthians 6:7 and 10:4 mention the weapons that believers possess; finally, Ephesians 6:12 reminds us that "our battle is not against flesh and blood, but against the rulers, against the authorities, against the world powers of this darkness, against the spiritual forces of evil in the heavens."

Every Christian is involved in a spiritual war, and his or her faith may be under attack in any number of ways. Sometimes the battle is for a marriage. Sometimes the battle is between a parent and a child. For many men today, their mind is a battleground for purity. As we saw in the previous section of 1 Timothy 6, there's a battle to be fought against materialism in our consumer-driven culture. And, of course, there's always the battle with unbelief and doubting God. Worry and despair seem to be unrelenting for some people. Needless to say, the Christian life is not an exercise in simply coasting along. And don't think this struggle doesn't apply to non-Christians. A spiritual battle is raging for their souls as well.

Followers of Christ should not take this spiritual battle lightly, for **the enemy in this spiritual war is formidable**. Martin Luther, in his well-known hymn "A Mighty Fortress," said of Satan, the prince of darkness, "on earth is not his equal." Satan aims to defame God's glory, distort God's gospel, and destroy God's people. He wants to wreck your marriage, destroy your relationships, abolish your purity, attack your integrity, and at all costs keep you from knowing the glory of God and spreading the gospel of God. First Peter 5:8 describes the Devil as "a roaring lion, looking for anyone he can devour." While it's true, Christian, that your foe is not all powerful, you are still no match for him, regardless of how strong or smart you are. This enemy cannot be taken lightly.

We not only need to see that the enemy in this spiritual war is formidable but also that **the scope of this spiritual war is universal**. This battle is cosmic. It involves every language, every people, every nation, every tribe, every family, and every life, which means that **involvement in this spiritual war is inevitable**. You do not choose whether to be involved in it; your involvement began the day you were born. So you can't just ignore it and hope to make it out alive. The Bible doesn't say, "Ignore the Devil, and he will flee from you." No, it says, "*Resist* the Devil, and he will flee from you" (Jas 4:7). If you try to avoid this war, pretending there is no struggle to be had, then you will not stand. Spiritual retreat only leads to spiritual defeat. Don't let that be you.

This war is universal and inevitable, and it's critical that we prepare for it because **the stakes in this spiritual war are eternal**. The casualties are so much more than merely losing an arm or a leg; a casualty in this war means losing everything, even your own soul. It's not too extreme to say that casualties of this war plunge into a hell of everlasting torment. That may sound overdramatic, but consider these realties: there is a God over this world who wants all people to be saved, and there is a god in this world who wants all people to burn in hell. There is a battle raging for your friends, coworkers, neighbors, and for all the peoples of the world. How we fight this battle has eternal implications. Satan does not want us to believe, live out, or spread this gospel. Is he succeeding in your life? Are you even aware that you're at war?

Fight the Good Fight
1 TIMOTHY 6:11-21

In light of the battle that is waging all around us, Paul tells us in verse 12 to "fight the good fight for the faith." This is a good fight, and the fight is for eternal life. It's a fight for peace, confidence, and hope—not just for you but so that others too will escape everlasting torment and receive eternal life. This is a good fight, but that doesn't mean it's easy.

Recently I agreed to join two men in my church for a workout program. The program only lasted for 12 minutes, so I thought to myself, "How hard could this be?" Ironically, they were inviting me on "Friend Day," which was a complete misnomer. I experienced the longest 12 minutes of my life, running and doing ball tosses, squats, and push-ups. After it was over, I was lying on the floor with my legs threatening to explode, unable to move, and I could hear the hushed tones of people walking around me saying, "Is that guy OK?" Friend Day had clearly gone awry. The next day, looking back on my workout, even though I was extremely sore, I thought, "That was good; my body clearly needed that." The benefits of getting in shape require effort, even painful effort. Our spiritual life is a lot like that—it's not an easy fight, but it's a good fight. And the reward, which God has secured for us, is more than worth the effort to continue fighting.

Think about where the battle is raging in your life—whether it's your marriage, your parenting, your relationships, or your emotions—and be encouraged from our text to persevere. Let the Word comfort and strengthen you in this fight of faith. Peacetime is coming, be assured of that, but it is not now. So Paul tells us that we must fight, and he begins with this exhortation: "But you, man of God, run from these things" (v. 11). **Flee evil that pulls you from God**. In this instance we fight by fleeing. Now that may sound more like running from a fight than fighting, but let me remind you that running is sometimes the best way to avoid defeat. If I meet a three hundred-pound football player in the street who wants to demolish me, hand-to-hand combat is not going to be my best strategy. Running is.[15] This is why Paul says we should "flee," or run away from, "these things." By "these things" he probably means things like materialism, quarreling, slander, and arrogance, the things he's just mentioned in verses 3-10. Consider three different ways in which we should run from evil.

First, **run from sinful actions**. Run from every temptation to sin. Beware: sin usually starts slowly and subtly, with just a glance or a thought or a kiss or a purchase. Don't flirt with the danger—run! But remember, sin goes deeper than actions. We should also **run from sinful desires**. In verses 9-10 Paul talks about sinful desires, such as the desire for riches and the love of money, cravings that pull you away from God. But there's an even deeper step to take: **Run from sinful thoughts**. This is the good fight of faith! The Bible is telling us to fight in order to believe God. Why is it that we run after materialism and earthly possessions? Because we do not believe God is enough for us. Paul is telling us to fight the desire for more stuff with the belief that God is enough for us. Our spiritual struggles with sin are, at the core, struggles to believe God. Consider the following questions:

- *Why do you lie?* Because you believe things will go better for you if you do. You believe yourself more than you believe the God who said, "Do not lie" (Col 3:9; Exod 20:16).

---

[15] The mistake alluded to previously is ignoring the fact that there is a battle. If I ignored the belligerent football player, I would certainly be demolished. Running is not denying warfare; it is one strategy within warfare.

- *Why do you give in to sexual impurity?* Because you don't believe that purity is the best thing for you. You don't believe God's plans are best in this area of your life.
- *Why do you struggle with doubt and despair?* Because you don't believe God will take care of you, He is good, and His promises are true.

Follower of Christ, God's Word is your weapon in this fight of faith. If you are struggling to believe God is with you, fight unbelief with verses like Joshua 1:5 and Matthew 28:20, where God promises us His presence. Think, "He has promised to be with me; He *is* with me." Believe it. Bank on it. If you're struggling to believe that God is in control, meditate on Psalm 31:15, "The course of my life is in Your power," or Romans 8:28, "We know that all things work together for the good of those who love God: those who are called according to His purpose." Be confident in God's promise.

The fight of faith is a fight to believe. Therefore, run from sinful thoughts, which produce sinful desires, which lead to sinful actions. But don't just run *from* these things; run *to* something. Paul said to "pursue" six different (but related) things in verse 11: "righteousness, godliness, faith, love, endurance, and gentleness." "Righteousness" here refers to **righteous thinking and living**. "Godliness," one of Paul's favorite terms in 1 Timothy, refers to **godly belief and behavior**. Next, Paul said to pursue faith, which is to say we should seek a **deeper trust in God**. Malcolm Muggeridge talks about how afflictions have played a part in this process of seeking to rely on God:

> Contrary to what might be expected, I look back on experiences that at the time seemed especially desolating and painful, with particular satisfaction. Indeed, I can say with complete truthfulness that everything I have learned in my seventy-five years in this world, everything that has truly enhanced and enlightened my existence, has been through affliction and not through happiness, whether pursued or attained. (Muggeridge, *Homemade*, July 1990)

Muggeridge expresses well the truth of Romans 5:3-4: "We rejoice in our afflictions, because we know that affliction produces endurance, endurance produces proven character, and proven character produces hope."

It's no surprise that Paul also mentions love, or **greater affection for God**, as something we should strive after. In John 15:9 Jesus said to "abide" in His love. Christian, have you considered the wonder of God's love for you? Does it not make you want to dwell in such an infinitely sweet love? When you do, you'll find that you are also growing in love for others, your wife, your kids, and everyone around you. After love Paul mentions endurance, which we might refer to as **patience amidst difficult circumstances**. The words *steadfastness* and *perseverance* come to mind when we think about endurance. We press on even when times are tough and it seems as if the end is nowhere in sight. Scripture speaks repeatedly of faith as a battle of endurance. After Jesus warns His disciples in Matthew 24 that difficult times are coming, He promises that "the one who endures to the end will be delivered" (v. 13). Likewise, Hebrews 3:14 says, "For we have become companions of the Messiah if we hold firmly until the end the reality that we had at the start." Finally, Paul exhorts us to pursue gentleness. We might think of this as **kindness toward difficult people**. What an interesting way to put this—we fight the fight of faith with gentleness. So, yes, we must have strength, but gentle strength, humble strength that overflows in kindness.

Although we pursue holiness and fight the good fight, don't get the impression that followers of Christ gain their own righteousness merely through self-effort. Our initial righteousness as well as the godliness, faith, and every other aspect of our ongoing sanctification have been bought for us by Christ. Only as we are in Christ do these things become a reality for us by the power of the Spirit (Phil 1:6; 2 Pet 1:3). Paul said in 1 Timothy 6:12, "Take hold of eternal life that you were called to and have made a good confession about in the presence of many witnesses." Eternal life is freely given, for God has "called" us to it, but we fight to take hold of it by faith. In effect, Paul instructs believers to **experience the life you have been given**. Timothy had already received eternal life when Christ called him, but that wasn't the end of the story. This is true for all followers of Christ. You are in Christ and you have His life in you, but you struggle on a daily basis to experience the fullness of this supernatural life. Until that day in the future when you are completely free from sin and the spiritual battles of this life are over, you must continue in this day-to-day battle to experience the life Christ has bought for you.

To every brother or sister in Christ who feels as if the battle of the Christian life is too daunting, Paul offers a number of encouragements and exhortations. First, **He has called your name**. You are His child. You are not fighting against God; He is fighting for you. Second, **you have confessed your faith**. You have taken your stand with the Lord Jesus, and this has been demonstrated most notably in your baptism, when you stood before witnesses and said, "My life is in Jesus; I have died to sin, and I have been raised to new life" (see Rom 6:3-4). In view of these truths, **live in light of God's presence**. Paul charged Timothy "in the presence of God" (1 Tim 6:13). **He is with you**, Christian, so fight this battle knowing that the Creator of all things is on your side.

As believers, we should also **live in view of Christ's faithfulness**. Paul said that Christ "gave a good confession before Pontius Pilate" (v. 13). When the life of the Son of God was on the line before Pontius Pilate, He made the good confession. Jesus confessed His kingship, and it cost Him His life. **He is the Savior who died for you**, and He stands beside you in battle. So what do you have to fear? Moreover, **He is the King who is coming for you**. Verse 14 says we are to walk in obedience "until the appearing of our Lord Jesus Christ." We fight with our eyes on the sky, looking and longing for the appearing of our Lord Jesus Christ. We pursue godliness because we know Christ is returning. He is coming back for the faithful, not the faithless.

And when you feel overwhelmed, **live in awe of God's greatness**. In verses 15-16 Paul erupted into one of the most majestic and glorious hymns of praise to God in all of Scripture. Consider what Paul tells us about God here:

- **His rule is universal:** God is sovereign over everything.
- **His reign is invincible:** He is the King of kings. No one can match Him.
- **He is immortal:** He is beyond time, from everlasting to everlasting.
- **He is unapproachable:** God lives in an atmosphere of blinding holiness.
- **He is inconceivable:** No one can fathom His greatness. He is utterly transcendent.
- **He possesses all power:** Eternal, omnipotent might is His.
- **He deserves all praise:** To God belongs honor and glory.

In verses 17-19 Paul returned to the issue of materialism, the very thing he addressed earlier in verses 5-10. So why did Paul talk about materialism, then fighting the fight of faith, and then return to materialism again? I think there is a method to what Paul was doing here. Follow Paul's reasoning: the contentment that comes along with godliness (v. 6) is something that we must fight for (vv. 11-14), and one way in which we fight for contentment is to give away what we have (vv. 17-19). After all, God is gain, so we have no reason to crave the passing pleasures of this world. Maybe you're wondering, "But what do I do with the stuff I already have?" Paul answers this question in verses 17-19 as he addressed the rich in Ephesus. And don't think he is simply referring to the upper-income bracket in America. The large majority of us, in comparison to the rest of the world and to the rest of humans who have ever lived, could be considered a part of the "rich" Paul is addressing. He urged them, and he urges us to **give for eternal gain**.

We live for eternal gain by fleeing certain things. First, Paul tells us to **flee self-confidence**. In verse 17 he says to Timothy, "Instruct those who are rich in the present age not to be arrogant or to set their hope on the uncertainty of wealth." It should come as no surprise that possessions produce pride. We like to think our security is not based on our stuff, but as soon as we think about giving our stuff away, our insecurities quickly surface. Second, Paul says we are to **flee self-centeredness**. Riches not only lead you to be haughty, but they can also cause you to hope in yourself. You begin to look at all you've acquired, and you get a certain sense of self-worth based on your accomplishments. Don't be deceived: That kind of thinking will kill you! Flee self-confidence and self-centeredness.

The third thing Paul tells us to do is to **focus on God**. We need more of the Giver, not more gifts. In the second half of verse 17, Paul says that we are to set our hope on God, the One who "richly provides us with all things to enjoy." Did you catch that? **He gives good things for our enjoyment**. Things in and of themselves are not bad. They were created to be enjoyed as God's good gifts. In turn, we should use God's gifts to do good, for He commands us "to be rich in good works, to be generous, willing to share" (v. 18). In response to God's goodness, **we give good things for others' enjoyment**. If you want to be rich in something, be rich in giving! The biblical antidote to materialism is extravagant giving. **We invest good things in our and others' eternity**. We set our sights on giving, not hoarding; on sacrificing, not indulging. We store up treasure for ourselves as a good foundation "for the age to come," so that we "may take hold of life that is real" (v. 19). One way we lay hold on eternal life is by the way we use our money.

In verses 20 and 21, Paul gives his closing charge to Timothy. As one who was helping to shepherd the church at Ephesus, Timothy must **guard all spiritual truth**. Paul is direct: "Timothy, guard what has been entrusted to you." That which had been entrusted to Timothy was the whole of the Christian faith, at the center of which is the gospel, the good news of Christ's death and resurrection. These foundational truths were under attack in Ephesus, and they have continued to be under attack throughout the church's history at all times and in all places. In light of such attacks, **we fight to be faithful to the gospel**. Paul returns to the exhortation he began with, and the theme he had touched on throughout the letter—hold fast to the truth of the gospel. Consider some of the ways in which this theme has been woven throughout these six chapters. Timothy had been instructed in the following ways:

- Stop others from teaching "different doctrine" (1:3).
- Hold on to faith and a good conscience (1:19).
- Appoint elders who can teach the Word (3:2).
- Devote himself to the public reading of Scripture, exhortation, and teaching (4:13).
- Keep watch on himself and his teaching (4:16).
- Fight the good fight and keep the commandment without fault or failure (6:12, 14).

So why is it so important to hold on to the gospel and not waver? What's at stake? First, **for our sake** we must remain in the truth. Paul talked about those who had wandered from the truth; some had been delivered to Satan (1:20), while others had been pierced with many pains for departing from the faith (6:10). We should not be so arrogant as to think that this could never happen to us. We will be tempted every day to let go of this gospel. No one is immune from Satan's attacks. That's why Paul referred to the Christian life as a fight (6:12).

The second reason we must hold fast to this gospel is **for others' sake**. We might think of this on two levels: we remain faithful for those outside the church and for those inside the church. For those outside the church, individuals who are separated from God, we must preach and share the true gospel. We must fight fear and timidity and distractions in order to make this good news known so that people will be saved. For those inside the church, clinging to the truth is essential. If we don't, we can easily become like so many churches in our day, churches that have ceased to exist as true New Testament churches. The church landscape in Western Europe and across the United States is littered with churches that once used to preach the gospel but have since left that gospel behind. These churches have doubted the glory of God, questioned the character of God, and either diminished or altogether ignored the Word of God. There are scores of churches where the truth of God has, at best, a minimal role. These are churches filled with man-pleasing sermons and ideas that appeal to the world, all the while ignoring God's Word. If a pastor rejects the authority of God's Word or departs from the truth of the gospel, the church should remove him from his role. If anyone, Paul said, even an angel, preaches another gospel, then that person stands under God's judgment (Gal 1:8-9). We must hold tightly to the Word of God.

If all of this talk about fighting has you feeling weak, there's good news. Paul's final words in verse 21 were, "Grace be with all of you." Fellow believer, **we fight as we're filled with God's grace**. Paul knew Timothy was not able to do this on his own, and the same holds true for us. In Colossians 1:28-29 Paul talks about working hard in his ministry, and he says, "I labor for this, striving with His strength that works powerfully in me." Notice that Paul strived, but God was the one who provided the strength. It is reassuring to know that **we are never alone in this war**. Now this may sound like old news to some Christians, but consider how the closing to this letter communicates this point. When Paul says, "Grace be with all of you," he is speaking to a plural "you." This seems odd at first, considering that Timothy was addressed in the book's opening greeting (1:2). The entire letter had, in one sense, been aimed at Timothy as the pastor of the church at Ephesus. Yet, when Paul closed the letter, he had the entire church in mind. It is comforting to know that as we read 1 Timothy and any other book of Scripture that God has us in mind. He is with us, and we are never alone in the fight of faith.

If you have put your trust in Jesus Christ as your Savior and Lord, be encouraged in this spiritual battle: **we do not fight this war *for* victory; we fight this war *from* victory**. Our ultimate triumph in this battle is assured because Christ Himself has conquered sin and death. The second verse of Luther's hymn "A Mighty Fortress" serves as a fitting conclusion to Paul's letter:

> Did we in our own strength confide,
> our striving would be losing;
> Were not the right Man on our side,
> the Man of God's own choosing:
> Dost ask who that may be?
> Christ Jesus, it is He;
> Lord Sabbaoth, His Name,

from age to age the same,
And He must win the battle.

Reflect and Discuss

1. How is life different in a country that is at war? What does it look like for a Christian to have a (spiritual) wartime mind-set?
2. For Christians, on what fronts is spiritual war being waged? Where are most of your own battles fought?
3. Historically, what has happened to nations that were not prepared for war? How can a Christian prepare for spiritual war?
4. What are the temptations in your life from which you should flee? Are there some areas where the temptation of overconfidence blinds you to the prudence of flight?
5. How do righteousness, faith, trust, love, patience, and kindness function as weapons in spiritual warfare?
6. How can our possessions work against us in spiritual warfare? How can they be put to good use for the cause? How do we move from one attitude to the other?
7. What are the dangers of simply trying to avoid sin without intentionally pursuing righteousness?
8. Do Paul's instructions to the rich have an application to those we might consider to be (financially) lower- or middle-class in our culture? Explain.
9. What does Paul mean by "the uncertainty of wealth" in verse 17?
10. Does Paul condemn wealth? If not, how does he instruct the rich to view their wealth?

2 Timothy

The Making of a Gospel-Centered Leader

2 TIMOTHY 1:1-7

Main Idea: God calls us according to His will and shapes us by His grace.

I. **A Gospel-Centered Letter**
II. **A Gospel-Centered Leader (1:1-7)**
   A. Paul: Called by the will of God (1:1)
      1. The origin of Paul's apostleship (1:1b)
      2. The purpose of Paul's apostleship (1:1c)
   B. Timothy: Shaped by the grace of God (1:2-7)
      1. A personal mentor (1:2-4)
      2. A godly mother (1:5)
      3. The Spirit and the gifts (1:6-7)

Paul wrote 1 Timothy while traveling, hoping that he would soon be able to visit Timothy in Ephesus (1 Tim 3:14-15). He provided instruction on the nature and practice of the church, addressing matters such as ministerial offices, widows, and public worship.

In 2 Timothy, Paul focused on the personal ministry of Timothy himself more than the ordering of the church. According to tradition, Paul wrote this second letter from an underground chamber in Rome's Mamertine prison. Based on the end of 2 Timothy, it seems Paul had already received a court hearing (2 Tim 4:16-18) and expected to be executed soon (4:6-8). Even though Paul mentioned that Luke was with him (4:11), we still picture the war-torn apostle alone and cold.

He wanted his cloak, his scrolls (especially the parchments!), and to see Timothy. In light of his writing context, the passion and personal tone of 2 Timothy is understandable.

A Gospel-Centered Letter

Paul's words in 2 Timothy are not only deeply personal, but they are also deeply theological. This letter to Timothy is saturated with gospel-centered content. John Stott says, "Paul's preoccupation in writing to Timothy was with the gospel, the deposit of truth which had been revealed and committed to him by God" (Stott, *Message*, 20). With this dominant theme in mind, Stott outlines 2 Timothy in four parts:

- Guard the gospel (chap. 1).
- Suffer for the gospel (chap. 2).
- Continue in the gospel (chap. 3).
- Proclaim the gospel (chap. 4).

Indeed, this letter is both timely and timeless. For what can be more important today than to rightly guard and give the gospel to the next generation? It is often said that we are one generation away from losing the gospel. If the gospel is assumed in one generation, it will be neglected, ignored, and/or abandoned in the next. We must keep guarding, suffering for, continuing in, and proclaiming the gospel.

This gospel-centered focus speaks loudly to us, teaching us to fix our eyes on the issues in ministry that are of first importance. At the end of life, what was Paul most passionate about? The gospel. It was, after all, "most important" (1 Cor 15:1-3).

So what is the gospel? From this letter, we could describe the good news of Jesus with six shorthand descriptions. First, the gospel is *christological*. It is about Christ. There is no gospel apart from Jesus—He is the Hero of the gospel (2 Tim 2:8).

Second, the gospel is *biblical*. God has presented the saving work of Christ in Holy Scripture. Paul said that the Scriptures "are able to give you wisdom for salvation through faith in Christ Jesus" (3:15).

Third, the gospel is *historical*. Christ has appeared in human history (1:10) and will come again to usher in His heavenly kingdom (4:18). This grand narrative begins in Genesis and ends in Revelation, as the themes of creation, fall, redemption, and new creation unfold. And all of it points to the Savior who appeared in the incarnation and will soon appear again to complete the final stage of the redemptive drama.

Fourth, the gospel is *doctrinal*. Christians treasure the wonderful truths of the gospel. Second Timothy speaks of many important doctrines: the promise of life (1:1), sovereign grace (1:9), Christ's victory over death (1:10), the Spirit's indwelling (1:14), the person and work of Christ (2:8), election (2:10, 19), glorification (2:10), union with Christ (2:11), repentance (2:25), and future rewards (4:8).

Fifth, the gospel is *personal*. It must be received personally by faith, just as Timothy, his mother, and his grandmother received it (1:4-5).

Finally, the gospel is *practical*. It has to do with all of life, from our families to our finances, from our schooling to our purity. Our relationships in the church, our ministries of word and deed, our affections and our fears—the gospel has practical implications for all of these things.

The gospel is practical for both the believer and the unbeliever. To the lost, the gospel is the message of salvation and hope. It proclaims that this world and the people in it are broken, but Jesus has offered Himself as the payment for sin and the redemption of the world. What could be more practical?

For believers, the gospel reminds them of their position before God, their present power, and their eternal future. The gospel gives the believer strength to endure suffering and the trials of ministry. One reason Paul was preoccupied with the gospel in this letter is that he knew Timothy's one hope for persevering until the end was found in the grace of Christ Jesus. We too will finish our leg of the race only as we rely on the benefits of our union with Christ. It is this gospel that Timothy was called to treasure, love, and proclaim. I want to consider our exposition of this letter in seven parts:

1. The Making of a Gospel-Centered Leader (1:1-7)
2. Gospel-Centered Bravery (1:8-18)
3. Images of Endurance (2:1-13)
4. Images of a Faithful Teacher (2:14-26)
5. Godly Examples (3:1-13)
6. Faithful to the Word (3:14–4:4)
7. Faithful to the End (4:5-22)

A Gospel-Centered Leader
2 TIMOTHY 1:1-7

In these initial verses we are introduced to the key figures of the letter: Paul and Timothy. Paul begins by describing the origin and purpose of his apostleship and then describes some of the background of Timothy's life and ministry. As we observe verses 1-7, we learn how God calls us according to His will and shapes us by His grace. We gain important insight as to how God builds a gospel-centered leader.

Paul: Called by the Will of God (1:1)

Paul says that he was "an apostle of Christ Jesus." By claiming this title, Paul placed himself in the same camp as the Twelve who were selected by Jesus as apostles (Luke 6:13). Like these Paul had the privilege of learning directly from Jesus. He was sent by the Master with unique apostolic authority to teach in Jesus' name. Of course, Paul's apostleship was slightly different from the others' because he was somewhat of a late addition. On the Damascus Road the risen Lord commissioned him with a particular call to proclaim the gospel to the Gentiles (Acts 9:15-16; 26:12-18). Even though Paul humbly called himself the "least of the apostles" (1 Cor 15:9), he was indeed part of this select group.

Therefore, this letter comes to us with divine authority because it comes from a divinely inspired apostle. It is a letter not just for Timothy in the first century but for Christians of all times in all places. May the Lord "give [us] understanding in everything" regarding this book of sacred Scripture (2 Tim 2:7).

The origin of Paul's apostleship (1:1b). Paul's apostleship was not owing to anything in and of himself. He states that his position was established "by God's will." Paul did not volunteer for it. He was summoned to it! He did not make a career move. He was "appointed" (1:11). Elsewhere, Paul describes his calling with pronounced awareness of God's sovereign grace and divine will:

> *Paul, an apostle of Christ Jesus* by the command of God *our Savior and of Christ Jesus our hope: . . . I give thanks to Christ Jesus our Lord who has strengthened me, because He considered me faithful,* appointing me *to the ministry.* (1 Tim 1:1, 12; emphasis added)

> *Paul, an apostle*—not from men *or by man, but by Jesus Christ. . . . But when God, who from my birth set me apart and* called me by His grace, *was pleased. . . .* (Gal 1:1a, 15; emphasis added)

> *Paul, an apostle of Christ Jesus* by God's will. *. . . I was made a servant of this gospel* by the gift of God's grace. (Eph 1:1; 3:7; emphasis added)

Of course, God did not shape Paul into a gospel-centered leader apart from Paul's own spiritual sweat. The apostle was a worker; he writes that he "worked more than any of them." But Paul's work was preceded by God's work of calling him, and Paul's work was made possible by the enabling grace of God: "Yet not I, but God's grace that was with me" (1 Cor 15:10).

God shaped Paul into a mighty leader by first calling him by grace and then empowering him with divine strength. While we are not apostles in the same sense as Paul and the Twelve were, we do share some common experiences with them as those who trust in Christ. Like Paul, God calls us to Himself by His own will and pleasure, and by His power He enables us to live faithfully before Him for His glory.

The purpose of Paul's apostleship (1:1c). Paul said that this calling was according to "the promise of life in Christ Jesus." Paul was commissioned to communicate the gospel, which he described as "the promise of life." As Paul awaited death, he knew there was the promise of life for those who are in Christ Jesus. The gospel gives life because at the heart of our message is a person, Jesus Christ, who is Himself "the way, the truth, and the life" (John 14:6). John says, "The one who has the Son has life" (1 John 5:12). Paul also writes that Jesus "abolished death and has brought life and immortality to light through the gospel" (2 Tim 1:10). Indeed, this theme runs throughout the Bible, for in Genesis and later in Revelation, we read of people eating of the tree of life and drinking from the water of life.

The gospel is like water: man did not invent it, and man cannot live without it. Therefore, faithful servants of Jesus will take the water to thirsty men and women. Are you showing the thirsty where you found everlasting water?

Timothy: Shaped by the Grace of God (1:2-7)

Next, let's note three shaping influences in Timothy's life. Like us, Timothy was still a work in progress! Paul mentions three means of grace that God used to transform this servant: a personal mentor, a godly mother, and the Spirit and the gifts.

A personal mentor (1:2-4). It is possible that Timothy met Paul and embraced the gospel on Paul's initial visit to Lystra (Acts 14). By the time Paul visited Lystra a second time, we know that the brothers there spoke highly of Timothy, referring to his spiritual growth and maturity. Paul then took Timothy with him on his mission (Acts 16:1-5). We see several snapshots of Timothy's ministry leading up to the writing of 2 Timothy. Consider the following time line:[16]

- Timothy ministers with Paul and Silas in Philippi (AD 50).
- Paul flees Berea; Timothy and Silas continue the work (AD 51).
- Timothy rejoins Paul in Athens and brings word of the work to Macedonia (AD 51).
- Timothy returns to Thessalonica to encourage the new believers (AD 51–52).
- Timothy joins Paul in his ministry in Corinth, bringing word of progress in Thessalonica (AD 52).
- Timothy comes to Ephesus to work with Paul during Paul's three-year ministry (AD 54–56).
- Paul sends Timothy with the 1 Corinthians letter to the disordered church in Corinth (AD 56).
- Paul comes to Corinth in person and from there he and Timothy write Romans (AD 57).
- Timothy is with Paul during Paul's first imprisonment in Rome (AD 60–62).
- Upon his release from his first imprisonment, Paul goes to Ephesus and appoints Timothy as pastor (AD 62).
- Paul writes 1 Timothy and Titus (AD 62–64).
- Major persecutions of the Christians in Rome begin, following the great fire (AD 64).
- Paul returns to Rome, is arrested, and writes 2 Timothy from the Mamertine Prison (AD 67?).
- Paul's martyrdom in Rome (AD 67?).

Paul viewed Timothy as his own spiritual child (cf. 1 Cor 4:14-17). He introduces Timothy in verse 2 as his "dearly loved son" and says many other wonderful things about his loyal disciple. Commending Timothy to the Philippians, Paul confesses, "For I have no one else like-minded who will genuinely care about your interests; . . . you know his proven character, because he has served with me in the gospel ministry like a son with a father" (Phil 2:20, 22). And Paul extends a greeting to his son: "Grace, mercy, and peace from God the Father and Christ Jesus our Lord" (2 Tim 1:2). In this triad Paul highlights the indescribable

---

[16] *HCSB Study Bible* (Nashville: Holman Bible Publishers, 2010), 2082–83.

love of God. God gives grace to the desperate, mercy to the guilty, and peace to the restless—all of it through Christ.

In verse 3, Paul expresses his love for his disciple by thanking God for him. Paul mentioned that he thanked God like his "ancestors." Paul was not being disloyal to his Jewish ancestors by believing in Jesus. His faith was the fulfillment of their faith and hope. When Jews come to Christ, they are, in a sense, coming home—all the way home.

Not only does Paul thank God for Timothy, but he also intercedes on his behalf: "I constantly remember you in my prayers night and day." We know that Paul urged believers to "pray constantly" (1 Thess 5:17)— that is, to be in a continuous state of prayer—but perhaps he is referring here to periodic times of prayer. I draw this from the fact that Paul said "prayers" (plural). Paul's other references to his "prayers" (for example, Rom 1:10; Eph 1:16; 1 Thess 1:2) suggest that he set aside designated times for prayer, apparently as Jesus did (Luke 5:16). Should we pray without ceasing? Absolutely! Live in communion with God! But setting aside specific times for intercession is both wise and beneficial.

Paul was locked in a prison, but his heart was free to seek the living God in prayer. These prison prayers remind me of Arnold Dallimore's description of the First Great Awakening, a movement that swept across Britain and the Americas in the 1730s and 1740s. He notes how the prayers of imprisoned English believers preceded this revival:

> Legislation was enacted which distressed the Puritan conscience, and in 1662, on one of the darkest days in all British history, nearly two thousand ministers—all those who would not submit to the Act of Uniformity—were ejected from their livings. Hundreds of these men suffered throughout the rest of their lives, and a number died in prison. Yet these terrible conditions became the occasion of a great volume of prayer; forbidden to preach under threat of severe penalties— as John Bunyan's Bedford imprisonment bore witness—they yet could pray, and only eternity will reveal the relationship between this burden of supplication and the revival that followed. (Dallimore, *George Whitefield*, 19–20)

Paul was not finished yet. Though imprisoned in harsh conditions, he still had important work to do: praying for his disciple, Timothy. Oh, the privilege of having faithful saints praying for us! Paul's thankfulness, thoughtfulness, and prayerfulness were driven by two dynamics: his **peaceful condition** before God, and his personal **love** for Timothy.

Paul's condition before God is noted with the phrase "a clear conscience" (v. 3). Paul was not sinless, but he was guiltless. That is because Jesus had taken Paul's guilt through His substitutionary death on the cross. God cleansed Paul's guilty heart from an evil conscience through the work of Christ (see Heb 10:22).

Paul experienced the wonderful blessing that every true believer shares: peace with God through faith in Jesus Christ. As we approach our deaths, Paul shows us that there is nothing greater than knowing that our sins are forgiven. Is there anything more important than having a "clear conscience" before dying? The hymn writer says:

> My sin—oh, the bliss of this glorious thought:
> My sin—not in part, but the whole
> Is nailed to the cross and I bear it no more,
> Praise the Lord, praise the Lord, O my soul![17]

That's the song of one who possesses a clear conscience. Is it well with your soul?

Next, Paul's love for Timothy in particular is expressed beautifully in verse 4: "Remembering your tears, I long to see you so that I may be filled with joy." Evidently, the last time Paul and Timothy were together there were tears—maybe before Paul was taken off to the Roman prison. Now he wanted to see Timothy that he might be "filled with joy." This is the picture of a faithful believer's confidence before death and a loving mentor's attitude toward his disciple.

How important is *life-on-life* discipleship to you? As a pastor, it is often easy to overlook or neglect this Pauline model. In 2 Timothy 2:2, Paul instructs Timothy to invest in other men the way Paul invested in him. Do you have a Paul in your life? Do you have a Timothy in your life? Who is your spiritual son or your spiritual father?

What exactly do you do in a mentoring relationship? Verses 3-4 show us two essentials behind the act of mentoring: **love and prayer**. A true mentor must start here. From this starting point, I see some lessons for us who desire to mentor others. Paul helped Timothy in three areas: **calling, character, and competency**. In terms of calling, Paul encouraged

---

[17] Horatio G. Spafford, "It Is Well with My Soul"; public domain.

Timothy to use the gifts God had given him to live out his calling (2 Tim 1:6). As for character, Paul urged Timothy to pursue godliness, endurance, love, and other Christlike qualities (3:10-12). As for ministerial competency, Paul coached Timothy on how he should respond to people appropriately (2:16, 23-26; 3:5), study the Word diligently (2:15), preach the Word faithfully (3:16–4:2), and do the work of an evangelist constantly (4:5). If you are an older leader, invest in a Timothy. Help him fan the flame of his calling, develop Christlike character, and grow in his competency.

A godly mother (1:5). Timothy not only had the privilege of a mentor, but he also had the gift of a godly mother (Eunice) and grandmother (Lois). In verse 5 Paul mentions the "faith" of all three individuals. He says Timothy, like these ladies, has a "sincere" faith, the genuine article. By Paul's statement, "I am convinced [this faith] is in you also," we are reminded of how every child must do his or her own believing. Timothy had the blessing of having a Christian mother and grandmother, but he still had to believe for *himself.*

While it seems that Timothy's father was an unbelieving Greek, these two ladies were vibrant Christians. Who knows? Maybe all three were converted from Judaism to Christianity through Paul's visit to Lystra. What we do know is that these godly ladies' faith was observable to Paul. Probably before they were believers, they taught Timothy the Old Testament (3:15), but now their understanding of these Scriptures was Christ centered. Timothy and these godly mothers came to know and love the fact that the Scriptures make us wise for salvation because they point us to the Savior Himself, who is the fulfillment of the Scriptures (see Luke 24:44).

From a parental perspective, having children is a wonderful gift. But with the gift comes responsibility. Are you teaching your kids the Scriptures? Do they see in you, mom or dad, a "sincere faith" in Christ? One cannot overstate the importance of living out the Christian life before watching children. I want to say to my kids, "[Follow] my teaching, conduct, purpose, faith, patience, love, and endurance" (see 2 Tim 3:10).

The Spirit and the gifts (1:6-7). Finally, and most significantly, God shaped Timothy into a leader through the presence and gifting of the indwelling Holy Spirit. Paul says, "Therefore, I remind you to keep ablaze the gift of God that is in you."

Judged by the surrounding context of 1 and 2 Timothy, Timothy was not a spiritual rock. He appears to be physically weak (1 Tim 5:23), personally timid (2 Tim 1:7), and relatively young (1 Tim 4:12). But

God delights in using the weak and the ordinary in order to demonstrate His mighty power. Thankfully, God uses "clay jars" so that only He can get the glory (2 Cor 4:7)!

Knowing the reality of God's power in the life of Timothy, Paul urges him to "keep ablaze" his gift. What is this gift? We do not know for certain. It seems connected to the phrase "through the laying on of my hands" (v. 6; cf. 1 Tim 4:14). This phrase seems to refer to an ordination or commissioning in which Paul affirmed God's call in Timothy's life. If so, then this "gift" is probably related to the spiritual endowment necessary for the work of ministry. Paul is reminding Timothy that God equips His servants to fulfill their ministry by granting them spiritual power and gifting.

How encouraging it is to remember that God gives His people the authority and enablement to carry out their assignments! Not everyone will have a personal mentor or a godly mother, but God does invest spiritual gifts in every believer (1 Cor 12:7). The fourth stanza of Martin Luther's hymn captures the wonder of the Spirit and the gifts:

> That word above all earthly powers, No thanks to them,
>   abideth;
> The Spirit and the gifts are ours Through Him who with us
>   sideth.
> Let goods and kindred go, This mortal life also;
> The body they may kill; God's truth abideth still:
> His kingdom is forever.[18]

Praise God, for the Spirit and the gifts are ours through Him who is for us!

The gifting of the Spirit not only encourages us and inspires worship, but it also inspires hard **work**. Paul reminded Timothy of his personal responsibility in becoming a gospel-centered leader. He told him (1) to **develop and use his gifts** (v. 6) and (2) to **maintain spiritual discipline** (v. 7).

First, we see that the gift is like **fire**. This Greek verb *anazopureo* ("fan into flame" or "rekindle") is in the present tense, emphasizing ongoing action. Paul was urging Timothy to keep the fire alive—indeed

---

[18] Martin Luther, "A Mighty Fortress Is Our God," trans. Frederick H. Hedge; public domain.

ablaze—by making full use of it! He was to do this, then, by **exercising his gift passionately**. God gave Timothy gifts to be used and developed.

There is no room for sluggishness in the Christian life. Rest? Yes. But laziness, passiveness, and timidity should not characterize the believer. Jim Elliot's prayer captures well the spirit of this verse:

> God, I pray Thee, light these idle sticks of my life and may I
>   burn for Thee.
> Consume my life, my God, for it is Thine.
> I seek not a long life, but a full one, like you, Lord Jesus.
>   (Elliot, *Shadow*, 247)

Are you using your gifts passionately? Often I talk to Christians who are "waiting on a church to call so they can preach" or for some other ministry job to open up before they begin serving. While I understand their thought, we need to be careful not to overprofessionalize the ministry. If God has gifted you for gospel proclamation, then go proclaim! Maybe you do not have a brick church building to preach in, but there are people everywhere! Go preach to one, or two, or three. As Martin Lloyd-Jones says, go "gossip the gospel"—go share it with one person in a coffee shop, in a park, or in your neighborhood (Lloyd-Jones, *Preaching*, 24). Better yet, go overseas and gather up some kids in Africa and tell them the good news. You need to be developing and using your gifts, even if it is not in a glorious setting. Fan it into flame! That requires work, effort, and intentionality.

Second, Paul tells Timothy to maintain discipline, "for God has not given us a spirit of fearfulness, but one of power, love, and sound judgment" or self-discipline (1:7). Paul here addresses Timothy's shyness and weaknesses and reminds him that his fear did not come from God. What comes from God is a "spirit" of power and love and discipline.

There is a discussion on whether or not "spirit" should be translated as "Spirit" with a capital *S* (meaning Holy Spirit) or as "spirit" with a lower case *s* (implying an attitude). While Paul may have referred to "a spirit" (not the "Holy Spirit"), that does not mean the Holy Spirit is not in view here. The word "for" in verse 7 alludes back to verse 6, where the reference is to the Spirit's gifting *in* Timothy (Paul also made a connection with the Spirit and gifts in other places, like 1 Cor 12:4). Additionally, the words "love" and "power" are used especially for the work of the Spirit elsewhere in Scripture. Boldness, not cowardice, is a mark of the Spirit's work in believers (Acts 4:31).

The object of Timothy's fear remains unclear. Perhaps it was evangelism, proclamation, or pastoral leadership. Whatever its cause, we know that this fear did not have to be paralyzing to Timothy. Interestingly, even Paul faced fear. When he planted the church in Corinth, the Lord appears to him in a vision and says,

> *Do not be afraid, but go on speaking and do not be silent, for I am with you, and no one will attack you to harm you, for I have many in this city who are my people.* (Acts 18:9-10 ESV)

Do you see this? The Lord tells Paul to fight fear with His promises. He promises to be with him, to protect him, and to use him to bring people into the kingdom. Now Paul is directing Timothy to the same source of hope. He says essentially, "Timothy, in your fear, remember that God is with you, in you, and for you; His Spirit produces the power you need to endure and the love you need to minister. Be disciplined. Be diligent. Be brave, for God is with you."

Who has not experienced timidity and fear in ministry? If you have ever been a part of a church plant, you understand the fear of the unknowns. If you have ever done street evangelism, perhaps you know this feeling. If you have ever been in a tense meeting where people oppose you, even gang up on you, perhaps you have experienced timidity. Remember: fight fear with the promises of God. The Spirit of God empowering the people of God is sufficient to accomplish the mission of God.

Therefore, there is no excuse for not performing our mission with diligence. God has given us everything we need. The Spirit and the gifts are ours! God has given us spiritual gifts to execute our ministries and Spiritual power to enable our ministry.

How then is a gospel-centered leader formed? From this passage we see the mysterious combination of God's provision and man's humble responsibility. For Paul, clearly God appointed him and enabled him, but his appointment did not mean Paul was to be passive. No! He was to proclaim the promise of life actively! In the life of Timothy, God provided a mentor, mothers, and (most of all) the Spirit and the gifts to make him into an instrument for noble purposes. But Timothy had the responsibility of using these gifts. What about you? Do you recognize the gifts God has given you? Are you resting in His promises, relying on His power, and serving Him with passion?

Reflect and Discuss

1. How is our calling different from Paul's? How is it the same?
2. In what way is the gospel like fresh water? Is it necessary to convince people they are thirsty?
3. Do you have a spiritual mentor? Do you know someone for whom you could be a mentor?
4. What is the difference between being in a continuous state of prayer and setting aside specific times of prayer?
5. How does a Christian maintain a clear conscience?
6. Are Paul's three areas of calling, character, and competency relevant in spiritual mentoring today?
7. What is a mother's role in raising godly children when her husband is not a Christian? What is her role if he is a Christian? What if she is a single mother?
8. What assignment has God laid on your heart? How has He equipped you to fulfill it?
9. How can you use God's gifts in your life in between the major tasks He assigns you?
10. What aspect of your assignment from God makes you nervous or anxious? Which of God's promises addresses this particular fear?

Gospel-Centered Bravery

2 TIMOTHY 1:8-18

Main Idea: When we are not ashamed to share the gospel and we fulfill our responsibility to guard the unchanging gospel, we should expect to suffer for the gospel.

I.   **Exhortation 1: Do Not Be Ashamed of the Gospel (1:8a).**
II. **Exhortation 2: Suffer for the Gospel (1:8b-12a).**
    A.   How we suffer: by the power of God (1:8c)
    B.   Why we suffer: because the gospel is worth it (1:9-12a)!
        1.   The greatness of God in salvation (1:9a,10b)
        2.   The grace of God in salvation (1:9b)
        3.   The ground of our salvation (1:10)
    C.   When we should expect suffering: as we make the gospel known (1:10c-12a)
III. **Exhortation 3: Guard the Gospel (1:12b-18).**
    A.   The ultimate guardian (1:12b)
    B.   Guardians of the gospel (1:13-14)
    C.   The ashamed and the unashamed (1:15-18)

After charging Timothy to develop and use his gift fearlessly and earnestly (1:6-7), Paul continues in the same vein by giving Timothy three challenges in verses 8-14. He charges him with three imperatives:

- "Don't be ashamed of the testimony about our Lord." (v. 8a)
- "Share in suffering for the gospel." (v. 8b)
- "Hold on to the pattern of sound teaching that you have heard from me." (v. 13a)

Following these exhortations, Paul then provides examples of individuals who either turned away from him (Phygelus and Hermogenes) or supported him (Onesiphorus).

As we examine the exhortations and examples, we sense the passion of the apostle Paul. We also feel the reality of suffering for the cause of Christ. Many around the world endure great opposition and even death for the gospel. We need to feel the weight of these words and at the same time feel the wonder of Jesus, who is a great Savior! He is worthy of worship and of our very lives.

Exhortation 1: Do Not Be Ashamed of the Gospel
2 TIMOTHY 1:8A

What should we do with the gospel? First, we should not be ashamed of it! Paul's use of "so" in verse 8 connects this passage to the previous section, where he reminds Timothy of God's mighty work in him to overcome timidity. Now he says, "Don't be ashamed of the testimony about our Lord." Here we see that our witness is about *Christ*. We are not commending an idea or a society but a Savior.

Picture Timothy in the tough city of Ephesus, where there are competing religious systems and worldviews. Ephesus was a city full of idols, and according to Acts, a riot ensued following Paul's ministry in this city. Like the Corinthians, there undoubtedly were those in Ephesus who believed the cross was foolishness. There will always be cross mockers. Interestingly, the earliest known picture of a crucifixion comes from Rome. Called "The Alexamenos Graffito," the sketch is of a human figure on a cross, but the crucified man has the head of a donkey. A young man is beside the cross looking at the crucifixion, and the caption reads, "Alexamenos worships God!" This image illustrates the widespread mockery of Christ's crucifixion both in the past and today.

Do not be ashamed of your Lord. Instead, embrace the passion of Polycarp, who refused to renounce Christ in the face of impending martyrdom. He said, "Eighty and six years have I served Him, and He never did me any injury; how then can I blaspheme my King and my Savior?"[19]

Today we have all kinds of conflicting and competing ideologies. One of the more prevalent worldviews cultural analysts have recently described is "moralistic, therapeutic deism" (Smith and Denton, *Soul Searching*). This is the belief that if people "do good," "feel good," and "believe in a god" (one who created the universe but is not really involved in the affairs of life), then there is a heavenly future awaiting them. The idea that we are actually "bad" and in need of a Savior is viewed as ignorant, primitive, or simply foolish.

---

[19] *The Martyrdom of Polycarp*, chapter 9.

Other worldviews have emerged, such as the new atheism. This militant brand of atheism rejects not just God but even rejects *a respect* for belief in God. Further, the continued growth of other world religions, many of which are hostile toward Christ followers, makes Paul's charge to Timothy in verse 8 all the more relevant. Remember Jesus' own words:

> *For whoever is ashamed of Me and of My words in this adulterous and*
> *sinful generation, the Son of Man will also be ashamed of him when*
> *He comes in the glory of His Father with the holy angels.* (Mark 8:38)

Notice that the Savior says not to be ashamed of Him or of His words. Many will mock both the person and the words of Jesus. Gospel-centered bravery, on the other hand, requires that we take our stand with Jesus and His teachings and let the chips fall where they may.

Paul goes on to include himself in this charge to Timothy: "or of me His prisoner." Many were scoffing not just at the gospel but also at this particular messenger. Oftentimes, cowardly believers refuse to associate with their brothers and sisters who are taking a stand for Christ. This may happen in a school, where a believer speaks up with a word of witness and the "Christians" show little support. It may also happen on a sports team, when a player refuses to take part in sinful postgame activities and the "Christians" leave him to stand alone. Or it may happen on a business trip, when an employee does not join the guys in immoral activity and the "Christians" turn their backs on him to have a "little fun." In the context of this letter, Paul was in chains, and people were leaving him. He urged Timothy not to join their number. But even if everyone would abandon him, Paul was not looking for their approval. He identified himself as Christ's prisoner. He was not in chains to earn the popular praise of men but rather to honor the Savior through obedience to God's perfect will.

Exhortation 2: Suffer for the Gospel
2 TIMOTHY 1:8B-12A

Not only must we be unashamed of the gospel, but Paul adds that Timothy (and we) should also join with him in suffering for the gospel. Suffering for Christ is a major theme in this letter. In verses 8c–12a, Paul explains (1) **how** we suffer, (2) **why** we suffer, and (3) **when** we can expect suffering.

How We Suffer: By the Power of God (1:8c)

Like Timothy, we are weak, common vessels, but by God's power we endure hardship. Indeed, there is a marvelous mystery in the biblical concept of **strength through weakness**. Jesus supplies sufficient strength to His followers so they can endure opposition, weakness, and persecution. Paul says elsewhere:

> But He said to me, "My grace is sufficient for you, for power is perfected in weakness." Therefore, I will most gladly boast all the more about my weaknesses, so that Christ's power may reside in me. So I take pleasure in weaknesses, insults, catastrophes, persecutions, and in pressures, because of Christ. For when I am weak, then I am strong. (2 Cor 12:9-10)

Jesus is enough. If and when you suffer for the gospel, remember that you have the privilege of sharing in the sufferings of Christ and enjoying the special power of Christ.

Perhaps the reason Paul found it necessary to tell Timothy to suffer by "the power of God" is that he knew of believers' tendency to do everything but rely on the power of God. Let this verse remind you that apart from Him we can do nothing (see John 15:5). Abide in Jesus. Remain in Jesus. Rely on Jesus and experience His supernatural strength.

Why We Suffer: Because the Gospel Is Worth It! (1:9-12a)

In a few verses Paul concisely exalts God's gospel. When he finishes with this awe-inspiring description, he says, "And that is *why* I suffer these things" (v. 12; emphasis added). The reason Paul was willing to lay down his life in this mission was that he believed the gospel was worth it; Christ was worth it! Paul found Christ to be more desirable, enjoyable, and beautiful than anything else. Even dying was gain for Paul because of this vision of the Savior. Religious people find God **useful**, but cross-bearing disciples find him **beautiful**. You can endure suffering when you see what Paul saw.

What did Paul see when he contemplated the gospel? From these verses, notice how Paul spoke of the greatness of God in salvation, the grace of God in salvation, and the grounds of our salvation. This is why he suffered.

The greatness of God in salvation (1:9a,10b). Three phrases in these verses capture God's great work of salvation from beginning to end:

He saved us, *He* called us with a holy calling, and *He* brought life and immortality to light. First, God **saves** us. What a concise description of the gospel: God saves. In His sovereign grace, God rescues sinners from their awful condition and places them into His kingdom forever. In the words of Jonah, "Salvation is from the LORD" (Jonah 2:9).

Next, God **sanctifies** us. Paul reminds us that God calls us to holiness. God saves us to sanctify us. We are called to live clean lives to the glory of God.

Finally, God **glorifies** us. Notice the "immortality" that is promised in verse 10. Paul agrees with Jesus' words in John 11:25-26: "I am the resurrection and the life. Everyone who lives and believes in Me will never die—ever." Praise God that He promises us life forever!

Marvel at the greatness of God in your salvation. He rescued you. He is making you holy. He assures you that you will never die. Justification, sanctification, and glorification—all three of these aspects of salvation are essential in our understanding of what God has done for us. **Justification**: God saved us from the penalty of sin. **Sanctification**: God is saving us from the power of sin. **Glorification**: God will save us from the presence of sin. Only this gospel will sustain you in great suffering. Preach it to yourself daily!

The grace of God in salvation (1:9b). When Paul meditated on the gospel, he mediated on grace. He assures Timothy and us that we are not saved by our "works" but by the grace of God (cf. Eph 2:8-9; Titus 3:4-7). God did not save us and call us to holiness because of anything in us, "but according to His own purpose and grace, which was given to us in Christ Jesus before time began" (2 Tim 1:9). Oh, the wonder of grace! God gave us grace before time began! He gave us grace in the person of Jesus (cf. Titus 2:11), and He gave it to us according to His sovereign purposes. Paul reminds us, "So then it does not depend on human will or effort but on God who shows mercy" (Rom 9:16).

The source of our salvation, then, is not our merit but God's unmerited favor. It is not grace with a mixture of works. You must take your pick: Is your salvation based on your effort or God's grace? Scripture assures us it is all of grace. Paul says, "Now if by grace, then it is not by works; otherwise grace ceases to be grace" (Rom 11:6). And not only did He save us in spite of our inability to do enough good works, but He did so *before* we could even attempt them! His grace goes back before history, into eternity, and it will extend throughout eternity (see Eph 2:7).

This teaching shows a critically distinctive point about the Christian message. Many false gospels are built around the idea that if you are basically moral then God will save you. But Christians believe God does not owe us anything! We deserve judgment because we are sinners. Our only hope is grace. We cannot make ourselves alive; we cannot atone for our own sins; we cannot cleanse ourselves. We need that which we do not deserve—saving grace. We cannot "do it," but there is One who has already "done it!" By God's grace, believe in the One who cried out, "It is finished!" and be saved.

This teaching is a powerful encouragement, for there is great freedom and joy in this salvation. Charles Spurgeon—in a sermon entitled "Salvation Altogether by Grace" from this one verse (v. 9)—said when Paul wanted to encourage Timothy he did not "attempt to persuade him by mere appeals to feelings" but rather by "remind[ing] him of solid doctrinal truth, which he knew Timothy believed" (Spurgeon, *Grace*, 31–32). To be sure, feelings are important. But feelings follow the facts of the gospel driven deeply into our minds and hearts. Because of this, we need to work the grace of God into our hearts regularly. Remind yourself daily—especially in your suffering—that you were chosen by grace, you are kept by grace, and you will see the Savior one day by grace.

The ground of our salvation (1:10). Our great salvation is rooted in the person and work of Christ. Paul shows us that Christ appeared in His incarnation and then "abolished death and . . . brought life and immortality to light through the gospel." Not only did God give us grace in Christ before time began but also in the historical appearing of Jesus. Paul said that the Savior "abolished death," meaning He overthrew death. He defeated death. He rendered our physical death powerless (cf. 1 Cor 15:54-57). Though we will all die **physically** (unless Christ returns first), we do not all have to die **ultimately**. Instead, as believers, when we die we enjoy the presence of God forever (see 2 Cor 5:6-8; Phil 1:21).

This is no vain wish. Our hope is rooted in human history. It is grounded in the person and work of Christ, the Messiah who lived, died, and was raised on our behalf to the glory of God the Father.

Such hope is crucial for believers. In Eric Metaxes's wonderful biography of Dietrich Bonhoeffer, the last hours of this martyr's life are particularly moving. Evidently, just 24 hours before Bonhoeffer was executed, he performed the work of a pastor. He gathered some prisoners and held a worship service. He chose Isaiah 53 and 1 Peter 1:3, two passages that speak of God's glorious salvation and the perfect work of Christ, as his texts for reading and exhortation. Almost immediately after his closing prayer, two men came and said, "Prisoner Bonhoeffer. Get ready to come with us." All the prisoners knew what these words meant: the scaffold. Bonhoeffer told his friend, "This is the end. For me the beginning of life" (Metaxas, *Bonhoeffer*, 527–28). Jesus, our atoning sacrifice and risen king of Isaiah 53, took the sting out of death so that we too can face our death—even if by hanging—with a sense of indescribable peace.

As Bonhoeffer told his friend in prison on that day, so Paul, the Lord's prisoner, told Timothy that death is only the beginning because Christ "brought life and immortality." The communion with God that Bonhoeffer and other believers shared in this life only continued in the next; indeed, it got sweeter. As Paul pondered *death*, he was reminded that there really is no such thing for the believer. As John Stott quips, "The proper epitaph to write for the Christian believer is not a dismal uncertain petition, 'R.I.P.' . . . but a joyful and certain affirmation 'C.A.D.' ('Christ abolished death')" (Stott, *Message*, 39).

When We Should Expect Suffering: As We Make the Gospel Known (1:10c-12a)

Paul says this glorious good news was "brought . . . to light." This implies that we must make it known so people can hear and believe in our gracious Savior. In this one passage we can observe how God has not only ordained the end of salvation but also the means. While salvation is all of grace, it is also experienced through the presentation of the gospel. God saves people through, not apart from, the proclamation of the good news. Paul brought the gospel to light by living out his appointment as "a herald, apostle, and teacher" (v. 11). As a herald, Paul announced the gospel. As an apostle Paul was sent with the gospel. As a teacher Paul explained the gospel. While we know there are no apostles today who measure up to Paul, we want to maintain the idea that all believers are sent into the world to herald and teach the good news of salvation by God's grace alone in Christ alone. Through faith we share this same commissioning and this same message. We are to shine this gospel light in this dark world.

We are most likely to suffer for the gospel when we proclaim it. While it is important to live out the gospel in deed, it is absolutely essential that we speak the gospel in word. And in the speaking of the good news, we should expect opposition. We do not go looking for suffering, but we should not be surprised by it when we give verbal witness.

Paul says, "That is why I suffer these things" (v. 12). Paul suffered because he spoke boldly, and he spoke boldly because he believed the gospel was worth it!

Exhortation 3: Guard the Gospel
2 TIMOTHY 1:12B-18

In addition to the duty of standing tall and suffering for the gospel, in these verses Paul urges Timothy to guard the gospel.

The Ultimate Guardian (1:12b)

Before Paul charges Timothy with this responsibility, he reminds the young pastor that God Himself is the ultimate guardian of the gospel. Paul says, "But I am not ashamed, because I know the One I have believed in and am persuaded that He is able to guard what has been entrusted to me until that day." The word for "guard" here is a military term used of a soldier on watch. Paul is saying that God is watching His gospel and no one can match the power of this Guardian! Paul reminds Timothy to trust His security.

Paul was confident that because of God's faithfulness, not only was his personal future certain but also was the preservation of the gospel. Paul believed that "the good thing" (the gospel, v. 14) would be guarded until that day because his confidence was this: "I know Him." Christ had entrusted the gospel to Paul, and Paul was certain Christ would see to it that it was passed on through the generations. Now Paul was passing on the gospel to Timothy, and he wanted Timothy to be reminded that Christ is faithful to His servants. Timothy was not left to himself in guarding this gospel. Not only is verse 14 true—namely that we guard the gospel "through the Holy Spirit who lives in us"—but it is also true that we guard the gospel with the sure promises of God that He will keep what has been entrusted to us until that day. Stott says,

> We may see the evangelical faith, the faith of the gospel, everywhere spoken against, and the apostolic message of the New Testament ridiculed. We may have to watch an increasing apostasy in the church, as our generation abandons the faith

of its fathers. Do not be afraid! God will never allow the
light of the gospel to be finally extinguished. True, he has
committed it to us, frail and fallible creatures. He has placed
his treasure in brittle, earthenware vessels. And we must play
our part in guarding and defending the truth. Nevertheless, in
entrusting the deposit to our hands, he has not taken his own
hands off it. (Stott, *Message*, 47)

Guardians of the Gospel (1:13-14)

In light of this rock-solid confidence, Timothy is charged to "hold on to
the pattern of sound teaching that you have heard from me, in the faith
and love that are in Christ Jesus. Guard, through the Holy Spirit who
lives in us, that good thing entrusted to you" (1:13-14). The word choice
in these two verses shows us how precious and unchanging the gospel
is and why we must guard it faithfully. Notice these words and phrases:
"the pattern," "sound teaching," and "the good thing."

The word "pattern" in verse 13 can be translated as "outline." Just
as an architect might sketch a pattern before adding the details, or as
an artist might sketch the design of a painting before completing it, or
as a writer may start with an outline of a paper before writing the manu-
script, so Timothy was to follow Paul's outline—and then expound and
apply it. Timothy was not told to make up his own outline, add to it, or
take away from it. He was to take what Paul taught and teach it to others.
There is no other gospel than the one Paul passed along to Timothy: the
gospel contained in the Word of God. While we may apply its implications in various ways to our people today, we may not adjust the message
of the gospel. Our outline is written with the red blood of Jesus.

The word for "sound" means "healthy." The gospel makes spiritually sick people whole in Christ. Just as I try to give my kids healthy food
so they can grow, Timothy was to give God's people healthy teaching
so they can grow up in the faith. Timothy was also told to stay true to
this pattern "in the faith and love that are in Christ Jesus." Here is the
wonderful balance of this passage. Timothy was to be unashamed, bold,
and brave in gospel ministry, but he was also to be faithful to the gospel
in love and faith. Paul was not just interested in **what** Timothy preserved
but also in **how** he preserved it. This faith and love come only from
being "in Christ."

The gospel is not just healthy words and the outline for all our
teaching, but it may also be thought of as the "good deposit" (v. 14 ESV).

The word for "good" can also be translated as "beautiful." The gospel is beautiful, and it is to be "guarded" with such care that it is not damaged. The word for "guard" is used of protecting a palace from intruders and possessions from thieves (Luke 11:21; Acts 22:20). Because of the presence of heretics, Timothy was called, like us, to protect this beautiful gospel.

In the *The Archer and the Arrow*, Jensen and Grimmond illustrate this sacred trust of protecting the gospel with the Mona Lisa painting. This most famous painting resides in a purpose-built, bullet-proof case in the Louvre. It is considered so valuable that it has only been exhibited outside the Louvre on two occasions in the last century. Jensen and Grimmond ask about those who would have transported it: "Can you imagine what might have happened if those responsible for delivering the painting decided that the Mona Lisa was a little short in artistic merit? What if they had whipped out a brush in transit and added a nice floral pattern to the border or updated the dress to duck-egg blue fashion of the day?" The authors rightly say, "Their job was not to improve the painting, but to deliver it in its original condition. How much more the Word of God!" (Jensen and Grimmond, *The Archer*, 13).

For those who are called into ministry, this passage is especially relevant. We have been called to protect this gospel. We must protect the gospel from intruders, wolves, and heretics who want to add to or take away from the purity of it. We must keep studying the gospel; we must keep exemplifying the gospel; and we must keep teaching the gospel, all so that our people may know it and communicate it to a world that so desperately needs to receive it.

This task is humbling. Where do we find strength to stand for the gospel in the face of suffering and protect it from marauders? Paul's words are encouraging here: we stand "through the Holy Spirit who lives in us" (v. 14). Once again we are not alone in our mission. God is with us, in us, and for us. And if God is for us, then who can be against us (Rom 8:31)?

The Ashamed and the Unashamed (1:15-18)

The connection of verses 15-18 with the preceding passage is clear. Paul provides negative and positive examples in order to reinforce his exhortation to Timothy to be **unashamed**. To begin, he mentioned two men who "turned away" from him in Asia, "Phygelus and Hermogenes" (v. 15). We know nothing else about these two men because they are not mentioned anywhere else in the New Testament. Perhaps they were leaders of a particular group within the church. Whoever they were, they obviously disappointed Paul. They also represented others who turned away from the apostle. Paul says, "All those in Asia have turned away from me." Asia was the name of the Roman province in which Ephesus was located, and apparently many from there had abandoned Paul.

In contrast to the deserters, Paul mentions his refresher, Onesiphorus. Paul longs for the Lord to "grant mercy to the household of Onesiphorus" because he refreshed Paul often and "was not ashamed of [his] chains" (v. 16). He actually prays for him to receive mercy again in verse 18: "May the Lord grant that he obtain mercy from Him on that day!"

Clearly Paul loved this servant. He represented a host of people for whom Paul was grateful. Though Paul was a scholar, a preacher, and a missionary, it seems he was also a relational individual. He knew the value of godly friendships. In the final chapter of Romans, Paul's closing comments include 33 names. He prayed for his friends constantly, recognizing that they were gifts of grace.

Why did he admire and pray for Onesiphorus? Onesiphorus refreshed Paul, was unashamed of Paul, and searched earnestly for Paul. The refreshment that he brought refers mainly to his presence. He may have met some of Paul's physical needs, but undoubtedly he refreshed Paul by his loyal support. And notice that he refreshed Paul "often." Onesiphorus was not a fly-by-night guy; he was a loyal friend.

He was unashamed of Paul's chains, which again points us to the previous section. If this guy could do it, so could Timothy. Hearing the stories of bold Christians helps inspire and motivate others to equally bold witness. Onesiphorus was one such bold Christian. Even when Paul was bound up with a chain, he was not ashamed to come to Paul.

Finally, Paul says, "He diligently searched for me" (v. 17). The language suggests that Onesiphorus searched with the singular intent of finding Paul. This prison situation seems to be worse than the one described in Acts 28:23, 30-31 since it was necessary for him to search for Paul diligently. Paul was grateful to his friend for his steadfast pursuit. Now he prays for Onesiphorus, the one who found him, to "obtain mercy." We can believe that he did, if we keep in mind Jesus' words: "The merciful are blessed, for they will be shown mercy" (Matt 5:7).

The merciful and faithful servant, Onesiphorus, illustrates what unashamed, sacrificial service looks like. This passage leaves us with the question, Which example are you? Do you line up with Phygelus and

Hermogenes, who are ashamed of the gospel? Are you quick to flee when faithful obedience and boldness are required? Or are you a loyal servant, like Onesiphorus, who works hard to refresh others? We are reminded here that all types of faithful servants are needed in the kingdom: the Pauls and Timothys (leaders) as well as the Onesiphoruses (encouragers). May our sovereign God, who saves us and calls us, raise up an army of such faithful kingdom servants.

Reflect and Discuss

1. In what way is the crucifixion mocked today?
2. Who among your acquaintances or family has expressed antipathy toward the gospel? What is that person's underlying philosophy behind the rejection?
3. What situations have you encountered in the last month where it has been difficult or unpopular to take a Christian stance?
4. How might you remind yourself daily of your need for God's grace?
5. How would you explain the resurrection as the ground for your hope of salvation when speaking to a Christian who is struggling with doubt? How would you explain it to a seeker who asked you about it?
6. How does the fear of suffering affect your intention to speak the gospel boldly?
7. How would you express the "pattern" or outline of the gospel in three short sentences?
8. What do people today want to add to the gospel? What do they want to take away from it?
9. Do you have a friend you would call spiritually "refreshing"? Do you know someone who needs a refreshing friend?
10. Have you ever been tempted to abandon a fellow Christian? What kinds of situations give rise to such temptations for you?

Images of Endurance

2 TIMOTHY 2:1-13

Main Idea: Because of the importance of preserving and passing on the gospel, we must endure in the grace of God.

I.   **Challenge 1: Live in the Gospel (2:1).**
II. **Challenge 2: Pass On the Gospel (2:2).**
III. **Challenge 3: Endure for the Gospel (2:3-7).**
    A. The dedicated soldier (2:3-4)
    B. The disciplined athlete (2:5)
    C. The hardworking farmer (2:6)
IV. **Challenge 4: Remember the Hero of the Gospel (2:8-13).**

What pictures come into your mind when you think of ministers and ministry? Do you view vocational ministry as a comfortable, inside job that does not require sweat or heavy lifting? Is it something of marginal importance or that which is eternally significant? Have you ever thought of pastors as spiritual athletes? How about spiritual Green Berets or spiritual surgeons?

In 2 Timothy 2, Paul gives a number of metaphors for Christian ministry. His first topic in 2:1-13 is **endurance**, and he provides three images to illustrate: "a good soldier," "an athlete," and a "hardworking farmer" (2:3-6). All convey the idea of work, discipline, endurance, and even suffering. He tells Timothy in verse 3 to "share in suffering" or (ESV) "endure hardship" (NIV). He also speaks of endurance in verse 10 to refer to himself and again in verse 12 as an expression for all the saints ("if *we* endure"; emphasis added).

In the next section (2:14-26), Paul provides three additional images to describe a **faithful teacher**: an approved worker, an instrument, and "the Lord's slave." From all six of these images, we clearly sense the intense nature of Christian ministry. It is not a walk in the park. It is work. It requires effort. It is war.

In addition to these images, we should also pay attention to the continued emphasis on **the gospel** in 2 Timothy, which illustrates **why** ministry demands all we have (2:8-9; cf. 1:8, 12). Because of the importance of preserving and passing on the gospel, we must endure; and because of the hope we have in the gospel, we can endure. In these verses we see four challenges for gospel-centered endurance that must be overcome if we are to stand firm in the faith.

Challenge 1: Live in the Gospel
2 TIMOTHY 2:1

Paul begins his exhortation to Timothy by alluding to the previous examples of the defectors in Asia and of Onesiphorus's terrific exception. In light of these, Timothy is "therefore" to resist the trend of the former and instead follow the example of the latter.

If Timothy was going to endure, it would be because he was strengthened "in the grace that is in Christ Jesus" (2:1). Paul urges him to **live in the gospel**, that is, to abide day by day depending on the enabling grace that flows from our union with Jesus. Paul does not tell Timothy simply to "be strong" or "pull yourself up by your bootstraps." That is of no help. He tells him to be inwardly strengthened by the grace that is in Christ. The grace of Christ empowers all of the exhortations of chapter 2. We cannot live out these charges apart from *His* strength.

One of the refreshing things we find in the life and writings of Paul is his constant emphasis on grace. To the Corinthians he describes how Christ's grace is sufficient in his weakness (2 Cor 12:9). In his earlier letter he declares, "By God's grace I am what I am" (1 Cor 15:10). Interestingly, the only description we have of Paul's physical appearance is from the (noninspired) book *Acts of Paul and Thecla* written in the second century. In this account Onesiphorus is said to be looking for Paul based on the description given to him by Titus, portraying the apostle as "small in size, bald-headed, bandy-legged, well-built, with eyebrows meeting, rather long nose, full of grace" (Roberts, Donaldson, and Coxe, *Ante-Nicene Fathers*, 487). Whether the account is of any historical value is unlikely, but what we do know is that the Corinthians said of Paul, "His letters are weighty and powerful, but *his physical presence is weak*" (2 Cor 10:10; emphasis added). In other words, he was more like George Costanza than Vin Diesel!

While his bodily presence may have been unimpressive, we see him in Acts enduring afflictions all over the Mediterranean world! How did Paul endure? The same way he was telling Timothy to go on: by "the grace that is in Christ Jesus." If Timothy, a fragile vessel, was going to last in Ephesus—the city with blatant heresy, widespread disbelief, and an overall difficult church—it would be by the strength of Jesus.

How can we endure? We have the same source. "Be strengthened *by the Lord* and by His vast strength" (Eph 6:10; emphasis added). Our strength is not in how long we have been Christians, in how much we know about the Bible, or in how long we have been in ministry. Our strength, this very moment, is in the grace that is in Christ Jesus. Our strength is derived from our union with Jesus and is supercharged by our daily communion with Jesus.

If you find yourself desperate for strength, you are in a good place. You are a great candidate for grace. You are in the number of those faithful servants in Hebrews 11 who "gained strength after being weak" (Heb 11:34). Perhaps you are dealing with wayward children, fatigue, discouragement, betrayal, or illness. My friend, remember that there is a fountain of grace in Jesus. Join the prayer of Jehoshaphat, who confessed, "For we are powerless before this vast number that comes to fight against us. We do not know what to do, but we look to You" (2 Chr 20:12). So, if you are looking for strength to endure in the midst of hardship and suffering, look in the right place and to the right person—Jesus.

Christians who make an eternal difference in this world are those who have learned to rely on God's strength, not their own. David Livingstone once commented on all the work Charles Spurgeon would do in a typical day (and Livingstone was no sluggard!). He asked the prince of preachers how he could do it all. Spurgeon said, "You have forgotten, there are two of us" (Piper, "Spurgeon"). God's presence in us supplies what we need to endure.

Realize what you already possess as a Christian (2 Pet 1:3), and seek the Father in prayer, asking "to be strengthened with power in the inner man through His Spirit" (Eph 3:16). Also, remember that another means of grace is meditating on God's Word. Paul opened many of his letters by saying, "Grace to you." When you open the Bible, there is grace coming to you—through personal devotion, hearing the Word read and preached, and singing it. Meditate on the gospel daily because you never outgrow your need for it. Paul concluded his letter to the Romans saying, "Now to Him who has power to strengthen you *according to my gospel*" (Rom 16:25; emphasis added). Go to the gospel daily and find strength.

Challenge 2: Pass On the Gospel
2 TIMOTHY 2:2

Paul picks up the idea previously explained in 1:13-14, that is, guarding the gospel, only now it was taken to the next step of passing it on to others. Paul notes four stages of this gospel handoff.

First, Christ gave this message to Paul (1:12). Paul did not make up this message (Gal 1:11-12); he was given this message. It was entrusted to him through divine revelation, not human invention.

Second, Paul passed on the good deposit to Timothy. He says that this message was "what you have heard from me in the presence of many witnesses." This was the basic message Paul taught publicly in churches everywhere. In Stott's words, this phrase refers to

> the totality of Paul's instruction over the years . . . not a secret
> tradition handed on privately to Timothy (as the Gnostics
> were claiming) . . . but a public instruction, whose truth was
> guaranteed by the many witnesses who heard it and who could
> therefore check Timothy's teaching against the apostle's.
> (Stott, *Message*, 50–51)

What Timothy heard was what Timothy is now to speak.

Third, Timothy is to entrust the message to other men. The word "commit" is the same word Jesus used when He cried out from the cross, "Into Your hands I entrust [or commit] My spirit" (Luke 23:46). Just as the Son knew His life was safe in the Father's hands, so Timothy was to put the gospel into safe hands. Such men possess two essential qualifications. They must be "faithful men," and they must be "able to teach." These two qualifications speak directly of the life of pastors who are called to be men of godly character and have the ability to teach (1 Tim 3:1-7). Despite the large number of defectors in Asia, apparently there were still a few faithful men in Timothy's sphere of influence, and he is called to invest in them intentionally.

Finally, Timothy is to entrust the message to faithful men so that they could "teach others also." Think about it. Paul's message went from a hole in the ground in Rome to where I am writing from in North Carolina roughly two thousand years later! How did that happen? Simple—some faithful men practiced 2 Timothy 2:2. They did not let the gospel die with them.

Every Christian leader needs to be looking for some faithful believers who can do the same. As Phil Jensen says, we need a category of men that he calls "Blokes Worth Watching" (Dennis, "Multiplying Men"). It is our responsibility as stewards of God's Word to guard the deposit entrusted to us and then invest it in some "blokes worth watching" who are able to teach others also. Could anything be more important than passing on the message of salvation to qualified teachers?

Timothy is charged later in this letter to "teach" (2:24; 4:2) and "preach" (4:2 ESV). We understand the importance of public teaching and preaching to both believers and unbelievers. But this exhortation to "commit to faithful men" seems to be a third type of instruction. It is more personal and intimate. It is closer to mentoring, or what we sometimes call "discipleship." Whatever we call it, it is certainly true that one of the biggest weaknesses in the church today seems to be the absence of 2 Timothy 2:2 ministry.

You could think of teaching like the three types of golf clubs. You have woods, irons, and a putter. The woods are big, showy, and impressive. That is like preaching publicly. You are able to cover a lot of ground, talking to lots of people. Then you have irons. They require finesse and accuracy. Irons are like classrooms or smaller groups, where you get feedback and dialogue. Then there is the putter! This is the club that poor golfers misunderstand and so often fail to practice with! It is personal. It is for short distances. I liken it to this third way of teaching described in 2 Timothy 2:2. Which of the three clubs is most important? While you need all three clubs in your bag, my observation has been that many pastors have a pulpit ministry (a driver), and sometimes a classroom (irons), but few use their putter (mentoring a few "faithful men"). But good golfers remind poor golfers (like me) that "you drive for show and putt for dough." An important lesson from the book of 2 Timothy for Christian leaders is that we should remember the importance of all our clubs. Do you have a few "blokes worth watching" in whom you are investing your life and instruction?

Why are many not practicing 2 Timothy 2:2? I am sure there are several reasons, but a few in particular come to my mind. Mentoring is about relationships, and therefore many do not pour into others because it requires time, vulnerability, and trust—and the acceptance of the fact that inevitably someone will hurt you. Others do not practice this multiplying ministry because it is viewed as bonus work. How many pastors are asked by inquiring search committees, "Will you train other elders/pastors?" How many denominations keep count of mentoring relationships? Because we do not submit these things on our numbered lists, they are not deemed important. But what did Jesus do? Did He not pour His life into the Twelve? Sure, He occasionally used His irons and driver too, on hillsides and in the synagogues, but Jesus was not building buildings. He was building men. And these faithful men turned the world upside down.

Have you ever considered the fact that perhaps the greatest thing you might do with your life is to pour into a future leader? In 1606, William Perkins wrote a book entitled *The Calling of the Ministry*. In it he has a chapter entitled "The Scarcity of True Ministers" in which he says, "Good ministers are one in a thousand." He advises, "If ministers are few in number, then all you can do is increase their number. . . . So let every minister both in his teaching and conversation work in such a way that he honors his calling, so that he may attract others to share his love for it" (Perkins, *Art of Prophesying*, 96–98). We need a vision for multiplying the gospel beyond us!

How do you do this? I do not think there is a perfect plan. But what is clear from this verse is that it requires **careful observation**. Timothy was to find some "faithful men," just as he himself was "well spoken of by the brothers" before Paul took him as his spiritual son (Acts 16:2 ESV). Every pastor should not just have a "to-do" list but also a "to-be" list, a list of potential leaders to mentor. It also requires **relationship development** after these particular prospects are selected. Develop relationships by meeting regularly, going on ministry trips together, or going to conferences. Paul took Timothy with him. He did not just hand him a book. Finally, it involves **pastoral coaching**. Help these faithful men teach and lead well. Help them discern their **calling**, cultivate godly **character**, and increase their level of **competency** by giving feedback and support in their teaching.

I am indebted to Dr. Jim Shaddix who lived out this verse while I was in school in New Orleans. Dr. Shaddix selected a few men to join his Emmaus Road Group. This group met at his house once a month to eat, watch a sermon, pray, and just have a great time talking about life and ministry. Our wives also joined us for these meetings (but they went to a separate room during the sermon!). Then periodically he would ask us to go on trips with him where he was preaching. There we heard his preaching "in the presence of many witnesses." We would also run errands, make airport runs, edit his books, and participate in many other activities that stoked our fires. In short, we had a relationship with a caring pastoral coach.

My friend Joel also models 2 Timothy 2:2. He was a music minister for 35 years before he and his wife left for Ukraine at age 57! For nine years now, Joel has been training and equipping a handful of "faithful men" to plant churches in the former Soviet Union. When I first met him in Kiev in 2006, he said, "This is the most meaningful ministry of my life." I think Joel discovered what many also discover: the joy of pouring into younger leaders who will teach others. This ministry reinvigorated my older brother, and I find great hope knowing that when I am 65, I too may find such joy in ministry.

Challenge 3: Endure for the Gospel
2 TIMOTHY 2:3-7

To inspire Timothy for faithfulness in ministry, Paul uses three simple but powerful images: the soldier, the athlete, and the farmer. These are some of Paul's favorite images, and he uses them elsewhere to illustrate various truths.

The Dedicated Soldier (2:3-4)

Paul was familiar with Roman soldiers since he was in prison more than once! He notes that a "good" soldier is known for his focus and his willingness to suffer. He tells Timothy to "endure hardship" (2:3 NIV), not "get mad in hardship" or "quit in hardship" or "expect no hardship." Suffering and hardship are part of the life of every Christian. For a pastor-minister, these are only increased.

Ministers often joke about how many times they have resigned on Monday morning! I mean, it would be great to be the guy on the TV show, *Diners, Drive-ins, and Dives* (who gets to drive around and eat great food!), instead of enduring constant criticism, unpredictable giving patterns, the burden of reconciling marriages, or the weekly pressure of sermon preparation—not to mention having your life threatened on the mission field! However, Christ has not called us to a life of ease but a life of endurance. By the grace that is in Jesus, we are called to put a helmet on and stay in the battle until our commander says the war is over! We need Green Berets for Jesus!

Paul adds in verse 4 that the good soldier does not get "entangled in the concerns of civilian life; he seeks to please the recruiter." Soldiers live with the awareness that a war is going on. There is a sense of concentration, austerity, self-denial, and disregard for trivial matters.

Of course, this does not mean that Christians in general or pastors in particular should neglect family life or healthy vacation time. Paul was speaking here of a mind-set and a mission. How easy is it for us to get distracted by things that simply do not matter? Are any good things keeping you from doing the main things? Are you entangled with stuff that is keeping you from making disciples among all nations? We remedy this problem by remembering that our chief aim must be to please Jesus. Fight the good fight—the one Jesus has called you to fight.

Later Paul tells Timothy not to "fight about words" (2:14), to "avoid irreverent, empty speech" (2:16), and to "flee from youthful passions" (2:22). What is entangling you? Augustine said, "The love of worldly possessions entangles the soul and keeps it from flying to God." Are you all tied up with greed, a quest for control, senseless controversies, or youthful passions? Let your passion be singular: to please the One who enlisted you.

The Disciplined Athlete (2:5)

Once again Paul draws on an analogy with which he was familiar. As a leatherworker (or tent-maker), Paul would have been around the Greek games often. He did not point out a particular sport but simply spoke of "an athlete" to make his point about discipline. In every sport the athlete must compete "according to the rules" if he is to be "crowned." To receive the evergreen wreath of the Greek games, the athlete must avoid unfair tactics. Perhaps if Paul were alive today, he would have added, "Athletes cannot use performance enhancing drugs" or, "Baseball pitchers cannot scuff the baseball."

To be a winner, you must play by the rules. And to be a winner, you must train. Paul tells Timothy elsewhere, "Train yourself in godliness" (1 Tim 4:7). There are no shortcuts in sports. It requires discipline. Millions admire athletes, but few imitate them. Many enjoy their performances, but few watch and attempt their training. And many Christians want God's blessing on their life without playing by His rules. Please understand, Paul was not talking about rule-keeping *to earn* salvation. He was talking about the desire of every true believer: to walk in godliness in accordance with God's Word. We have "rules" by which we are to live; our lives are to be governed by the Bible. For example, God tells believers to marry other believers. He tells us to share our faith, to pray, to give financially to His mission, and more. We cannot take shortcuts, either redefining God's truth or disobeying it. If we want the reward of faithfulness, we must compete according to God's standards (cf. 2 Tim 4:7-8; 1 Cor 3:10-15; 9:24-27). Once again, we do this by "the grace that is in Christ Jesus" (2 Tim 2:1). If athletes can train and compete for trophies and men's applause, how much more should we train and sweat for that which is eternal!

The Hardworking Farmer (2:6)

Just as with soldiers and athletes, farmers cannot take any shortcuts either. They must toil every day. The difference with this illustration is that farming, unlike athletics and sometimes the military, is not glorious or exciting. The farmer is not applauded by fans or civilians. He does not call a press conference when he bales his hay!

This is a good analogy for ministry. Pastoral work is not glamorous. It involves sowing, planting, plowing, and monitoring. Farming is also like pastoral work in that it is endless. The farmer does not clock in and clock out. He gets up early, he works the field, he cares for the animals, . . . and he shoots wolves! He is devoted to his work.

Paul adds that the hardworking farmer deserved the first "share of the crops." The farmer gets to enjoy some of the fruit of his labor. This is the other side to farming and likewise to pastoral work. There are tremendous blessings involved in watching people grow in holiness, seeing skeptics converted, and watching mission projects develop. Slow, careful, faithful pastoral ministry eventually produces because we reap what we sow (Gal 6:7-8). Therefore, "we must not get tired of doing good, for we will reap at the proper time if we don't give up" (Gal 6:9). If the famer does not plow, he will not reap. Paul told Timothy (and us) to "keep plowing."

Paul concluded these examples by saying, "Consider what I say, for the Lord will give you understanding in everything" (v. 7). Here is Bible Study 101! Students of Scripture must "consider" God's Word carefully in order to understand it. Students of Scripture should also study with this promise in view: "The Lord will give you understanding in everything." Do not be lazy in Bible study. Work hard and believe that God will help you uncover its truths. To be a great student of Scripture, you need hard work and a heart of humility.

Challenge 4: Remember the Hero of the Gospel
2 TIMOTHY 2:8-13

In order to endure to the end, through the good seasons and the difficult seasons, believers must never lose sight of Jesus. Paul says, "Keep your attention on Jesus Christ" (v. 8). At first glance this may seem like an unnecessary statement. How could you possibly forget Him? However, Stott reminds us, "The human memory is notoriously fickle: it is possible to forget even one's own name!" (Stott, *Message*, 61). Israel suffered from spiritual memory loss, which led them down a pitiful path of unfaithfulness and idolatry (see Ps 106:19-21). Certainly, there are many occasions in which the church and her leaders have forgotten whose people they are and whose mission they have joined. One must be careful not to make ministry a mere profession in which the person of Jesus Christ is pushed to the fringes of importance. Christ is to be central and preeminent in ministry.

Remembering Jesus involves keeping both His person and His work central. Paul says that Christ is "risen from the dead and descended from David." Here Paul affirmed Christ's person as fully *divine*, "risen from the dead" (cf. Rom 1:4), and fully human, "descended from David." He also affirmed Christ's work. Jesus died in our place for our sins, He rose from the grave, He conquered our enemies, and now He sits at the Father's right hand.

When your tank is empty, remember that the tomb is empty and the throne is occupied. You can endure anything if you have sufficient motivation. A lofty vision of the person and work of Christ will keep us in the war, in the game, and on the farm.

Paul adds that this is "according to my gospel" (v. 8). His gospel was occupied with the Hero of the gospel. And this was not a mere theological exercise for Paul. He personally experienced the transforming power of Jesus. Paul went from a terrorist to an evangelist! It is for the Hero of the gospel that he was suffering to the point of "being bound like a criminal" (v. 9). Paul encouraged Timothy with the reminder that he was enduring suffering with this vision of Christ, even as he penned this letter.

Paul knew that the Hero of the gospel is also powerful enough to keep His word advancing despite imprisonment. He says, "But God's message is not bound." Paul alluded earlier to the fact that God is the ultimate guardian of the gospel who will keep what was entrusted to Paul (1:12). Not only will God preserve His Word, but He will also make sure that it is not bound. Opponents may chain the messengers, but the sovereign Christ will make sure they cannot chain the message.

Further, Paul writes that because of this gospel and the glory of Christ, he would "endure all things for the elect: so that they also may obtain salvation, which is in Christ Jesus, with eternal glory" (v. 10). The doctrine of election did not make Paul's preaching of the gospel unnecessary, but rather it made it essential! God has ordained that people find salvation in Christ by means of a gospel presentation. Some people will believe if you will preach the gospel faithfully. And our gospel witness will require varying degrees of suffering, but we suffer that they may experience "eternal glory."

Finally, Paul quotes a popular saying of his time, which reinforces the idea that all believers must endure hardship. This trustworthy saying in 2 Timothy 2:11 may have been the fragment of an early hymn. It consists of two pairs of sayings, which are general truths of the Christian's life. The first pair relates to those who endure faithfully; the second pair describes those who are unfaithful. First, "If we have died with Him, we will also live with Him; if we endure, we will also reign with Him" (vv. 11-12). The idea of dying with Him to live with Him probably refers to dying to self, as we take up our cross to follow Jesus. Jesus said, "Whoever wants to save his life will lose it, but whoever loses his life because of Me and the gospel will save it" (Mark 8:35). In order to truly live, believers must die. This view certainly fits the context, in which Paul was telling Timothy to lay down his comfort for Christ and His gospel. But not just for Timothy. All believers are called to a life of dying. If we do endure, then, as Paul quotes from the hymn, "We will also reign" with Christ. However, only if we share in Christ's sufferings now will we reign later.

The next pair of statements describes the awful picture of denying Christ, proving faithless: "If we deny Him, He will also deny us; if we are faithless, He remains faithful, for He cannot deny Himself" (vv. 12-13). This first statement also seems to echo the teaching of Jesus in the context of a discourse on persecution: "But whoever denies Me before men, I will also deny him before My Father in heaven" (Matt 10:33). The meaning of Paul's statement in 2 Timothy 2:12b, then, in light of this connection with Matthew 10, is clear: we must not deny our Lord.

But what about the next statement—"If we are faithless, He remains faithful"—how are we to understand this expression? Some take verse 13 to refer to the idea that even if we turn away from Jesus, He will not turn away from us. Others find this to mean that if we are unfaithful, He remains faithful . . . to His own **character**, which in this case would include rejecting the faithless. One group sees this verse as a word of **comfort**, the other as a word of **warning**. While it is certainly true that God is not fickle, and His faithfulness is new every morning for believers who have moments, like Peter, of denying Christ, that is not what this hymn appears to be saying. I think the best way to understand this hymn (though I hold this position loosely) is to take it as a warning for those who persist in a state of faithlessness. These statements appear to be parallel, pointing in this direction: "If we deny Him" is parallel to "if we are faithless," and "He also will deny us" is parallel to "He remains faithful." "He will deny us" helps us understand the phrase about His faithfulness. God is faithful not just to extend blessing to those with genuine faith but also faithful to His warnings.

However one wishes to interpret this last phrase of the hymn, it is clear and wonderfully encouraging that "He cannot deny Himself." God cannot act contrary to His nature. He is faithful. He is the God of mercy and justice. He is the same yesterday, today, and forever.

Remember Jesus Christ! Remember the One who conquered our enemies is seated at the Father's right hand and gives sufficient grace that we may endure hardship. If we endure through Him, we will reign with Him. And when your faith ends in sight and you hear the Savior say, "Well done," I promise that you will not regret living in, passing on, and suffering for the gospel as a good soldier, a disciplined athlete, and a hardworking farmer.

Reflect and Discuss

1. What pictures come into your mind when you think of ministers and ministry? Have you ever thought of pastors as spiritual athletes? How about spiritual Green Berets or spiritual surgeons?
2. Why is a simple exhortation to "be strong" or to "buck up" insufficient?
3. Which source provides you the most encouragement: prayer, Bible reading, listening to sermons, meeting with other Christians, worshiping through music, or reading Christian books?

4. Does your church have a mentoring ministry? Which person would you talk to if you wanted to learn or teach? Do your gifts include the ability to organize a discipleship ministry in your church?
5. Do you have a few "blokes worth watching" in whom you are investing your life and instruction?
6. Why are many not practicing 2 Timothy 2:2?
7. How are Christians and soldiers alike? How are they different?
8. Are any good things keeping you from doing the main things? Are you entangled with stuff that is keeping you from making disciples among all nations?
9. How does your understanding of election fuel your desire to share the gospel?
10. How is God's unchanging nature both a comfort and a warning?

Images of a Faithful Teacher

2 TIMOTHY 2:14-26

Main Idea: We are all commissioned and empowered to be faithful teachers of the one, true gospel.

I. **Image 1: The Unashamed Workman (2:15-19)**
   A. The good workman (2:15-16)
   B. The bad workman (2:17-19)
II. **Image 2: The Clean Vessel (2:20-22)**
III. **Image 3: The Lord's Servant (2:23-26)**
IV. **Who Is Sufficient for These Things?**

Adding to the **soldier**, **athlete**, and **farmer** illustrations from the preceding verses, Paul introduces three more metaphors to describe the nature of ministry. They each highlight aspects of **teaching** in particular: (1) the unashamed workman (vv. 14-19), (2) the clean vessel (vv. 20-22), and (3) the Lord's servant (vv. 23-26). Paul speaks of the act of teaching (e.g., "remind them," "able to teach," "correcting opponents"), the character of a faithful teacher (e.g., "a worker," "holy," "patient"), and the danger of false teachers and their teaching (e.g., "their word will spread like gangrene," "deviated from the truth").

Paul enters this subject with the charge, "Remind them of these things" (v. 14). The phrase "these things" occurs several times in 1 and 2 Timothy. It probably refers to the previous section most directly, where Paul urged Timothy to pass on the **gospel** (2:1-13), but it may also refer more generally to Paul's entire instruction to Timothy. In either case Timothy is not to make up his content. He is simply urged to tell and retell what he received from Paul, who himself received it from Jesus.

As faithful teachers, our job is always to preach and teach **these things** (sound doctrine) not **our things** (personal opinions). We are commissioned with the task of reminding people over and over of God's Word (see also Rom 15:15; Phil 3:1; Jude 5; 2 Pet 1:12-15; 3:1-2). When you are preaching something that is from God, rather than simply a word from man, it is worth repeating! Paul constantly reminded people of the crucified and risen Christ (1 Cor 2:1-5; 15:1-5). This does not mean we should say it the same way every time but only that we must keep repeating the same gospel. As John Newton put it in his hymn "Amazing Grace," "Redeeming love has been my theme, and shall be till I die."

The unacceptable alternative to teaching and reteaching "these things" is quarreling over "words" (v. 14). Timothy is told to avoid such practice because it is not profitable and it will "ruin" the hearers.

The teacher who abandons Scripture as the primary source of instruction will end up damaging people and creating division. This is because once a teacher leaves **biblical revelation** for **human speculation** the final court of authority has been removed. People will fight over all kinds of issues if they have no common source of authority for evaluating experiences, opinions, and traditions.

Now that the substance of Timothy's content, the true gospel, has been explained, Paul provides three metaphors to describe the character of a faithful teacher.

Image 1: The Unashamed Workman
2 TIMOTHY 2:15-19

In these verses there is sharp contrast between two types of teachers or two types of workmen. There are **good workmen** and **bad workmen**. The good workmen are devoted to "the Word of truth." The good workmen are also "approved," having been tested like metals or coins, being recognized as "sterling" (Stott, *Message*, 66). In contrast the bad workmen are not devoted to the truth (vv. 16-18). They are not approved because they fail the test of authenticity. Consequently, the good workmen stand unashamed whereas the bad workmen should be deeply ashamed.

Timothy is to stand as a model for the unashamed workman (if he followed Paul's instruction) who handled the Word of truth rightly and was thus approved by God. Hymenaeus and Philetus were examples of those who were unapproved because they were not devoted to the Word of truth and their teaching damaged people. Let's look a little deeper into these two contrasting types.

The Good Workman (2:15-16)

Paul alluded to three marks of an unashamed workman. First, **the good workman is a hard worker**. Like the "hardworking farmer" analogy in verse 6, this metaphor pictures the ministry as something that will require spiritual sweat. Paul says, "Be diligent" (v. 15). There is no room for slackers in the ministry, especially those who are giving the words of life! It has been said, "Holy shoddy is still shoddy!"

Word work is hard work. Any teacher that is worth his (or her) salt will toil in the preparation and delivery of God's Word. Before there is success in the classroom or in the pulpit, there must be diligence in the study.

Paul told Timothy earlier that those who "work hard at preaching and teaching" are "worthy of an ample honorarium" (1 Tim 5:17). Several things make biblical teaching labor intensive. It is hard work to rightly understand the teaching of Scripture and then present it in a way that is clear and understandable to the hearers. Teaching is also difficult because oftentimes your product is **invisible**. You cannot always see results from your teaching. It is also work because you are handling material that is by its nature **controversial**. A teacher is not handling ideas that are mere topics for small talk but rather the Word of God that is death to some and life to others (2 Cor 2:15-17). This reality will cause the teacher to feel the burden of sermon/lesson preparation weekly, and critics will arise because of the bold truth claims that have to be made by the faithful teacher.

Next, **the good workman is God centered**. The internal warfare experienced by a biblical teacher never goes away. There is constantly more to be done, more questions to answer, more critics to silence, and more waves of discouragement to endure. For these reasons and more, a faithful teacher must keep eternity in view. He or she must live for the approval of God and not of people. God-centered workmen desire to stand unashamed before their God as ones who rightly taught His Word. Teachers must keep in mind that God places them in ministry positions and they must give an account to God. This God-centered vision will sustain teachers in difficult times because it will place their trials in proper perspective. God-centered teachers want to be faithful, not flashy or famous.

Finally, **the good workman is careful and accurate in his teaching**. The Greek word *orthotomeo*, translated as "correctly teaching" or "rightly handling" (ESV), is a word that means to "cut straight." The "straight" part is a word from which we get words like "orthodontist" and "orthodoxy." The orthodontist is one who realigns teeth, and orthodoxy is teaching or belief that rightly aligns with Scripture and the historic Christian faith.

But what is Timothy metaphorically to cut straight? Commentators suggest several options, such as "a father slicing bread for children," "a stonemason cutting stones to fit a building," "a surgeon making an incision," or from Paul's own trade, "a tent-maker cutting leather." Perhaps the best description (though not certain) is "a road-maker cutting a straight path." Timothy is to keep the hearers on the way of truth by clearing out a straight path on which they may walk. The idea of road-making or plowing a straight furrow seems to fit the verses in Proverbs where this same word is used (Prov 3:6 and 11:5). The idea is clear: Timothy must teach the Word carefully and clearly to help the hearers stay on the path of life.

Faithful teachers are unlike Elymas, who was guilty of "perverting the straight paths of the Lord" (Acts 13:10). There is plenty of perverse or crooked Bible teaching today! We need an army of accurate handlers of God's Word. Perverse teaching leads people down a dead-end path. And those who teach false doctrine will not receive God's approval but rather God's judgment.

The teacher has neglected his path-giving assignment if he exchanges careful exposition for "irreverent, empty speech" (v. 16). Timothy is charged to "avoid" the temptation to get caught up in irreverent and irrelevant distractions because such things would damage his hearers. Paul said that they would "produce an even greater measure of godlessness." Faithful teachers have the goal of godliness, not godlessness. Godliness is cultivated as the Word of God is taught and changes people from the inside out. Godlessness comes when people exchange the beauty and truth of God's Word for the pettiness and falsehood of merely human ideas.

The Bad Workman (2:17-19)

The word picture for the bad workman was taken not from road construction or agriculture but from *archery* (Stott, *Message*, 68). The truth was likened to a marksman's target. Hymenaeus and Philetus were among those who had been led into empty talk and had thus "deviated from the truth" or "swerved from the truth" (v. 18 ESV). The word for "deviate" or "swerve" is the Greek verb *astocheo*, which is the negated verbal form of the noun *stochos* meaning "target." Bad teachers miss the mark.

These particular teachers deviated from one specific truth: the resurrection. They taught that "the resurrection [had] already taken place" (v. 18). Of course, Jesus has risen from the dead, and those who are true believers have been raised up with Christ (Eph 2:6). But the resurrection of believers' **bodies**, along with the glory of the new heavens and new earth, is still a future expectation (Acts 17:32; Rom 8:18-25; 1 Cor 15:12-58). These false teachers were leading others down the wrong path by denying a future bodily resurrection. They could have been early Gnostics who taught that the body was basically evil, and therefore a bodily resurrection was unnecessary and counterproductive. For them hope was found in losing our mortal bodies. Similarly, some today simply want to believe in the **idea** of the resurrection but not an **actual** bodily resurrection. Paul says these had all missed the mark. The resurrection, both Jesus' and our own, is no small thing. It is foundational to our faith (1 Cor 15).

What is the result of such heretical teaching? Paul says false teachers, such as Hymenaeus and Philetus, were "overturning the faith of some" (v. 18). The result of false teaching is **deadly**. It leads people away from God. Moreover, false teaching spreads throughout the community with ravaging effects. The illustration used could hardly be more graphic and appropriate. He said false teaching spreads like **gangrene**, which is the decay of tissue in a part of the body where the blood supply is blocked due to an injury or disease. The decay spreads continually. Just as gangrene progressively spreads throughout the body bringing death, so does erroneous teaching. It will slowly eat through the individuals and the body of Christ.

This is different from the modern worldview. Today is the age of "tolerance" and "relativism." "Whatever is true for you, is true for you," people say. Really? Paul shouts in our ears today: there is a true path and a false path; there is a mark you can hit or you can miss; there is truth that can nourish; and there is falsehood that kills.

What should Christians do in light of the presence of false teaching? They should "avoid irreverent, empty speech" (v. 16). They should stay on the path of truth, revealed in Holy Scripture. And they should do one more thing: they should avoid despair. Despite living in a world filled with Hymenaeuses and Philetuses who deny the Christian essentials, Paul reminds us of the comforting truth that "God's solid foundation stands" (v. 19).

The "foundation" probably refers specifically to the church as a whole. Paul is saying, "Do not despair, Christian! The church will go marching on because God alone is sovereign, and He has a people for Himself!" We know God has a people for two reasons, one invisible and the other visible. First, drawing on the story of the rebellion of Korah,

Dathan, and Abiram in Numbers 16, Paul reminds us, "The Lord knows those who are His" (2 Tim 2:19). God knows the hearts of people. He knows who His true people are. As awful as the episode of Korah's rebellion was, it did not totally destroy the people of God. And as destructive as the false teaching is, it will not **ultimately** devastate the church. God has a people that He has chosen for Himself, and no false teacher will ultimately steal away the church of God.

Second, while we cannot see the hearts of people, we can see the lives of believers. Those who claim to be believers are urged to "turn away from unrighteousness." This exhortation reflects the sentiment of Psalm 34:14 and Proverbs 3:7. God's action in salvation results in a life of fruitful obedience. His people avoid wickedness and bear fruit.

Both of these realities, the doctrine of election and the fruitfulness of God's people, are glorious and mysterious, and they also remind us that God's church will endure. Christians should fear false teaching and run from false teachers, but they should not think the church would ever crumble, for no false teacher has that kind of power. The truth of God's sovereignty and the testimony of true believers tell us otherwise. This subject of godliness leads to the next image of a faithful teacher.

Image 2: The Clean Vessel
2 TIMOTHY 2:20-22

Paul moves to household images to describe the lifestyle of responsible Bible expositors in these three verses. The illustration is simple enough. Houses are filled with utensils. There are pots and pans, cups and glasses, forks and dishes, and more. The gold and silver vessels are "for honorable use." The wood and clay vessels are used for "ordinary" or "dishonorable" use. The Master of the house uses the honorable vessels for special occasions. The dishonorable vessels are used for other menial tasks (and sometimes thrown away with their contents).

This "large house" (v. 20) seems to be the visible church ("God's household," 1 Tim 3:15). These "bowls" seem to be two types of teachers, not two types of believers (see Stott, *Message*, 71). Paul himself was described as a chosen "vessel" or "instrument" set apart for the special purpose of making Christ known among the Gentiles (Acts 9:15). These two types of vessels represent two types of teachers present in the first-century church at Ephesus and also in the church today. There are the good workmen and bad workmen or honorable vessels and dishonorable vessels, the Timothys and the Hymanaeuses. Faithful teachers are honorable vessels used by the Master of the house.

What then characterizes such privileged individuals? Paul says there is one indispensable condition: he must purify himself (v. 21). If the vessel is clean, it will be an honorable vessel used for special purposes.

The cleansing in view here is of both **life and doctrine**. Paul says, "If anyone cleanses himself from *these things*" (v. 21 NASB; emphasis added), and in this passage "these things" seems to refer back to the corrupt teaching of Hymenaeus and Philetus and the consequent result: "godlessness" (vv. 16-18). Paul also shows the connection between impure doctrine and impure living (see 1 Tim 1:19-20; 6:3-5). Another clue that a pure life (not just pure teaching) is in view is that the clean vessel metaphor is sandwiched between two verses that speak of personal holiness: "turn away from unrighteousness" (v. 19) and "flee from youthful passions, and pursue righteousness" (v. 22). To be an honorable vessel, one must pursue pure doctrine and pure living. This charge is consistent with Paul's qualifications for pastor-elders (1 Tim 3:1-7; Titus 1:5-9). A clean vessel heeds the exhortation, "Pay close attention to your life and your teaching" (1 Tim 4:16).

While God has chosen impure vessels for His purposes in redemptive history (such as Nebuchadnezzar and Cyrus), we should remember that these were exceptional cases. The consistent command and expectation of God is for His people to be holy as He is holy (Lev 11:45; 1 Pet 1:16).

Paul gives three descriptions of this clean vessel. First, it must be "set apart" from unrighteousness and for righteousness. Second, clean vessels must be "useful to the Master," knowing He owned them and may do with them as He pleased. Third, clean vessels are also "prepared for every good work," meaning that they were willing and eager to be used of God for His glory.

In verses 22-23, Paul tells us specifically how to purify ourselves. He states both the negative and positive elements. Negatively, we must "flee from youthful passions." Often this phrase "youthful passions" is interpreted as **sexual sin**. While Scripture indeed teaches we must avoid this type of sin (see 1 Cor 6:18), the command in this context is not limited to sexual sin. What are these youthful passions, then? If we glance at verses 23-25, it seems best to understand these desires as the temptation to quarrel, be unkind, or be harsh. The remaining words in verse 22 also point us in this way, as we note how Timothy was to pursue love and peace. Young leaders have the temptation to indulge the flesh in a variety of ways including impatience, arrogance, stubbornness, recklessness, harshness, and unkindness.

I am personally challenged by this command because it is not just limited to sexual passions. It would be easy for a young leader to think that he is growing in maturity if he is abstaining from one particular temptation. But Paul will not allow us to reduce sanctification to abstaining from looking at pornography or engaging in adultery. Honorable vessels are clean vessels. Clean vessels flee from **all** that is not Christlike.

Positively, Paul tells Timothy to "pursue righteousness, faith, love, and peace, along with those who call on the Lord from a pure heart" (v. 22). The contrast could not be greater. The word "flee" is the term *pheugo*, from which we get our word *fugitive*. Paul is saying, "Run like Harrison Ford away from youth's passions!" But the term "pursue" (*diako*) is about running in the opposite way—toward something. (Paul makes the same "flee/pursue" challenge in 1 Tim 6:11.)

While believers are urged to flee certain things like idolatry, materialism, and sexual sin, they are not simply to say no to sin. They are also to say yes to God! They are to turn their minds away from sin and to meditate on the person of Christ and on their position in Christ. They must savor the Savior. They must delight in Jesus' finished work. And as they behold the glory of Christ, they will grow in godliness and experience His peace.

Do you want to be useful to the Master? By Christ's grace and through His power, you must pursue practical holiness. To a young ministerial student, the Scottish Pastor Robert Murray M'Cheyne (young himself!) said,

> I know you will apply hard to German, but do not forget the culture of the inner man—I mean of the heart. How diligently the cavalry officer keeps his saber clean and sharp; every stain he rubs off with the greatest care. Remember you are God's sword, His instrument—I trust, a chosen vessel unto Him to bear His name. In great measure, according to the purity and perfection of the instrument, will be the success. It is not great talents God blesses so much as likeness to Jesus. A holy minister is an awful weapon in the hand of God. (Bonar, *Memoirs*, 95)

If we neglect the priority of being a clean vessel, we will forfeit the privilege of being used by God. Still, many fail to take this call seriously. I have watched friends fall every year because of moral failure (mostly sexual sin). These were gifted men. They were theologically bright. They could teach systematic theology, parse Greek words, define "contextualization," provide a philosophy of multisite churches, and preach great sermons. Yet they failed to take care of the inner man.

Remember, the condition for usefulness is not skillfulness but holiness. Spurgeon said, "But let a man once become really holy, even though he has but the slenderest possible ability, and he will be a fitter instrument in God's hand than the man of gigantic accomplishments who is not obedient to the divine will, or clean and pure in the sight of the Lord God Almighty" (Spurgeon, *Soulwinner*, 41). Are you fleeing from sin and pursuing Christ?

Image 3: The Lord's Servant
2 TIMOTHY 2:23-26

Paul's final word picture is a "slave" or servant (*doulos*). Before getting to it, notice again that Paul mentions the need to avoid word battles. This time Paul refers to them as "foolish and ignorant disputes" (v. 23). The word for "disputes" (*zetesis*) occurs once in each of the three Pastoral Epistles, with 1 Timothy 6:4 and Titus 3:9 being the other two. Paul seems to be alluding to foolish debates about speculations, myths, and genealogies (see 1 Tim 1:4). Of course, pastor-teachers must not avoid all controversy. In fact, they cannot escape it if they are teaching the Bible since everything a faithful teacher presents is by its nature controversial! These controversies refer to things that do not deserve time and energy. Senseless arguments only breed division and quarreling. Faithful teachers must be devoted to preaching revelation, not debating man's speculations.

The character of the Lord's servant is contrasted with false teachers who wished to quarrel about speculations. Fundamentally, the Lord's servant is to be **gentle**. Paul mentioned this twice in verses 24-25: "The Lord's slave must not quarrel, but must be *gentle* to everyone . . . instructing his opponents with *gentleness*" (emphasis added). Paul mentions this trait in his list of pastoral qualifications elsewhere (1 Tim 3:3). The faithful teacher is not to be hot tempered or violent (Titus 1:7). The easy road, the way of the flesh, would be to take our frustrations out on people with rash words or with a right hook! But the Lord's servant must pursue Christ, who by the Spirit produces the fruit of gentleness (Gal 5:23). Paul said to the Thessalonians that "we were gentle among you, as a nursing mother nurtures her own children" (1 Thess 2:7). What an image!

But do not miss what else Paul says. He does not tell Timothy to shrink back. That would be inconsistent with what has already been said in this letter. No, the Lord's servant was also charged to be "instructing his opponents" (v. 25). Gentleness does not mean timidity. It is strength under control. Timothy was called to correct his opponents but to do so gently.

The goal of such an attitude and such an approach is the opponents' salvation. Paul expresses the heart of an authentic evangelist with this phrase: "Perhaps God will grant them repentance leading them to the knowledge of the truth." Paul tells Timothy that the Lord's servant is not out to win arguments but to win souls. Faithful teachers want to see people turn from sin and to Christ ("repentance") and lay down their false doctrines for the truth of the gospel ("to know the truth").

Behind this is the belief that the real enemy is not the false teachers but the Devil, who has captured them to do his will. Paul wanted Timothy to share his desire in seeing that these opponents "may come to their senses and escape the Devil's trap." Notice the warfare. Those who oppose the gospel are in the grip of the evil one. They desperately need to come to the truth. Their hope is in the gentle gospel witness of the Lord's servant and in the Lord of grace, who may "grant them repentance," opening up their eyes to the person and work of Christ (cf. 2 Cor 4:4-6).

Who Is Sufficient for These Things?

The call in this chapter is weighty. Faithful teachers, as unashamed workmen, must be diligent in Bible study and accurate in Bible teaching. They must work hard to keep the hearers on the right path. Faithful teachers, as honorable vessels, must maintain purity in both life and doctrine if they want to be used by the Master. They must flee youthful passions and pursue Jesus. Faithful teachers, as the Lord's servants, must avoid foolish controversies. They must gently speak truth to their opponents, praying that God may grant them repentance.

These challenges make us cry out with Paul, "Who is sufficient for these things?" (2 Cor 2:16 ESV). Remember, "our competence is from God" (2 Cor 3:5). While we will fail at these tasks, we should take heart in the fact that there is One who fulfilled them all, and in Him and through Him we live out these exhortations faithfully.

Jesus was **the ultimate unashamed workman**, who perfectly taught God's Word. He taught with authority and not as the scribes, leading us on the path of eternal life. He could stand before the Father with no shame because He perfectly fulfilled the Father's will.

Jesus was **the ultimate honorable vessel**. He was set apart for the special occasion of rescuing sinners. Because of His perfect fulfillment of God's righteous requirements and His substitutionary death for sinners, we can be made righteous and are given the power to live out His character.

Jesus was **the ultimate Lord's servant**. He said He was "gentle and humble in heart" and that we can find rest if we come to Him (Matt 11:29). He is portrayed as both meek and majestic in the great Servant Songs of Isaiah. The suffering Servant endured the flogging of evil men and the mocking of sinners. He went to the cross like a sheep led to the slaughter (Isa 53:7). The Lord's Servant was wounded for our transgressions and crushed for our iniquities (Isa 53:5). "He was oppressed and afflicted, yet He did not open His mouth. . . . He bore the sin of many and interceded for the rebels" (Isa 53:7, 12). Jesus Christ, the Lord's Servant, is not only the model for all teachers, but He is also the person who gives us power to accomplish our mission of teaching the Word.

Reflect and Discuss

1. How is it possible to teach the same thing—the gospel—year after year without being monotonous or tedious?
2. How does the "hard work" of a pastor compare with that of a carpenter or farmer? In what ways would shoddy pastoral work show itself? In what ways does hard work pay off in a pastor's congregation?
3. Is the pastor the only spiritual "workman" in the body of Christ? In what ways do others toil in the work of the kingdom?
4. Why is bodily resurrection central to the Christian message?
5. Why does it seem that false teaching spreads more easily and quickly than sound doctrine?

6. What should Christians do in light of the presence of false teaching?

7. What undesirable "youthful passions" have you seen in yourself or in others? How does the Christian response to these things contrast with secular culture?

8. What kinds of "disputes" are worthwhile for Christians to engage in? What kinds are not worthwhile? Give examples.

9. What is the difference between gentleness and timidity? How can a Christian balance meekness and humility on one hand with boldness and confidence on the other?

10. Can winning an argument also win souls? What is the role of Christian apologetics—reasoned arguments to justify Christianity—in evangelism?

Godly Examples

2 TIMOTHY 3:1-13

Main Idea: Avoid ungodly examples, follow godly examples as they follow the Savior, and do it all by Christ's mighty power.

I. **Avoid Ungodly Examples (3:1-9).**
 A. Their lives are totally self-centered (3:2-4).
 B. Their religion is a show (3:5)
 C. Their proselytizing is evil (3:6-9).
II. **Follow Godly Examples (3:10-13).**
 A. Remember Paul's life (3:10).
 B. Remember Paul's persecutions (3:11).
 C. Remember Paul's precept (3:12-13).
III. **Example and Empowerment**

Children imitate superheroes. Elementary kids grow up and want to be like their favorite athletes. Little girls sing with their hairbrush in front of a mirror emulating their favorite singer. Teenagers follow the style and interests of pop culture. I have watched seminary students try to mimic the style of their favorite preacher. We have all observed the power of an **example**. In my opinion the most powerful form of persuasion is the spoken word. Just under it, and connected to it, is the persuasive power of example. Jesus Himself did both. His teaching explained His life; His life exemplified His teaching. He gave us both word and example.

Because of the importance of living examples, it is necessary for us to know whom we should follow. As leaders, there are godly examples to emulate and ungodly examples to avoid. In 2 Timothy 3:1-13, Paul shows us both extremes. In verses 1-9 he takes us to the moral sewer. He rattles off no fewer than 19 particular expressions of sin among godless people in just three verses (vv. 2-4)! He also describes the emptiness of godless religion (v. 5). He then discusses the corrupt nature of the false teachers, including their evil method of proselytizing (vv. 6-9). Paul gives Timothy the clear charge in light of this picture: "Avoid these people!"

Prior to this section, Paul holds out hope that some of Timothy's "opponents" might be granted repentance and come to the knowledge of the truth (2:25). But here we see that some people will never arrive at the truth (3:7). Such obstinate, disruptive individuals must be avoided. To "avoid" them might even mean completely to break fellowship with them. Of course, believers should not avoid contact with all unbelievers; the individuals in view here are those who are within the church, wrecking others' lives. Leaders must guard the flock against wolves, and believers must avoid the example of the ungodly.

In verses 10-13, Paul takes us to a godly example: himself. Timothy is told to remember his mentor's life and teaching and to continue on that course. Paul reminds Timothy that everyone who wants to live a godly life will face some degree of persecution (3:12). In verses 14-17 (which we will cover in the next chapter), he tells Timothy to continue focusing on and believing the truth found in Scripture rather than listening to the false teachers' message.

Therefore, this passage is very practical. Some important questions we need to ask ourselves based on these verses include: What kind of person are you, godless or godly? What kind of person are you becoming? Whom are you following? According to Paul, we must avoid ungodly examples and follow godly examples.

Avoid Ungodly Examples
2 TIMOTHY 3:1-9

Paul opens this catalogue of sins and description of corrupt teachers with the phrase, "But know this: Difficult times will come in the last days" (v. 1). The "last days" are not only the days immediately preceding Christ's second coming. Rather, they began at Pentecost and will continue until that day. In other words, we have been and still are living in the last days. The new age arrived with Christ's incarnation and the old age began to pass away, ushering in the last days. In his Pentecost sermon Peter said that "in the last days" God would pour out his Spirit on all humanity, and he proclaimed that this prophecy from Joel had now been fulfilled (Acts 2:16-17; cf. 1 Tim 4:1).

Paul is not telling Timothy about something that would eventually happen in the future but rather something that was happening in the present. Instead of being overly optimistic about his situation in

Ephesus, Paul tells Timothy to "know this" (v. 1). Timothy's battles with false teachers, his critics, his physical hardships, and his other sufferings should not surprise him. These are the realities of living in a fallen world, a world that awaits the final act of the redemptive drama: the glorious return of Christ. Until that great day, we will all have "difficult times." There will be dangers, storms, and stressful times for all Christians, in which we must rely on God's grace to endure.

What is the problem in the last days? The problem Paul notes here is simple: "people" (v. 2). Sinful people who live corrupt lives will create difficult times. Some of these people, under the influence of the Devil (2:26), will pose as teachers and lead other people astray. Paul describes this depraved situation in verses 2-9. The practices he mentions are characteristic of sinful humanity in general and the false teachers in particular (for two other lists of sinful vices see Rom 1:29-31 and 1 Tim 1:9-10). While it is almost impossible to try and organize this description of sinful humanity and false teachers, it seems that three general characteristics stand out.

Their Lives Are Totally Self-Centered (3:2-4)

The self-centered people described in these verses first had **misdirected loves**. Notice the descriptions: "lovers of self," "lovers of money" (v. 2), "unloving," "without love for what is good" (v. 3), and "lovers of pleasure rather than lovers of God" (v. 4). Observe how Paul brackets this list of sinful practices with statements of love in verses 2 and 4. Perhaps this is the best way to summarize the fundamental problem of these evil men. Everyone worships something or someone, and one's life is a spillover of that supreme love.

Putting this in contemporary terms, Paul notes three inordinate loves: **narcissism** (love of self), **materialism** (love of money), and **hedonism** (love of pleasure). These excesses lead people not to love what is good. In his first epistle to Timothy, Paul deals with the issue of the false teacher's inordinate loves, especially their love for money (1 Tim 6:5-10). The other two excessive loves are emphasized in this particular list, and several phrases may be grouped into the love-of-self and love-of-pleasure categories:

- Love of Self: "boastful," "proud" (v. 2), "conceited" (v. 4)
- Love of Pleasure: "unholy" (v. 2), "without self-control" (v. 3), "reckless" (v. 4)

Clearly, when love of God is replaced with other loves, all sorts of vices follow.

I was once blessed with the opportunity to sit with a small group of young pastors and speak with Rick Warren about lessons he'd learned in pastoral ministry. He was gracious and encouraging in sharing his time and wisdom with us, and at one point he gave a strong warning about the temptations of Satan. Pastor Rick said that pastors must prepare for three main temptations that plunge leaders into ruin: **narcissism, hedonism**, and **materialism**. He said the first temptation is the temptation "to be" (narcissism), the second is the temptation "to feel" (hedonism), and the third is the temptation "to have" (materialism). He said that every moral failure of pastors is due to one of these three traps. He added that virtually every television commercial is aimed at one of these three temptations. He said he used to ask his kids after each commercial, "Which of the three temptations was that commercial?"

Pastor Rick said that leaders must fight these three temptations by pursuing the opposite of each: **humility** (in contrast to narcissism), **integrity** (in contrast to hedonism), and **generosity** (in contrast to materialism). Indeed, we are to be "lovers of God" ultimately. Out of the overflow of love for God, we can live lives of humility, integrity, and generosity. The psalmist expresses the supreme love: "Who do I have in heaven but You? And I desire nothing on earth but You" (Ps 73:25). Godliness begins with adoration for God. What is your greatest love? When you are satisfied in Him and Him alone, then you will find these godly virtues present in your life.

In addition to these misdirected loves, these self-centered people have **corrupt relationships**. In verse 2 Paul said that people would be "abusive" (ESV; from *blasphemos*, "slanderer, blasphemer"), "disobedient to . . . parents," and "ungrateful." Sadly, one can witness these sins every day. Our day is plagued with abuse, disobedience to parents, and ingratitude. Not only is it observable; it is also the subject of entertainment in certain television shows.

Further, Paul notes their other relational sins. They were "unloving, irreconcilable, slanderers," "brutal," and "traitors" (vv. 3-4). Sin can cause people to be heartless and unforgiving. And a failure to love others leads to sinful acts such as backbiting, brutality, and treachery.

Seen together, these two groups of sins, **misdirected loves** and **corrupt relationships**, reveal that the underlying failure in fallen humanity is disobedience to the Great Commands (Matt 22:36-40): they love neither God nor people. Sin separates us from God and others. We are desperately in need of someone to cure this problem. Thankfully, Jesus Christ came to reconcile us to God through His death on the cross and to bring peace in our relationships with others (Eph 2:13-18). Only the gospel offers a deep enough solution to this radical problem created by sin. Behavior modification, rules, or the law are not enough. They may manage sin, but they cannot transform the heart. Only the gospel Paul and Timothy experienced can do that (1 Tim 1:13-15).

Their Religion Is a Show (3:5)

If these sinful practices are not enough, Paul went a step further and said that the same people who do these things may also be *religious*! Like the idolatrous practices of Israel in the Old Testament (e.g., Amos 2:6-8), Paul says that some merely have a "form of godliness" but their lives are not pleasing to God. They have external practices, but they are morally corrupt. Their religion is a show. They are spiritually power-less. Paul mentions showy religion earlier in his correspondence with Timothy (see 1 Tim 1:4; 4:1-3; 2 Tim 2:16-19), and these religious acts were full of empty form, empty talk, and empty sacrifices. The leaders of these religious systems were phonies. They were to be avoided because they had no substance.

Not only did these religious fakes lack spiritual power; they also denied it. That is, they stubbornly refused to believe in the truth of the gospel. By failing to embrace Christ, they failed to embrace the power. Apart from the gospel, people are just practicing dead religion. No Christ, no power. People can go to church their whole life, have their office in a church, even move their bedroom into the church; but if they do not have Christ, they do not possess spiritual life!

The Bible is full of examples of religious showmen, those who have an appearance of godliness but are actually ungodly. Through the prophet Isaiah, God gave a mighty rebuke to the people of Judah. He urged them to wash themselves, remove evil, and repent. Why? They had big religious feasts, prayers, and worship services but were not doing good, seeking justice, correcting oppression, defending the fatherless, or pleading for the widow (Isa 1:14-17). At which point God says, "I will not listen. Your hands are covered with blood" (1:15). In contrast James writes that "pure and undefiled religion" in God's sight involves caring for those in need, like widows and orphans in their affliction (Jas 1:27).

Similarly, Jesus reserved His most intense words for religious leaders. He tells them, "On the outside you seem righteous to people, but inside you are full of hypocrisy and lawlessness" (Matt 23:28). In this sermon Jesus called the scribes and Pharisees "hypocrites" (seven times), "fools" (once), "blind" (five times), and "snakes"/"brood of vipers" (once).

This should be a warning to all who are engaged in religious activities. Jesus is merciful to those whose lives are a mess and who admit they need Him, but to those who play the hypocrite, there is nothing but rebuke. While there is a fundamental difference between the people described in 1 Timothy 3:1-9 and Spirit-indwelled Christians, we should also remember that Christians can play the hypocrite as well. One example is Peter's failure to have fellowship with the Gentiles in Galatians 2:11-14. His conduct was not in line with the gospel (Gal 2:14). Similarly, we also must avoid practicing religion without godliness and faith without works.

Their Proselytizing Is Evil (3:6-9)

Finally, as if their corrupt lives and religious emptiness were not enough, Paul says that certain people would also try to win converts to their wicked religion. And the way they would try to add to their number was evil. Notice three parts: their tactics, their victims, and their mental corruption.

First, Paul says that they "worm their way into households" (v. 6). Their method was not out in the open. It was secretive and sneaky, like Satan himself. They also sought to "capture" their victims. Stott notes that this verb properly means "to take prisoner in war" (Stott, *Message*, 89). The location for their stealth mission was "households." The Greek text says "*the* homes," meaning that it might be spacious homes of the wealthy where the church often met.

Next notice their victims. Paul says these zealous false teachers went after "idle women burdened down with sins, led along by a variety of passions, always learning and never able to come to a knowledge of the truth" (vv. 6-7). Paul is not using this as a description of all women but rather those who are immature, childish, silly, weak, and especially those burdened down with sins. Because of their unclean consciences, they were open to hear anything, even the messages of these false teachers. The false teachers preyed on their intellectual weaknesses, their moral weaknesses, and their gullible nature. These women would listen to anybody, but they were never able to come to "a knowledge of the truth."

Stott adds that this method of preying on women is a timeless tactic of false teachers:

> Choosing a time when the menfolk were out (presumably at work), they would concentrate their attention on "weak women." This expedient, comments Bishop Ellicott, was "as old as the fall of man," for the serpent first deceived Eve. It was also employed by the Gnostics, and has been the regular ploy of religious commercial travelers right up to and including the Jehovah's Witnesses of our own day. (Stott, *Message*, 89)

Finally, Paul gives an example of spurious teachers in verse 8 as he relates the mental corruption of such men. He alludes to the Egyptian sorcerers who opposed Moses before Pharaoh (Exod 7:11-12). Though Jannes and Jambres are not mentioned by name in the Bible, they are in extrabiblical sources. When Aaron threw down his rod and it became a snake, they cast down their rods, which also became snakes. These sorcerers opposed Moses like the false teachers were opposing Paul and Timothy (and by extension those who proclaim God's Word today).

Paul says such men are "corrupt in mind" (v. 8). They are mentally warped. Consequently, they are "worthless in regard to the faith." Notice how we keep coming to the issue of truth in this letter. The war Paul describes here is a truth war. Paul talks about a "knowledge of the truth" (2:25; 3:7), those who "resist the truth" (3:8), and the false teachers' "lack of understanding" (3:9). People have always been prone to drift to every wind of doctrine, especially that which is new. We live and minister in this world. We must guard the truth that has been given to us in Holy Scripture (1:14) and pass it on to others (2 Tim 2:2). We need an army of good soldiers who will, by God's grace, preach and teach the Word with faithfulness because eternity is at stake.

The final thing Paul says in verse 9 is similar to what he has already said in 2:18-19. He reminds Timothy that even though the situation may look depressing, Christianity will not collapse. He says that just as the folly of Jannes and Jambres became evident to all and people realized that no one could match the power of God, so the false teachers in Ephesus would "not make further progress, for their lack of understanding will be clear to all" (v. 9). Paul believes that their error would eventually be exposed, and God would preserve His truth. This had to be an encouraging word to Timothy as he looked at the apparent success of the false teachers. Like Timothy, we must rest in God's promises and courageously keep teaching His truth in spite of opposition and false religious systems.

To summarize 3:1-9, Timothy and others were to avoid these men and these practices. They must avoid self-centered lives with misdirected loves and corrupt relationships, religious forms devoid of Christ's power, and the evil tactics of false teachers. There is a better way, and Paul describes it in the following verses.

Follow Godly Examples
2 TIMOTHY 3:10-13

In stark contrast to these false teachers just mentioned ("But you," v. 10), Paul gives Timothy the imperative to "continue" in verse 14. Paul urges Timothy to continue following Jesus by doing two things: remembering the past (vv. 10-13) and focusing on the Scriptures (vv. 14-17). Because verses 14-17 are so closely tied to 4:1-4, we will treat them in the next chapter.

In verses 10-13, Timothy reminded of Paul's example. The apostle's example was to be emulated in so far as he followed Christ (1 Cor 11:1). Every leader should be able to say, "Follow me, as I follow Christ." This is leadership 101. Leadership is not lordship. Peter said pastors should not be domineering but should set an example to the flock (1 Pet 5:3; cf. 2 Cor 1:24). Leadership is about following Jesus and inviting others to come along. Paul illustrated this as well as anyone. Paul tells Timothy (and us) to remember (1) his life, (2) his persecutions, and (3) his precept about godliness.

Remember Paul's Life (3:10)

Paul's lifestyle was unlike that of the false teachers mentioned in the previous section. He said that Timothy knew well of his "teaching," his "conduct," and his "purpose." His life was lived out in the open. Paul's teaching explained his life, and his life exemplified his teaching. Paul lived out his charge that he gave to Timothy earlier in his first letter: "Pay close attention to your life and your teaching" (1 Tim 4:16). And Paul's purpose was to live for something greater than pleasure, money, or personal fame. Paul expressed his single-minded passion to the Ephesians elders: "But I count my life of no value to myself, so that I may finish my course and the ministry I received from the Lord Jesus, to testify to the gospel of God's grace" (Acts 20:24). Paul's great aim in life was to finish his ministry of testifying to the gospel for the glory of Christ. He reminds us of that glorious purpose to which we must give our lives in our own ministry contexts.

Timothy also observed particular virtues in Paul's life: "Faith, patience, love, and endurance." These four qualities are at the heart of the Christian life. Timothy observed Paul's faithfulness in ministry (e.g., Acts 18:5-11). He knew of his patience toward others (e.g., the Corinthian church!). He witnessed his love for the churches (see Phil 1:7-8). He watched Paul's amazing endurance as he kept on going despite endless hardships (see 2 Cor 6:4-10). Of course, none of this was owing to Paul's ability but to God's transforming grace. These four characteristics mark Paul's life, and now in a prison cell he urges Timothy to follow them.

Which of these is most absent in your life? My guess is that most leaders would say "patience." Maybe because that is what I would say! Later Paul would tell Timothy (and us) to "proclaim the message . . . with great patience" (2 Tim 4:2). How do you cultivate patience as a leader? The type of patience we need only comes by the Spirit. Patience is a fruit of the Spirit. As we abide in Jesus, love Jesus, and treasure Jesus, the Spirit produces patience in us. As we reflect, as Paul did, on how Jesus has been patient with us (1 Tim 1:16), it should cause us to grow in our patience toward others.

Remember Paul's Persecutions (3:11)

Timothy also had intimate knowledge of Paul's "persecutions and sufferings." Interestingly, Paul mentions three particular locations: "Antioch, Iconium, and Lystra." Timothy knew of other experiences as well, including the persecutions in Philippi, Ephesus, and Rome. But Paul draws particular attention to these three locations probably because they surrounded Timothy's home region. Timothy knew of Paul's brutal beating by a hostile mob, when the apostle was left for dead (Acts 14:5-6, 19). Paul said, "What persecutions I endured!" These particular sufferings apparently had a great impact on Timothy, and Paul urged Timothy to remember his example as he continued to live out his calling.

Paul then reminds Timothy that "the Lord rescued me from them all." This is almost an exact quotation from Psalm 34:19 where David celebrates his deliverance from his enemies. God is the ultimate rescuer. He has delivered His people throughout the ages. Though He never promises us that this life will be easy, He does promise to be with His people and to rescue them either in this life or by bringing them to glory! As Paul was writing, he was awaiting the ultimate rescue (see 2 Tim 4:17-18).

Timothy is called to endure by the strength God supplies, trusting in God's great faithfulness to His people. Paul is not just giving Timothy an example to follow; he is pointing him to the source of power by which to live.

Remember Paul's Precept (3:12-13)

In verse 12, Paul reminds Timothy that everyone who seeks "to live a godly life in Christ Jesus will be persecuted." We should understand the inevitability of persecution as we consider the life and words of Paul. After Paul's stoning in Lystra, Luke says,

> *After they had evangelized that town and made many disciples, they returned to Lystra, to Iconium, and to Antioch, strengthening the disciples by encouraging them to continue in the faith and by telling them, "It is necessary to pass through many troubles on our way into the kingdom of God." (Acts 14:21-22)*

We will pass through many troubles as we live out the gospel. Therefore, Paul tells the Philippians, "It has been given to you on Christ's behalf not only to believe in Him, but also to suffer for Him" (Phil 1:29).

What is more, as we look at the life of Jesus, we should remember the reality of Christian suffering. Jesus says, "If they persecuted Me, they will also persecute you" (John 15:20). John echoes his Master's words, "Do not be surprised, brothers, if the world hates you" (1 John 3:13). Race car drivers should expect some crashes, football players are not surprised by injuries, baseball players know the ball will hit them sometimes, and soldiers expect to be shot at. Christians should expect some degree of persecution. What is amazing from 1 John 3:13 is that John says we may face persecution because we love one another! Some are drawn to Christ by the love of Christians, but others are enraged by their love. Instead of being surprised by opposition, we should be surprised when we do not face any!

If we are not facing any opposition in our ministry, chances are we are not living out our calling to the hilt. Of course, we do not look for opposition; we are not seeking enemies. But we must understand that opposition is inevitable for all who live godly lives. Some will experience physical oppression. Others will feel it in their hearts as they grieve over others lives. Most will be ignored, mocked, or rejected.

This sobering reality actually helps us. We know the world is not spinning out of control. No. This is what will happen in the last days. False teachers, like these mentioned in chapters 2 and 3, "will become worse, deceiving and being deceived" (3:13). Timothy is to remember this reality and to remember Paul's example as he continued following Jesus.

Example and Empowerment

As we read these verses, we sense our need for help. How can we possibly endure evil people, false teachers, and persecution? Paul was the mighty apostle. How can we possibly follow his example? How are we to persevere and maintain godliness? To find out, we should ask, "What is 'godliness'?" Paul tells us earlier that Jesus Himself is "the mystery of godliness" (1 Tim 3:16). Jesus gave us the ultimate example of godliness in His incarnation. Jesus was the ultimate picture of humility, integrity, and generosity. His religion was not a show but was a demonstration of power. His outreach was not evil but loving. He taught with authority. He walked by faith. He lived with an eternal purpose. He displayed love like no other. His patience is unparalleled. And the only truly innocent man suffered a criminal's death where He took our judgment and gave us His righteousness. Jesus gave us the greatest example of godliness.

But we need more than an example. We need empowerment. And that is exactly what our Lord provided. Through His victorious resurrection, Jesus triumphed over our greatest enemies, ascended to the Father's right hand, and poured out the Holy Spirit. Now, as believers in Him, we are united with Him. Notice that Paul identified the desire to live "a godly life *in Christ Jesus*" (2 Tim 3:12). We live this life through our glorious **union with Christ**, and we remind ourselves of our relationship with Him through our daily **communion with Christ**. We have been crucified with Him, raised with Him, and seated with Him. Christ now lives in us! By the power of the risen Christ, we press on in godliness, keeping our eyes on Him.

Avoid ungodly examples, follow godly examples as they follow the Savior, and do it all by Christ's mighty power.

Reflect and Discuss

1. When you were a child, who was your hero? Why did you admire that person?

2. How does awareness of the nature of temptation help us fight it? Which temptation—narcissism, hedonism, or materialism—is most difficult for you?

3. Why do therapy and rules ultimately fail to cause people to love one another? How else does secular society address this problem?

4. Why was Jesus more angry with religious hypocrites than with non-religious people? Why did He call them "blind"? Why "vipers"?

5. How does reading about Christians who have suffered bring you encouragement? Whose stories have been particularly helpful for you?

6. Have you ever seen non-Christians react negatively to our love for one another? Have you seen a positive reaction?

7. Are you experiencing opposition because of your Christian faith? Are there things you could do to avoid it? What are some things you might do that would likely cause more opposition? Which course of action should you take?

8. How does it help to know that the more closely we follow Christ, the more likely we will encounter opposition and persecution?

9. Why would it be counterproductive to teach that if you follow Christ, your life will be easy?

10. Which is more encouraging for you—finding a person who is a good example to follow or knowing that the Holy Spirit empowers you to follow that example?

Faithful to the Word

2 TIMOTHY 3:14–4:4

Main Idea: Every Christian is called to keep on learning and living God's Word, and everyone who preaches and teaches the Word is called to do so faithfully.

I. **Continue in the Word (3:14-17).**
   A. Continue in the Christ-centered Scriptures (3:15).
   B. Continue in the God-breathed Scriptures (3:16a).
   C. Continue in the totally sufficient Scriptures (3:16b-17).
II. **Preach the Word (4:1-4).**
   A. Preach the Word faithfully (4:1-2a).
   B. Preach the Word consistently (4:2b).
   C. Preach the Word pastorally (4:2c).
   D. Preach the Word patiently (4:2d).
   E. Preach the Word theologically (4:2e-4).

Kent Hughes tells the following story:

> Dr. William Evans, who pastored College Church from 1906–
> 1909, was an unusually accomplished man. He had the entire
> *King James Version* of the Bible memorized as well as the New
> Testament of the *American Standard Version*. Dr. Evans also
> authored over fifty books. His son, Louis, became one of the
> best-known preachers in America and for many years pastored
> the eminent First Presbyterian Church of Hollywood. When
> Dr. William Evans retired, he moved to Hollywood to be near
> his son, and when Louis was away he would substitute for him.
> One unforgettable Sunday Dr. William, as he was
> affectionately called, spoke on the virgin birth. All were
> amazed when he raised his Bible and tore out the pages that
> narrate the birth of the Lord. As the tattered scraps floated
> down toward the congregation, he shouted, "If we can't
> believe in the virgin birth, let's tear it out of the Bible!" And
> then as he drove home his point, he tore out the resurrection

chapters, then the miracle narratives, then anything conveying the supernatural. The floor was littered with mutilated pages.

Finally, with immense drama he held up the only remaining portion and said, "And this is all we have left—the Sermon on the Mount. And that has no authority for me if a divine Christ didn't preach it." After a few more words, he asked his listeners to bow for the benediction. But before he could pray, a man in that vast and sedate congregation stood and cried, "No, no! Go on! We want more!" Several others joined in. So Dr. Evans preached for another fifty minutes. (Baldwin and Benson, *Henrietta Mears*, 149)

This story illustrates the situation in which Timothy found himself and in which we find ourselves. Many do not believe in the inspiration of the Bible. Many discount the miracles. False teachers abound. Yet there are still cries from some saying, "We want more!" Or, as in Ezra's day, "Bring the book" (Neh 8:1). This passage describes for us the nature of Holy Scripture and the great need for preaching it in today's world.

In the previous section Paul describes the evil nature of false teachers and urges Timothy to be different. He begins verse 10 with a contrastive statement, "But you." Paul urges Timothy to stand apart from the imposters by following his own example and teaching. There is another contrastive statement in verse 14: "But as for you." Timothy is urged to be different by (1) continuing in God's Word (3:14-17) and (2) preaching God's Word (4:1-4).

Every Christian is called to continue in the Word, and everyone who preaches and teaches is called to proclaim the Word. The relevance of 2 Timothy 3:14–4:4 has made this text a treasured passage throughout the ages, but we should not let its familiarity keep us from feeling the force of its timeless challenges.

Continue in the Word
2 TIMOTHY 3:14-17

Paul's life was about to end, but he knew Timothy must continue the race. He tells his spiritual son to "continue in what you have learned and firmly believed" (v. 14). Timothy had learned "the sacred Scriptures" from "childhood" (v. 15). Both his grandmother Lois and his mother Eunice taught him from his infancy (1:5). He also learned from the apostle Paul (e.g., 1:13; 2:2), and now he is charged to keep on learning God's Word and living in God's Word.

Are you continuing to learn the Bible? I recently heard of a panel discussion that featured several top-shelf biblical scholars. They were discussing interpretive issues related to the Old Testament, specifically regarding the story of Joseph in Genesis. In response to a certain question, one of these premier Bible scholars said, "It may be that I need to do further study of the Old Testament. And I'm very certain of that." Does that response convict you? Even authoritative Bible scholars come to issues in the text and conclude that they need to spend more time in the Bible. Even the brightest of biblical minds "need to do further study." We should never stop studying the Scriptures!

Notice something else in verse 14. Paul says, "Continue in what you have . . . firmly *believed*" (emphasis added). The belief mentioned here carries the idea of being convinced. Timothy had become convinced of the truth of God's Word through these aforementioned messengers. Now Paul urges Timothy to continue trusting in God's powerful Word.

These verses show us the folly of overemphasizing what is novel. Paul in his dying days did not tell Timothy to be trendy. Paul knew God had given us something timeless: the sacred Scriptures. Timothy must hold firmly to these Scriptures and pass them on faithfully above all else. Paul goes on to tell us more about the nature of these sacred Scriptures in which we are to study and by which we are to live.

Continue in the Christ-Centered Scriptures (3:15)

When Paul says Timothy had heard the "sacred Scriptures" from childhood, he is referring to what we call the Old Testament. Later in life Timothy would come to understand the Scriptures in a fuller sense as he learned how the Old Testament points to Jesus. Paul consistently used the Old Testament to preach and teach the gospel (e.g., Acts 17:2; 18:4-5; 26:22b-23). The gospel Timothy heard was the biblical gospel of the prophets and the apostles. It was authentic and worth his very life.

Paul adds that these Christ-centered Scriptures are "able to give you wisdom for salvation through faith in Christ Jesus." The Bible is a book that leads us to salvation. Some are amazed that you could use the Old Testament to lead someone to Christ. But the apostles show us that the

Old Testament can indeed make one wise for salvation through faith in Christ! When they went to various cities, they did not pass out tracts like "Four Spiritual Laws" or "Steps to Peace with God." They taught the Old Testament, pointing people to Jesus. Regarding the gospel in the Old Testament, Paul says, "For I passed on to you as most important what I also received: that Christ died for our sins *according to the Scriptures,* that He was buried, that He was raised on the third day *according to the Scriptures*" (1 Cor 15:3-4; emphasis added). These "Scriptures" were the Old Testament. In Galatians, Paul reaches back to Abraham as a pattern of how people are saved: by grace alone through faith alone in Christ alone (Gal 3:6-14).

The Bible narrates the ongoing flow of redemptive history that moves ultimately to the person and work of Jesus. From Genesis to Revelation, the Bible is unashamedly Christian. God did not make a mistake giving us a whole Bible instead of just a pocket New Testament! Sidney Greidanus gives us the following reminders about why we should not neglect the Old Testament (Greidanus, *Preaching Christ,* 25–32). Consider the Christ-centered, redemptive nature of the Bible.

1. The Old Testament is part of the Christian canon.
2. It shows the history of redemption leading to Christ.
3. It proclaims truths not found in the NT.
4. It helps us understand the NT.
5. It prevents misunderstanding the NT.
6. It provides a fuller understanding of Christ.

The Bible is not like Aesop's Fables, merely teaching moral lessons. Andy Griffith reruns can do a fine job of teaching moral principles! To use the Bible for this purpose alone is to misunderstand both its purpose and its content. Yet some people seem set on exactly that. I once heard of a teacher who after reading the story of Noah drew one moral principle: go love animals like Noah! Is that what we are to learn from this story of judgment and salvation? I do not think so. Further, the Old Testament is not a sanctified superhero book. Many want to turn Samson, David, and Gideon into our version of Marvel comic-book heroes. These and other abuses abound in both our Christian literature and in our preaching.

The Bible is a "Him Book." The Old Testament anticipates Christ, and the New Testament explains Christ. He is promised in the beginning,

He is there in the middle, and He is held up at the end as our object of worship for all eternity. Themes like creation, fall, redemption, and new creation unfold this redemptive drama. Yet sadly, many Christians know the stories of the Bible well but know nothing of its wonderful Christ-centered story line.

To be clear, I am not suggesting we ignore the historical setting of Old Testament texts. I am saying we read the Bible as Christians, not as Jewish rabbis. We should honor the historical context of the Old Testament *and* make *legitimate* Christ-centered connections—by observing the story line of the Bible, tracing theological themes, noticing where a passage stands in relation to Christ, and other justifiable interpretive methods (see Greidanus, *Preaching Christ,* for some ways to do this rightly).

As we consider the big redemptive story, we can see that Jesus is the Hero of the Bible. As preachers, we must make the Hero of the Bible the Hero of every sermon! Paul said, "We proclaim Him" (Col 1:28). A quick read through Acts shows us the apostles' pattern of pointing people to Jesus from the Old Testament (Acts 2:14-34; 3:18-21; 4:11, 25-27; 7:52; 8:32-35; 10:42-43; 13; 17:2-3; 18:5; 20:24, 27; 24:14; 26:22; 28:23-31). I believe the apostles viewed the Bible with a Christ-centered focus because of Jesus' own teaching. Christ showed them that the Scriptures were about Him (e.g., Luke 24:27, 44; John 5:39, 46).

Bruce Ware notes the nature and the message of the Bible, saying, "For although the Spirit is primarily responsible for producing the Bible as the inspired Word of God, the Bible is not primarily about the Spirit but rather it is about the Son" (Ware, *Father, Son, and Holy Spirit,* 110). Thus, Timothy was to continue in the Christ-centered Scriptures, which are produced by the Holy Spirit.

Continue in the God-Breathed Scriptures (3:16a)

This verse highlights the divine inspiration of Scripture. Paul states that the Scriptures are inspired or "breathed-out by God" (*theopneustos*). The Spirit worked through biblical writers to pen God's Word entirely and exactly as He intended. Just as God spoke the universe into existence, so also He breathed out His Word in Scripture. In fact, a better word than inspiration might be "expiration." God breathed out His holy Word. What a gift we have in the Bible!

Paul also affirms the *total* inspiration of Scripture saying that "all Scripture" is breathed out by God. This means we cannot simply pick and choose which parts of the Bible we like, which commands we wish to obey, and which doctrines we will believe. All of it is from the Spirit of God, and therefore all of it is good, binding, and true.

Peter describes how God revealed His Word to men: "First of all, you should know this: no prophecy of Scripture comes from one's own interpretation, because no prophecy ever came by the will of man; instead, men spoke from God as they were moved by the Holy Spirit" (2 Pet 1:20-21). Peter also affirms the inspiration of Scripture in the selection of Matthias: "Brothers, the Scripture had to be fulfilled that *the Holy Spirit through the mouth of David* spoke in advance about Judas" (Acts 1:16; emphasis added). This divine-human process is validated by the witness of writers and prophets throughout the Old Testament (e.g., 2 Sam 23:2; Isa 8:11; Jer 30:4; Amos 8:11).

We should not miss Jesus' emphasis on the divine nature of Scripture either. He quoted Scripture frequently as divine and authoritative. He said many powerful truths about Scripture: "Man must not live on bread alone but on every word that comes from the mouth of God" (Matt 4:4) and "Heaven and earth will pass away, but My words will never pass away" (Matt 24:35). Jesus also affirmed the authority of the Old Testament by His own use of it. And, as already mentioned, He taught that He was the fulfillment of it (Luke 24:44).

Regarding the God-breathed nature of the New Testament, Peter says that Paul's letters were like "the rest of the Scriptures" (2 Pet 3:16). They were in the same category as the Old Testament writings. Additionally, Paul writes, "For the Scripture says: Do not muzzle an ox while it is treading out the grain, and, the worker is worthy of his wages" (1 Tim 5:18). His first quote comes from Deuteronomy 25:4, and the second quote is found in Luke 10:7. Paul called both of these Old and New Testament references "Scripture." Paul's self-awareness of the inspiration process also led him to write, "What I write to you is the Lord's command" (1 Cor 14:37). Further, the early church made a practice of reading Paul's letters aloud. They would have been read alongside the Old Testament, showing their authority and continuity (see Col 3:16; 1 Thess 5:27; 1 Tim 4:13).

Indeed, a fundamental question is, What is the nature of Scripture? Many believe the Bible is one good book among many other religious texts. Some skeptics believe that only about 20 percent is historically accurate. Other influential agnostics contend that one cannot *know* if the Bible is God's Word. In every age the nature of Scripture is questioned. Like Timothy, we must continue learning and believing in the God-breathed nature of the Bible and build our lives on it.

Continue in the Totally Sufficient Scriptures (3:16b-17)

We have many today who say they believe in the inspiration of Scripture but deny their belief by their practice. Do not just *believe* Scripture. Use it! If Christians believe the Bible is God's inspired Word, then they should naturally see it as profitable. Paul has already told us the Bible is profitable for making us wise for salvation (v. 15). But now he adds that it is profitable "for teaching, for rebuking, for correcting, for training in righteousness" (v. 16).

The Bible shapes our beliefs as well as our lifestyle. It relates to both doctrine and conduct, and it is totally sufficient to shape us into the image of Christ by the power of the Spirit. The Bible addresses us in a variety of ways. It gives us doctrinal truth. It rebukes us for ungodly behavior or false beliefs. It corrects us when we stray from Christlikeness. It trains us in righteous living. The incredible scope of Scripture's power and the need to preach it is stated in 2 Timothy 4:2: "Proclaim the message; . . . rebuke, correct, and encourage with great patience and teaching."

God's Word meets our deepest needs. It transforms us from the inside out. People need God's Word more than man's observations and practical suggestions. Sure, there may be times to offer some practical suggestions and council or to read from a contemporary writer. However, we must distinguish between "good stuff" and "God's stuff." If you are a preacher/teacher, give them God's stuff: God-breathed Scripture!

Paul adds to his point on the sufficiency of Scripture, saying, "So that the man of God may be complete, equipped for every good work" (v. 17). Scripture is also profitable for **equipping us**. Hughes says, "Though we cannot see it in English, Paul here uses two forms of the Greek word for *equip* (an adjective and a participle) to make his point. The man of God is super-equipped by the Word of God" (Hughes and Chapell, *1 & 2 Timothy and Titus*, 239). I love that idea: "super-equipped" by the Scriptures! Stott says, "Scripture is the chief means which God employs to bring 'the man of God' to maturity" (Stott, *Message*, 103).

While the Scriptures equip all Christians, it seems that Paul had Timothy in mind specifically when he says "the man of God" (cf. 1 Tim 6:11). By extension, those who have leadership responsibility in the church should pay close attention to this verse. The Bible grows us personally as we live in it. We should have the spirit of the psalmist: "How I love Your instruction! It is my meditation all day long" (Ps 119:97); "My heart fears only Your word" (119:161b). The Bible also equips us as we seek to lead others to Christ, teach sound doctrine, counsel people, or grow a church. Indeed, it prepares us for "every good work." Let us pray like John Wesley: "At any price give me the book of God. . . . Let me be a man of one book" (in Gordon, *Evangelical Spirituality*, 36).

This charge to continue learning, trusting, and believing the Christ-centered, God-breathed, totally sufficient Scriptures is followed with the charge to proclaim this life-changing message of God, the gospel, the written and living Word declaring the truth about the incarnate Word.

Preach the Word
2 TIMOTHY 4:1-4

If the chapter division were not here in our Bibles, we would not be distracted from seeing the logical progression: a high view of the Bible (3:14-17) should lead to a high view of biblical preaching (4:1-4). Unfortunately, some hold to the inspiration of Scripture, but their actual preaching is not rooted in the Scriptures. I think the best approach for applying verse 2, "Preach the word!" (NKJV), is **expositional preaching**. Expositional preaching is Word-driven preaching. It is preaching in such a way that the main point of the selected **passage** is the main point of the **sermon**. It is taking the listeners for a swim in the Bible. Notice five ways we should do Word-driven preaching.

Preach the Word Faithfully (4:1-2a)

The proper motive of preachers is a desire for faithfulness to God, not worldly fame. This God-centered motive is noted here in verse 1 as Paul set up his exhortation with this stunning introduction. Nowhere else did Paul give this type of preface to a charge: "I solemnly charge you before God and Christ Jesus, who is going to judge the living and the dead, and because of His appearing and His kingdom" (v. 1). Feel the force of this verse. Paul put preaching in a holy context with these words.

Timothy is to remember that he preached *before God*. No preacher ultimately goes unnoticed. Unnoticed by people? Sure. Overlooked for big speaking engagements? Yes. But he is never out of the eyes of God. This should give all of us who preach a correct perspective on our task. Our audience first and foremost is God Himself. Because of this, the unpopular, "unknown" pastor should not be discouraged by his lack of fame and recognition. He should remember that his ultimate call is faithfulness to God and that his ministry is eternally important even if his church is small. The popular, "famous" pastor should not be arrogant. His ultimate evaluation is not from people but from God.

The questions that should concern every pastor-preacher are questions like these: Is God pleased with my treatment of His Word? Is He pleased with my motive? Is He pleased with my attitude and care for the flock? In a day filled with those who preach for the applause of man, we need faithful preachers who preach for the pleasure of God. God told Jeremiah, "The prophet who has only a dream should recount the dream, but the one who has My word should speak My word truthfully" (Jer 23:28).

Paul also reminded Timothy of *the coming of Christ* with three images: "appearing," judgment, and "kingdom." In 2 Timothy 4:8, he spoke of "all those who have loved His *appearing*" (emphasis added). Paul believed Christ will make a visible, glorious appearance (cf. Titus 2:13). When He does appear, He will judge the living and the dead. Christ the King will bring about His kingdom in its fullness.

We must live and preach in light of this holy accountability. James jolts us by reminding us, "Not many should become teachers, my brothers, knowing that we will receive a stricter judgment" (Jas 3:1). The author of Hebrews also puts the task of pastor-teacher in proper perspective: "Obey your leaders and submit to them, for they keep watch over your souls as *those who will give an account,* so that they can do this with joy and not with grief, for that would be unprofitable for you" (Heb 13:17; emphasis added).

In verse 2, Paul says, "Preach the word!" (NKJV). To "preach" means "to herald" or "to proclaim publicly" (cf. 1:11). As preachers, we "proclaim the message." For us today the message is the entire written Word of God. Throughout this section Paul uses various phrases to talk about the truth of God's Word, such as "sacred Scriptures" (3:15), "Scripture" (3:16), "sound doctrine" (4:3), and "the truth" (4:4). We have the holy responsibility and unspeakable privilege of heralding God's timeless truth to people. Like Ezra, let us study it, obey it, and teach it (Ezra 7:10; Neh 8). Paul told Timothy earlier, "Until I come, give your attention to public reading, exhortation, and teaching" (1 Tim 4:13).

Martin Luther said concerning the Reformation, "I simply taught, preached, wrote God's Word; otherwise I did nothing. . . . I did nothing; the Word did it all. . . . I did nothing; I left it to the Word. . . . But it brings him [Satan] distress when we only spread the Word, and let it alone do the work" (Luther, Jacobs, and Spaeth, *Works*, 399–400). Preach the Word faithfully, and believe that it will do the work.

Preach the Word Consistently (4:2b)

Next Timothy is told to persist in his faithfulness to God's Word "whether convenient or not," or as the ESV renders it, "Be ready in season and out of season." This speaks of urgency and readiness. There should always be a sense of urgency in light of the truth that we are communicating. We are preaching on matters of life, death, and eternity. And the preacher-soldier is always on duty! Let your ministry be known for readiness, not for laziness!

I remember being in a southern Nigerian leper colony a few years ago. This was my first time in a leper colony. It took me about 30 minutes to calm down. I was heartbroken by the poverty in this village, the physical effects of leprosy, the unbelievable conditions in which they were living, what the people were cooking, and most of all, by the people's desire for company and conversation. After our team of 12 guys visited with them for about an hour, our host announced, "Now Pastor Tony will preach. Everyone form a circle." I remember thinking, "I'm preaching? I wish I had known this beforehand! I don't even have a Bible, not to mention notes!" I immediately thought of these words: "Be ready in season and out of season." By God's grace I just began preaching Romans 8, talking about suffering and glory, about how we are all dying and need the Savior. The longer I preached, the bolder and more passionate I became. I still have a picture of a lady, who lost her fingers to leprosy, standing behind me with both arms raised in the air in praise to God. It was truly amazing. God's Word is powerful to change the hearts of people in all places at all times. Preach it consistently!

Preach the Word Pastorally (4:2c)

The pastor-preacher should apply the Word to the lives of his flock in a variety of ways. Paul gives us three ways of doing it: "Rebuke, correct, and encourage." Pastors need to know the condition of the flock and remain sensitive to how a particular passage is addressing them. Sometimes God's people need to be **rebuked** for their wrong beliefs or ungodly lifestyles. Paul illustrates this skill with his letters to the Corinthians (rebuked for their immorality) and the Galatians (rebuked for their failure to continue in the gospel of grace).

Other times God's people need to be **corrected** in order to get back on the path of righteousness. This means church discipline is actually done every week as the pastor teaches the Bible. We call this "formative discipline," with the other kind of discipline being "restorative discipline" (e.g., Matt 18:15-20; Gal 6:1). The Bible corrects us when we wander away from God's will.

Sometimes pastors need to **encourage** the flock when they are facing fear, anxiety, or great burdens. Pastors should apply the truths of the text to edify and build up suffering saints.

Of course, one may do all of these in one sermon. Because the scope of the Bible is amazing, we can address all kinds of people in all kinds of ways. Of course, our rebuke, correction, and encouragement should be Christ centered through and through. Show them their need and the Christ-centered solution.

Preach the Word Patiently (4:2d)

I overlooked the part of Paul's challenge for several years that commands "great patience"—that is, until I became a pastor! Then it became my favorite part of the verse! Sanctification (a Christian's growth in Christlikeness) is a slow process. Really slow! Sometimes pastors grow discouraged because they do not see immediate results from their sermons. Remember that there is a cumulative effect to your preaching. Over time there will be fruit. It may take a long time, but with patient biblical teaching you will see some progress.

Charles Simeon comes to mind whenever I think of pastoral patience. When he first came to Holy Trinity Church in Cambridge, no one wanted him to be the minister. For example, the "pew holders" locked the pew doors on Sunday mornings. They refused to participate in corporate worship and prevented any others from sitting down, allowing only standing individuals to worship. This lasted for about 12 years! They also would not allow him to preach the evening sermon! Yet Simeon—single his whole life—remained at this church for 54 years and eventually won the favor of many of his people (Piper, *Roots of Endurance*, 77–114). You can still read his faithful expositions in *Horae Homileticae*. How did Simeon endure? A friend said of him, "Simeon invariably rose every morning, though it was winter season, at four o'clock; and after lighting his fire, he devoted the first four hours of the day to private prayer and the devotional study of the Scriptures. . . . Here was the secret of his great grace and spiritual strength" (in Piper, *Roots of Endurance*, 106).

How can we grow in patience as pastor-preachers? Since patience is a fruit of the Spirit, then the simple answer is to walk by the Spirit. Commune with God. Abide in Jesus. As you spend time in God's presence, in unhindered and unhurried prayer and worship, meditate on God's patience. "The Lord is gracious and compassionate, slow to anger and great in faithful love" (Ps 145:8). Work the gospel deeply into your heart daily. Remember what patience God has shown you! Then, by His grace, display His fatherly patience to His people.

Preach the Word Theologically (4:2e-4)

Paul also adds that Timothy must proclaim the message "with . . . teaching" (v. 2). Interestingly, one of the most famous verses in the Bible about preaching also calls for "teaching." This is important to note because some want to make too sharp a distinction between preaching and teaching, saying preaching is for evangelism, while theological teaching is for the discipleship of believers. This is helpful, but it can be pressed too far.

We need to see how these two pastoral activities work together. Preaching is **heralding** the facts, while teaching is **explaining** the facts. When you say, "The tomb is empty! The throne is occupied!"—then you are preaching. You are declaring the news. Teaching must follow these news headlines and explain who Jesus is, why Jesus was crucified and buried, and what it means for Him to be the King. In other words, if we want to practice verse 2, then we will do both heralding and explaining throughout the sermon.

We desperately need a generation of preachers who preach the Word theologically. The spirit of our day is not unlike that of the first century. Paul says in the next two verses, "For the time will come when they will not tolerate sound doctrine, but according to their own desires, will multiply teachers for themselves because they have an itch to hear something new. They will turn away from hearing the truth and will turn aside to myths" (vv. 3-4). People drift from healthy teaching to suit their own passions. They wander away into myths. Jeremiah said of the people of Judah in his day, "The prophets prophesy falsely, and the priests rule by their own authority. My people love it like this" (Jer 5:31).

Today we have all kinds of preachers who "tickle the ears" of people. Some teach that one cannot believe the miracles of the Bible. Others draw attention as they deny the historical reliability of the Bible. Many fill stadiums with their corrupt health-and-wealth prosperity teaching. We must preach truth because there is an absence of it in every generation. We need courageous prophets who will declare, "Thus says the Lord" with power and grace. Remember, if you are a pastor-preacher, you are the church's theologian and apologist. Become a better theologian so you might become a better pastor-preacher-leader.

Continue in the Word. Keep learning it. Keep believing it. Keep preaching it!

Reflect and Discuss

1. Are you continuing to learn the Bible? How are you pursuing that study?
2. Thinking of your favorite Old Testament story, what does it teach about Christ?
3. How would you answer the question, What is the nature of Scripture? Would you give a different answer to a Christian or a non-Christian?
4. In what way are "rebuking" and "correcting" profitable?
5. Besides the Bible, what other books have you found helpful in your spiritual life? What are their strengths and limitations?
6. How should the warning in James 3:1 affect a teacher? How should it affect the attitude of those who learn from that teacher?
7. If you were asked to teach at this moment, what would you say? Do you have a favorite message that you would always be ready to share?
8. Which is easier for you to do—rebuke, correct, or encourage? Which requires the most conscious effort for you? Which is most required in your situation?
9. What aspect of the task God has assigned to you requires the most patience? Why? What gives you hope?
10. What do people want to hear? What do they need to hear?

Faithful to the End

2 TIMOTHY 4:5-22

Main Idea: As you pursue faithfulness to God, you can rest in the Savior's grace, remember God's perfect faithfulness, and rely on His strength to finish your course.

I. **Timothy's Call to Faithfulness (4:5)**
   A. Keep a clear head about everything (4:5b).
   B. Endure hardship (4:5c).
   C. Do the work of an evangelist (4:5d).
   D. Fulfill your ministry (4:5e).
II. **Paul's Example of Faithfulness (4:6-8)**
   A. The present (4:6)
   B. The past (4:7)
   C. The future (4:8)
III. **More Examples of Faithfulness (4:9-15, 19-21)**
   A. Nine examples (4:9-15)
      1. Timothy (4:9)
      2. Demas (4:10)
      3. Crescens, Titus, and Tychicus (4:10c, 12)
      4. Luke (4:11a)
      5. Mark (4:11b)
      6. Carpus (4:13)
      7. Alexander (4:14-15)
   B. Faithful old friends and new friends (4:19-21)
      1. Prisca and Aquila and Onesiphorus (4:19)
      2. Erastus and Trophimus (4:20)
      3. Eubulus, Pudens, Linus, Claudia, and the brothers (4:21b)
IV. **The Lord's Perfect Faithfulness (4:16-18, 22)**
   A. The Lord's presence (4:16-17)
   B. The Lord's rescue (4:18)
   C. The Lord's grace (4:22)

Recently one of our missionary friends showed us some pictures of a totally unengaged people group he and his family are going to minister among for the next three years. There has never been a church planted among this particular group of people in East Asia. We were struck by one notable photo. It was a picture of a casket. When individuals of this people group turn 65, they each build their own casket, and it just sits by their house. Our friends are going to share with these people "the promise of life in Christ Jesus" (2 Tim 1:1) so that when each one gets put in his or her casket, that person will be able to live forever in "His heavenly kingdom" (4:18). That picture of a casket is a reminder for everyone. We will all die. We must make this life count. We must be faithful to the end.

In this passage Paul gives Timothy (and us) his farewell message, emphasizing the subject of **faithfulness** in four main parts:

1. Timothy's Call to Faithfulness (v. 5)
2. Paul's Example of Faithfulness (vv. 6-8)
3. More Examples of Faithfulness (vv. 9-15, 19-21)
4. The Lord's Perfect Faithfulness (vv. 16-18, 22)

Timothy's Call to Faithfulness
2 TIMOTHY 4:5

The opening words are directed at Timothy with force: "But as for you." As in previous passages Paul once again contrasts the present situation in Ephesus with Timothy's call to be different. Even though many would be led into deception by false teaching (4:3-4), Timothy must do something else. He must keep a clear head in everything (v. 5). Because some did not want to hear the word of truth, Timothy must be prepared to "endure hardship" when people opposed his teaching. Since people were ignorant of the gospel, Timothy must "do the work of an evangelist." Even though some would abandon him for the false teachers, Paul told him, "Fulfill your ministry."

Timothy was in a challenging setting for ministry, but it is not unlike our own day. Indeed, these challenges are relevant for every Christian, especially pastor-leaders.

Keep a Clear Head about Everything (4:5b)

The commands to "be serious" or "be sober-minded" (ESV) have to do with "moral alertness" and "coolness and presence of mind" (Guthrie,

Pastoral Epistles, 179). Paul uses this word earlier in his list of qualifications for an overseer (1 Tim 3:2). The same verb is also used in 1 Thessalonians 5:6, 8 to denote a watchful attitude for Christ's coming. In colloquial terms you might say, "Don't freak out." We must not lose our heads when we face opposition or hang our head when we are discouraged. We must remain calm and sane like an airline pilot flying through rough air. Keeping a clear head is a challenge because of the pressure and problems of pastoral ministry. We need to be reminded of this challenge every day and pray for God's help. We might wake up and wonder, "What should I do today?" One answer is always, "I should keep a clear head about everything. Lord, grant me grace." This is an urgent directive. Sober-mindedness is absolutely necessary for pastoral faithfulness.

Similarly, Alistair Begg says we must avoid being "fat headed" (being puffed up with pride, 1 Tim 3:6; 6:4) or "bobble headed" (bouncing around to every doctrinal fad, 2 Tim 4:3-4; Begg, "Steady as You Go"). We might add empty-headed to the list (getting involved in ignorant controversies, 2 Tim 2:23). Paul also urges us to avoid being sick headed (having a mind filled with immorality, 2 Tim 3:1-4) or hot-headed (responding to critics with sinful anger instead of gentleness, 2 Tim 2:24-25). Instead, by the power of the Holy Spirit, we must be levelheaded. Self-control, stability, and steadiness are marks of a faithful pastor.

Paul himself exemplified this cool spirit later in the chapter. After saying that everyone deserted him in his first defense, he says, "May it not be counted against them" (4:16). Paul does not say, "I hope they all die and burn!" He is not reckless. He is self-controlled, sober, and merciful. Likewise, may the Lord give us strength to be sober-minded.

Endure Hardship (4:5c)

Once again the subject of endurance appears in 2 Timothy (cf. 1:8; 2:3, 9-10; 3:10-12). Timothy was to continue through conflict: "Endure hardship." He was to avoid being bitter in hardship, quitting because of hardship, or responding in violence to hardship. As Paul mentioned previously, Timothy was called to "share in suffering as a good soldier of Christ Jesus" by the grace that is in Christ Jesus (2:3).

No one will be able to say triumphantly, like Paul, "I have fought the good fight" (2 Tim 4:7) if they do not learn to endure hardship. In my short time as a pastor, I have encountered physical suffering, relational abandonment, demonic warfare, the burden of preaching, financial instability, a hurricane called Katrina, fear, discouragement, doubt, the loss of loved ones, parental challenges, wounding criticism, false accusations, and more. Christians who desire to obey Christ will inevitably face hardship (3:12). Let the hardships that come from following Jesus lead you to prayer and not to despair.

Do the Work of an Evangelist (4:5d)

Paul probably does not have the office or position of an evangelist in mind here. In Ephesians 4:11 and Acts 21:8 there seems to be a specialist ministry for "evangelists." The emphasis here in 2 Timothy has more to do with the "work" of an evangelist. Paul's focus was on the proclamation of the gospel. While Timothy was to teach the Word to those who belonged to Christ, he was also to reach the unbelieving world with the good news.

In a broader sense, all Christians are called to spread the word (Acts 4:31; 8:4). Whether it is one-on-one personal evangelism or public proclamation of the crucified and risen Christ, evangelism is "work." Spreading the gospel is not always easy. It takes hard work to see people come to know Christ. Jesus told His disciples to pray for "workers" to enter the harvest field because there were so few of them (Matt 9:37-38). He did not tell them to pray for "halfhearted slackers." Evangelism is labor! Like a hardworking farmer, we must keep sowing and plowing every day if we want to see fruit. Keep planting seeds, and pray for God to send the rain.

Acts 17:17-18 shows us a powerful picture of the work of an evangelist. Paul is waiting on his friends in Athens when he is provoked by the idolatry of the city. Because Paul longed for people to worship the Savior, he engages them with the gospel. In doing so, he interacts with three groups of people. First, he reasons with the religious people in the synagogue, pointing them to the Messiah. Second, he dialogues with those who were passing through the marketplace. Finally, he addresses the academic types at the Areopagus. We need laborers in all three fields today: those who preach the gospel to religious types, those who engage people on the street through conversation, and those who can give a reasonable defense of the faith to skeptical intellects. All of this takes work.

Do you need to improve in evangelistic faithfulness? If so (and who would not say this?), let me remind you of a few ideas. Remember that you do not work alone! The Holy Spirit is the great Evangelist who opens eyes for people to believe. Throughout the book of Acts, there is a magnificent picture of faithful evangelism and God's mighty work of bringing people to Christ (Acts 8:26-40; 16:14; 18:9-10). Further, remember that we speak out of the overflow of our hearts. Therefore, fill your own heart with the gospel daily. "Keep your attention on Jesus Christ," Paul told Timothy (2 Tim 2:8). Let us send "little evangelists" into our hearts every day, reminding ourselves of the gospel and who we are in Christ. Then let us arise and tell others about the Savior of our souls.

Fulfill Your Ministry (4:5e)

This exhortation is a summary of Timothy's calling. Paul urges him to complete his ministry. The same verb was used when Paul and Barnabas had completed their relief work in Jerusalem. Luke writes, "After they had completed [fulfilled] their relief mission, Barnabas and Saul returned to Jerusalem, taking along John who is called Mark" (Acts 12:25). Timothy is likewise urged to continue his work until it was completed.

The work Paul has in mind includes, broadly speaking, all he had already told Timothy to do in 1 and 2 Timothy. The immediate context, however, has to do with preaching the Word of truth in a truthless world (2 Tim 4:1-4). He wants Timothy to keep preaching the Bible, pointing people to Jesus, and loving Christ's church.

To fulfill our ministry, we must avoid foolish controversies and other silly matters. Nikolaus Zinzendorf, missionary count of the eighteenth century, said it this way: "Preach the gospel, die, and be forgotten." In other words, complete your assignment and then go home to your Savior.

Here then are four daily activities to perform: keep a clear head, endure hardship, do the work of an evangelist, and fulfill your ministry. Consistently pursue these tasks by God's grace. If you want to be faithful to the end, there are no shortcuts in the middle.

Paul's Example of Faithfulness
2 TIMOTHY 4:6-8

In 2 Timothy 4:6-8 Paul issues his charge in the light of his impending martyrdom. After urging Timothy to fulfill his ministry, he reflects on his own ministry. Here we find some powerful words to all Christians about loving and serving Christ until the end of our days.

The Present (4:6)

In verse 6, Paul speaks of dying and departing. The first subject is illustrated with a **sacrifice** and the second is perhaps the image of a **boat**. Concerning the former, he says, "I am already being poured out as a drink offering." About five years earlier he used this analogy in writing to the Philippians to describe the possibility of his death (Phil 2:17). Here it is no mere possibility. He speaks as though the process has already begun.

The image of sacrifice Paul uses is drawn from the Old Testament sacrificial system (Exod 29:40-41; Lev 23:13; Num 15:1-12; 28:7, 24). During the ritual of sacrificing a lamb, wine was poured out at the base of the altar. Perhaps Paul is using this image to refer to the type of death he expected. Because Roman citizens could not be crucified, he may have anticipated being beheaded, in which case his blood would splash like wine on the ground. This pouring out of his life would be an offering of worship to Jesus. The details of his death are not given in Holy Scripture, but this picture of being poured out for Christ's sake is still awe inspiring. Paul's entire life as a believer was about sacrificial service. When your life is over, will people be able to say, "He poured out his life for Christ's sake"?

Paul adds, "The time for my departure is close." The word translated "departure" is also used in Greek literature for the loosing of a ship from its moorings or a soldier loosing the stakes of his tent. The image of a boat is indeed a beautiful one. I love the image of Paul lifting the anchor, tossing aside the ropes, and joyfully sailing to a better place. The believer never really dies; she just departs. Paul longed for this final, ultimate voyage. He told the Philippians, "I have the desire to depart and be with Christ" (Phil 1:23). Why? Because it is "far better." This was Paul's dream. And now the ship was about to leave. Paul was ready. Are you?

Believers who approach their final days in this life can find comfort in these words. When we depart, we are better off. Consider how Paul puts present suffering in its place with this heavenly vision:

For our momentary light affliction is producing for us an absolutely incomparable eternal weight of glory. (2 Cor 4:17)

For I consider that the sufferings of this present time are not
worth comparing with the glory that is going to be revealed to us.
(Rom 8:18)

Another drink offering, Charles Spurgeon, said of his glorious departure, "To come to Thee is to come home from exile, to come to land out of the raging storm, to come to rest after long labor, to come to the goal of my desires and the summit of my wishes" (Spurgeon, *Morning by Morning*, 116). It is better to be with Christ. Far better.

The Past (4:7)

Paul looks back on his life with triumph, and he uses three more word pictures associated with victory. First, he uses the analogy of a **fight**. "I have fought the good fight," he says. Paul was a warrior. It is likely that he was not physically impressive, but he was a spiritual warrior. He had stood before Felix, Agrippa, and the officials of Rome with courage. He endured the riots in Ephesus and the opposition in Corinth. He endured all kinds of struggles on his missionary journeys. About 30 years had passed since Christ called him on the Damascus Road. On that momentous occasion he was told that he would suffer for Christ's name, and he did (Acts 9:16). Consider afresh some of Paul's past hardships:

> *Are they servants of Christ? I'm talking like a madman—I'm a*
> *better one: with far more labors, many more imprisonments, far worse*
> *beatings, near death many times. Five times I received 39 lashes from*
> *Jews. Three times I was beaten with rods by the Romans. Once I was*
> *stoned by my enemies. Three times I was shipwrecked. I have spent*
> *a night and a day in the open sea. On frequent journeys, I faced*
> *dangers from rivers, dangers from robbers, dangers from my own*
> *people, dangers from the Gentiles, dangers in the city, dangers in the*
> *open country, dangers on the sea, and dangers among false brothers;*
> *labor and hardship, many sleepless nights, hunger and thirst, often*
> *without food, cold, and lacking clothing. Not to mention other things,*
> *there is the daily pressure on me: my care for all the churches.* (2 Cor
> 11:23-28)

What is more, Paul said ultimately his fight is beyond what the human eye can see. He writes, "For our battle is not against flesh and blood, but against the rulers, against the authorities, against the world powers of this darkness, against the spiritual forces of evil in the heavens"

(Eph 6:12). Can you see the war-torn apostle writing this letter from a hole in the ground in Rome? It is a moving scene. Can you imagine being told to "endure hardship" (2 Tim 4:5) from this one who endured it to such a degree?

Second, Paul says, "I have finished the race." I love how Paul says that he simply "finished" his race, not that he won the race. Some years earlier he told the Ephesian elders that his goal was to finish his course (Acts 20:24). Now he could say triumphantly, "I finished it."

We all have a race to run. The author of Hebrews tells us to "run with endurance the race that lies before us" (Heb 12:1). He says that we run faithfully by remembering those who have gone before us, by throwing off anything that keeps us from faithfulness, and by fixing our eyes on Jesus, our victorious, seated King (Heb 12:1-2). Keep running!

Finally, Paul says, "I have kept the faith." Paul is probably emphasizing his role as a steward of sound doctrine. He was a guardian of the gospel. Earlier he told Timothy, "Hold on to the pattern of sound teaching" (2 Tim 1:13) and, "Guard what has been entrusted to you" (1 Tim 6:20). Paul held on to the truth and passed it on to Timothy and others.

Every Christian in general and leaders in particular should take heed. We too have a fight to endure, a race to run, and a treasure to guard.

The Future (4:8)

The final picture in verses 6-8 is that of a "crown," or garland. Again, an athletic analogy is used. Garlands won by the Greeks were greatly prized. Here Paul speaks of a crown of infinitely greater worth! He writes of a crown he would receive—the same crown we also will one day receive.

He says, "There is reserved for me in the future the crown of righteousness, which the Lord, the righteous Judge, will give me on that day." Notice that Jesus Christ is the righteous Judge (cf. 2 Cor 5:10). This righteous Judge had already given Paul His righteousness when he believed (Rom 3:21-22; 2 Cor 5:21). But now Paul awaits the crown of righteousness; that is, the ultimate, permanent state of righteousness. While Nero was about to declare Paul guilty and condemn him, Christ the righteous Judge was about to declare him righteous!

But Paul does not stop with his own crown. He says, "Not only to me, but to all those who have loved His appearing." The same crown of righteousness awaits all believers, not just the mighty apostle. Genuine believers are those who love Jesus' appearing. A sure evidence of saving faith is having your heart set on Christ. Unbelievers dread Christ's coming, but as believers we long for it. Jesus is our "blessed hope" (Titus 2:13).

This vision will keep you running your race. Do you see Jesus? There He is. You are getting closer. Keep running. Keep fighting. Keep guarding. Soon you will see Him as He is (1 John 3:2). Then you will see His scarred hands and look into His majestic eyes. His lips will move, and He will say, "Well done." He will place a crown on your head. On that day you will not regret fighting, running, and enduring for His name's sake.

More Examples of Faithfulness
2 TIMOTHY 4:9-15, 19-21

From Paul's final words here, we see the importance of relationships. What is on the mind of the apostle at death? Jesus and people! Paul was not a lone ranger. He always mentioned people in his letters. In chapter 1, he describes the sad desertion of Phygelus and Hermogenes and the exemplary service of Onesiphorus. In chapter 4, he mentions a number of individuals, both friends and foes. Some were faithful, and some were unfaithful. Some started well but departed. Others started poorly but were now exemplary. As we survey the individuals mentioned, we might ask ourselves if we are being faithful to God and one another. Are you like Demas or Mark? Are you an Alexander or a Luke?

Nine Examples (4:9-15)

In verses 9-15, Paul lists nine people. While we should not sit in judgment over them, it seems that enough is said about them to at least learn from them and examine our own faithfulness. Below is a chart that might help summarize this group of people. It may look like a battery, but it is not! The positive and negative signs reflect Paul's words. Some who are mentioned might receive a "positive, positive" while Alexander receives a "negative, negative." Others, like Demas and Mark, changed their course, according to Paul.[20] Of course, I do not mean to imply that the "positive, positive people" were *sinless*. I am only saying that Paul had good things to say about their lives and that we should all seek to emulate their faithfulness.

---

[20] This idea is taken from an audio sermon on 2 Timothy 4:9-18 preached by Mark Driscoll, though I never saw his chart.

+ +	Timothy Faithful Son	Titus Faithful Comforter	Tychicus Faithful Messenger	Crescens Faithful Unknown	Luke Faithful Friend	Carpus Faithful Host
- +	Mark Unfaithful Restored					
+ -	Demas Unfaithful Deserter					
- -	Alexander Faithless Opponent					

Timothy (4:9). Twice Paul urges Timothy to come to him quickly (vv. 9, 21). His desire for Timothy's urgent visit probably indicates that Paul believed his time was short, and soon the winter months would inhibit travel. It also shows the close bond between these two men. While Paul's ultimate desire was to see his Savior, he still wanted to see his spiritual son (cf. 1:4). John Stott notes that these two desires are not incompatible. He writes, "One sometimes meets super-spiritual people who claim that they never feel lonely and have no need for friends, for the companionship of Christ satisfies all their needs. But human friendship is the loving provision of God for mankind" (Stott, *Message*, 120). Timothy was a "positive, positive." He was there in the beginning, and he was there in the end.

Demas (4:10). While people can be wonderful sources of joy, they can also be sources of discouragement. Enter Demas. Paul says that he "has deserted me." The word "deserted" is a strong verb, meaning to "utterly abandon and leave someone helpless in a dire situation" (MacArthur, *2 Timothy*, 206). His desertion brought pain to Paul. According to other passages, Demas was previously a "coworker" (see Col 4:14; Phlm 24). In both passages, Demas's name is with Luke's. Demas had been "positive" but sadly went "negative."

Why did he desert Paul? Paul says it was "because he loved this present world." Instead of loving Christ's appearing (4:8), Demas loved "this present world" (cf. Rom 12:2; 1 John 2:15-17). It is hard to tell exactly what this means since the details are not given, but it is certainly not positive. We know it means he had misplaced affections. As noted earlier in this letter (3:2), when we have the wrong loves, we live a wrong life.

It is astonishing to think about a guy who hung out with Paul but later fell away. He not only went to "Bible studies," but he also sat with a guy who wrote part of the Bible! Demas reminds us of Judas. He was a fair-weather disciple. His desertion should serve as a warning to us: "Whoever thinks he stands must be careful not to fall" (1 Cor 10:12).

Crescens, Titus, and Tychicus (4:10c, 12). While Demas's desertion hurt Paul, three other departures seem to have received the apostle's blessing. Crescens and Titus appear to have been sent out on mission: "Crescens has gone to Galatia, Titus to Dalmatia." Dalmatia was across the Adriatic Sea, and Galatia was across the Aegean Sea. Nothing else is known about Crescens in the New Testament, but a tradition connects him with the churches of Mayence in Gaul (Guthrie, *Pastoral Epistles,* 183).

Titus is no stranger to us. Apparently, Titus finished his assignment in Crete and was now sent on a new assignment. Elsewhere, Paul calls Titus "my true son" (Titus 1:4) and speaks of him as an exemplary friend and gospel partner. Titus brought comfort to Paul and others (e.g., 2 Cor 7:6). He appears to be a strong equipper of leaders. Paul trusted Titus to lead struggling churches. Earlier Paul had told Titus that the reason he wanted him in Crete was to "set right what was left undone" (Titus 1:5). His mission in Dalmatia is probably similar. He is sent out to strengthen the church and build up its leaders.

Tychicus also seems to have been a "positive, positive" associate, demonstrating a consistent life of faithfulness. He was the loyal bearer of the letter to the Colossians and Ephesians (see Eph 6:21-22; Col 4:7-8). Think about that assignment! Hand delivering a book of the Bible! It is possible that he took this present letter to Timothy also: "I have sent Tychicus to Ephesus" (4:12). Another possibility is that he was going to serve as Timothy's (temporary) replacement in Ephesus, so that Timothy could visit Paul in Rome (see Titus 3:12).

Because these three faithful men were sent out, it increased Paul's need for Timothy's companionship.

Luke (4:11a). Paul says, "Only Luke is with me," but we should not read this as a disparaging comment about Luke. Paul is not saying, "Please come visit me! I have no real friend here, just Dr. Luke!" Luke, "the dearly loved physician" (Col 4:14), was a loyal friend and companion to Paul. He stands in contrast to Demas. Hughes says, "Luke was a tough friend for tough times. He was with Paul in prison from the first time to the last. He was Paul's biographer, and the 'we' passages in Acts indicate that he was with the apostle during some of the most difficult times" (Hughes and Chapell, *1 & 2 Timothy and Titus*, 260). Surely, Paul was glad to have Luke with him.

Mark (4:11b). Concerning (John) Mark, Paul writes, "Bring Mark with you, for he is useful to me in the ministry." Mark's story is encouraging. He started out with many incredible privileges and opportunities. His mother's home was one of the main places for the Jerusalem church. Peter joined the disciples in this home after miraculously getting out of prison (Acts 12:12). This home may also have been where the last supper was eaten. Mark was an eyewitness of Jesus and may have been the young man who ran away (naked!) at Jesus' arrest (Mark 14:51-52). He was familiar with the life and ministry of Jesus.

When Paul went on his first missionary journey, Mark went with him. For some reason, however, Mark went home (Acts 13:5, 13). Later Barnabas wanted to take John Mark with them on another trip, but Paul rejected the idea because he viewed Mark as a deserter. Barnabas and Mark went one way, and Paul and Silas went another.

But Mark gets restored and is later present with Paul during the apostle's first imprisonment (Col 4:10). Paul calls him a "coworker" (Phlm 24). Peter also mentions Mark as his "son" (1 Pet 5:13). Here in 2 Timothy, some 20 years after their separation, Mark makes the short list of reliable friends and companions of Paul.

Mark's story should give fallen Christians hope. Despite rejection, possible shame, hurt, and failure, Mark is restored and put back in the game. Mark not only was useful to Paul, but he was used by God to write the Gospel of Mark! Under the inspiration of the Spirit, Mark gives us the action-packed Gospel focusing on the suffering Messiah. This Messiah restored him and can restore us all by His grace.

Carpus (4:13). Paul mentioned Carpus in his request to Timothy: "When you come, bring the cloak I left in Troas with Carpus, as well as the scrolls, especially the parchments." As a pastor, few things are more important to you than your books! I would consider this guy a righteous man if he watched over my books and returned them safely! Apparently Carpus lived in Troas, and Paul had visited him. It is also possible that the church in Troas met in his house (see Acts 20:6-7). For some reason Paul left some important items there (due to an arrest?).

Paul's cloak is important because he was cold in Rome. This was probably an expensive item. His scrolls and parchments were also expensive and personally valuable. His "books" (ESV) were probably papyrus rolls, possibly being the Old Testament. Parchments were expensive. They were vellum sheets made of treated animal hides that were used for important documents like legal papers. These were possibly written accounts of Jesus' words and deeds. Or they may have simply been blank pages that Paul planned on using for other writing purposes. It is not outrageous to think that these parchments contained important Christian material. It certainly fits the idea of "guarding the truth."

We see a glimpse of Paul's humanness and need here. Stott says, "When our spirit is lonely, we need friends. When our body is cold, we need clothing. When our mind is bored, we need books. To admit this is not unspiritual; it is human" (Stott, *Message*, 121).

Alexander (4:14-15). Alexander was an obvious opponent to Paul and the gospel. Paul notes that he "did great harm to me" and that "he strongly opposed our words." He may have been involved in Paul's second arrest. As a "coppersmith," he may have been an idol maker who resented Paul (like Demetrius in Acts 19:24) because Paul was cutting into his bottom line. In 1 Timothy, Paul mentions an "Alexander," whom he "delivered . . . to Satan" (1:20). Whether this is the same Alexander we cannot know for sure.

Paul tells Timothy two things about Alexander. First, "The Lord will repay him according to his works" (v. 14). Paul says that the Lord, the righteous Judge, would render the ultimate judgment on this man (cf. Ps 62:12). Second, he warns, "Watch out for him yourself" (v. 15), and be on guard constantly against his evil opposition.

Faithful Old Friends and New Friends (4:19-21)

Prisca and Aquila and Onesiphorus (4:19). As we jump ahead to the final list of names, Paul first greets his friends in other places. Prisca and Aquila (wife and husband) befriended Paul in Corinth. Paul stayed with them and worked with them as tent makers (Acts 18:2-3). Paul called them his "coworkers" (Rom 16:3), and apparently, they were still in Ephesus, where they had accompanied Paul before he left for Caesarea (Acts 18:26). They exemplify steady faithfulness to Jesus. Paul also greets Onesiphorus's household. Even though this refreshing friend appears to be in Rome, Paul still mentions a word of greeting to his household.

Erastus and Trophimus (4:20). Two other mutual friends are included here. Paul says, "Erastus has remained at Corinth; I left Trophimus sick at Miletus." It may be that this is the Erastus spoken of in Romans 16:23, where he was known as the "city treasurer" and the same guy who was with Timothy on a previous trip to Macedonia (Acts 19:22). Trophimus, a native of Ephesus, was a companion of Paul on his third missionary journey. According to Acts 20:4, he was with Paul when he went to Miletus, and according to Acts 21:29, he went with Paul to Jerusalem. Trophimus knew of the hardships of Paul and undoubtedly experienced difficulty as well in laboring for the gospel. He may have been with Paul on this trip from Asia to Rome but had to remain in Miletus because of an illness. These individuals were loyal servants.

Eubulus, Pudens, Linus, Claudia, and the brothers (4:21b). Nothing is known of these three men and one woman. They appear to be part of the church in Rome since their names are joined with "all the brothers." One tradition places Linus as the one who became first bishop of Rome following the martyrdom of Paul and Peter.

These four new friends show how faithful saints through the years have blessed the body of Christ. While they are unknown to us, they were not unknown to God. Your service to Jesus does not go unnoticed either! The church has been blessed, enriched, and strengthened throughout the ages by unsung heroes.

The Lord's Perfect Faithfulness
2 TIMOTHY 4:16-18, 22

The Lord's Presence (4:16-17)

Paul's "first defense" (v. 16) may refer to a preliminary investigation that would precede the formal trial, roughly equivalent to a grand jury hearing (Hughes and Chapell, *1 & 2 Timothy and Titus,* 267). Paul says that no one stood with him during this trial. Some *could not* because of other tasks, and others *would not* because of fear or other reasons. This courageous missionary of the church did not have one single Christian alongside him. We do not know what charges were laid against him, but according to Pliny, Tacitius, and others, several claims were made about Christians. They were accused of atheism because they rejected Caesar-worship and of cannibalism because they spoke of eating the Lord's body (Stott, *Message,* 123).

Paul reminds us of Jesus. Previously Paul, like Jesus, went to Jerusalem knowing that he was walking into his death (Acts 21:11-14). Now here in 2 Timothy, Paul is in his own garden of Gethsemane. He says, "Everyone deserted me" (4:16; cf. Mark 14:50). And like Jesus, Paul says, "May it not be counted against them" (v. 16; cf. Luke 23:34), showing mercy and not anger or bitterness.

What is more, here during his dying days, it seems that Paul uses the language of Psalm 22 (vv. 16-18), which may indicate that he was meditating on this classic Christ-exalting psalm. This psalm also occupied the mind of Jesus during His dying moments. Take a moment to compare 2 Timothy 4:16 with Psalm 22:1 and 11; 2 Timothy 4:17 with Psalm 22:21 and 27; and 2 Timothy 4:18 with Psalm 22:28. Paul is certainly a model of faithfulness and devotion, worthy of our imitation because he points us to the Savior (1 Cor 11:1).

Paul also knew, like Jesus, that he was not ultimately alone. The Lord was with him! He says to Timothy, "But the Lord stood by me and strengthened me, so that the proclamation might be fully made through me, and all the Gentiles might hear. So I was rescued from the lion's mouth" (v. 17). By God's strength this Christlike apostle heralded the gospel to the Gentiles who were present. What an amazing illustration of 2 Timothy 4:1-2: "Proclaim the message; persist in it whether convenient or not."

Paul's dominant concern was not himself but the message of Christ! In front of this large crowd, before judges and perhaps the emperor himself, Paul publicly declared the gospel. He did not fear men because he preached "before God and Christ Jesus, who is going to judge the living and the dead" (4:1). When you recognize that you ultimately stand before God Almighty, you are freed from the fear of man. Remember that you preach in God's sight by God's strength.

The Lord also temporarily rescued him from death ("the lion's mouth"). The court could have easily decided to take his life, but instead there would be another hearing. In the end Paul would die, but the Lord would still provide the ultimate rescue to this faithful messenger.

The Lord's Rescue (4:18)

Though Paul was temporarily rescued, he knew death was certain. But he could face death with peace because of his relationship with his faithful Lord. He says, "The Lord will rescue me from every evil work and will bring me safely into His heavenly kingdom." He stood confident that the Lord would rescue him from evil and bring him to heaven.

Because God provides us the strength, gives us the message, protects us from evil, and will ultimately bring us to heaven, God deserves the glory: "To Him be the glory forever and ever."

The Lord's Grace (4:22)

We began this exposition of 2 Timothy by noting the gospel-centered nature of the letter. Now Paul ends it with a gospel-centered blessing: "The Lord be with your spirit. Grace be with you!" The apostle's final recorded thought is fitting: "grace." This war-torn apostle experienced God's amazing grace, testified to the gospel of grace, and closed by praying for the Savior's grace to strengthen and empower his "son."

As you pursue faithfulness to God, you can rest in the Savior's grace, remember God's perfect faithfulness, and rely on His strength to finish your course. Then when you are put in your casket, go join Paul and these others in the Savior's heavenly kingdom.

Reflect and Discuss

1. How are you most likely to lose your clear head—by becoming too excited or too discouraged?
2. How can a cool head and an intense passion for sharing the gospel go together?
3. What is the difference between the office of "evangelist" (Eph 4:11) and "the work of an evangelist" (2 Tim 4:5)?
4. Who would you rather discuss the gospel with—adherents of another religion, people on the street, or secular intellectuals? Why?
5. How does knowledge of the sacrificial system in the Old Testament help us grasp the meaning of Paul's words more deeply?
6. Are you convinced that "departure" is better than life? What feelings do you have when you contemplate death?
7. How does knowing about Paul's experience of suffering affect the way you understand his last words?
8. Are we called to win the race or to run the race? How does that affect our intention to give 100 percent?
9. What role do fellow Christians play in your spiritual journey? Do you grow more on your own or with a friend?
10. Besides the Bible, what three books would you want with you in prison? Why?

Titus

Saved to Serve

TITUS 1:1-4

Main Idea: The salvation we have received in Jesus Christ leads to a life of godliness and service to God our Savior.

I. **We Are Servants of Our Lord (1:1).**
   A. We are slaves.
   B. We are sent.
   C. We are selected.
   D. We are sanctified.
II. **We Are Secure in the Lord (1:2-3).**
   A. We have His witness (1:2).
   B. We have His word (1:3).
III. **We Are Separated unto the Lord (1:4).**
   A. We share a common faith.
   B. We are in God's family.

I t is a fortunate man who knows who he is and why he is here. Such a man was Saul of Tarsus, the man better known as the apostle Paul. A persecutor of Christians and an enemy of Christ, he stood in support of the murder of the first Christian martyr, Stephen. Acts 7:58 says those who killed Stephen "laid down their robes" at his feet. God, however, had a sovereign plan for this young radical. As Paul was traveling on the Damascus road with the intent of destroying Christian lives and homes (Acts 9:1-19), the risen and glorified Lord Jesus appeared from heaven and saved him. He saved him, not just to take him to heaven; He saved him, like He saved you and me, to serve.

Here in Titus 1:1-4, in one of Paul's longest introductions, the apostle begins a short three-chapter, 46-verse letter that weds in a beautiful duet the Christian sonnet of doctrine and deeds, belief and behavior, conduct and creed. Being sound in doctrine and zealous for good works are twin themes that tie this short, powerful epistle together.

This is a bargain-basement letter. You get more than your money's worth as Paul packed in so much truth and so much teaching in such a short amount of space.

We could consider the theme to be "An Apostolic Manual for Church Planting." Here is a blueprint for planting and building churches that will survive and thrive for the glory of God.

Paul begins by telling something about himself, something about salvation, something about preaching, and something about his son in the faith, a man named Titus. What then is his message for us today? What do we need to know about who we are and why we are here?

We Are Servants of Our Lord
TITUS 1:1

"Paul," which means small, little, or humble, was his Greek/Roman name and was perhaps taken in honor of his first Gentile convert on his first missionary journey, a man named Sergius Paulus (Acts 13:7-12). Paul, the greatest missionary-theologian who ever lived (he saw no difficulty in bringing the two together), was in his later years. While his eyes may have been growing dim at this time in his life, his spiritual vision had never been clearer. He saw clearly just who and what he was "in Christ."

We Are Slaves

Paul identifies himself as a "slave of God." Only here does he call himself a slave of God; normally it was "of Christ." For Paul there was no difference. He was God's slave, bought and paid for by the precious blood of Jesus (1 Pet 1:18-19). He was now no longer his own (1 Cor 6:19); he was a slave of God. This demonstrates the **humility** that should characterize our lives as servants of our Lord.

We Are Sent

Paul also calls himself an "apostle of Jesus Christ." **Apostle** is both a technical and a general term in Scripture. Technically, it refers to the Twelve, the disciples who were eyewitnesses of the life, death, resurrection, and ascension of our Lord. Paul was also an apostle, but "one abnormally born," one placed into the office at a different time and in an unusual way (1 Cor 15:8). The term **apostle** also has a general meaning that applies to every one of us, for we are "sent ones" as those who go on behalf of Jesus Christ. This speaks of our calling and **authority** as missionaries of our Savior.

We Are Selected

In the remainder of verse 1, Paul expresses the purpose for which he was called—a purpose that we too share as believers. Watch carefully! Don't miss it. He says his apostleship exists for "the faith" (here is human responsibility) "of God's elect" (here is divine sovereignty). Paul sees no dichotomy, no contradiction between the sovereignty of God and the human responsibility of man. Salvation from beginning to end is the sovereign work of the grace of God (Eph 2:8; Heb 12:2). And yet no one will be saved who does not repent and believe, and all who repent and believe will be saved (Rom 10:13).

I understand Paul to be a theological and soteriological compatibilist. He believed God elected and predestined people to be saved but did so in such a way as to do no violence to their free will and responsibility to believe the gospel. The great prince of preachers, Charles Haddon Spurgeon, once commented on this issue: "He saves man by grace, and if men perish they perish justly by their own fault. 'How,' says someone, 'do you reconcile these two doctrines?' My dear brethren, I never reconcile two friends, never. These two doctrines are friends with one another; for they are both in God's Word, and I shall not attempt to reconcile them" ("Jacob and Esau," in *New Park Street*, 5:120). And neither should we.

I am convinced Paul stood against anything that questioned the sovereignty of God and he stood steadfast against anything that would harm a red-hot passion for missions and evangelism. Here we see the purpose of our **ministry**. It is a ministry that exists for the salvation of the lost among all the nations through the proclamation of the gospel.

We Are Sanctified

The faith of those belonging to God was also for a purpose. Saving faith moves one to a full knowledge of the truth that results in a new life of godliness. A knowledge of the truth and godliness are intimately connected in Christianity. One commentator states this well: "A profession of the truth which allows an individual to live in ungodliness is a spurious profession" (Hiebert, *Titus and Philemon*, 21). The gospel should lead to godliness. In other words, what I believe will affect how I live, and how I live will demonstrate what I believe!

Vance Havner, commenting on the church's failure to move from faith to knowledge to godliness, said, "We are challenged these days, but not changed; convicted, but not converted. We hear, but do not; and thereby we deceive ourselves" (Hester, *Vance Havner*, 1963).

The child of God is to live a sanctified life, a holy life, a pure life, and a godly life. Here the genuineness of the truth of the gospel is lived out for all to see. This speaks of our **maturity** as followers of Christ and further describes the purpose of our ministry. As servants of God, we exist to seek both the salvation of the lost and growth in godliness in the life of the believer.

We Are Secure in the Lord
TITUS 1:2-3

We are not only servants of our Lord, but we are also secure in the Lord. Paul understood that radical service for the Lord Jesus Christ must be grounded in a security in Christ that sets us free to serve Him with an otherworldly abandonment that knows, no matter what: I am His! In verses 2-3, Paul places before us two avenues of a sure and certain security. One is God's witness; the other is God's Word.

We Have His Witness (Titus 1:2)

Paul here addresses one of the great promises of Scripture, placing all its weight on the character of God. Note the wonderful "chain reaction"! The saving faith of those who belong to God leads to a knowledge of the truth, which will lead to godliness, all of which rests on the hope of eternal life in a God who cannot lie! What a promise! What a hope!

Hope is a confident certainty and expectation of something that is not yet ours but will be. **Eternal life** is the very life of God. It is both a quantity of life (forever) and a quality of life ("Christ in you, the hope of glory," Col 1:27). This "hope of eternal life" is founded upon the character and integrity of the God "who cannot lie" (cf. 1 Sam 15:29; Heb 6:18). In stark contrast is Satan, who "is a liar and the father of lies" (John 8:44), as well as the Cretans, who are described as being "always liars" (v. 12). Paul points out that this hope of eternal life was "promised before time began." The plan of salvation, the promise of eternal life, looks both ways down "God's highway of grace"; it runs into eternity past and it lasts into eternity future (Hughes and Chapell, *1 & 2 Timothy and Titus*, 277).

Some theologians see in verse 2 an allusion to what is called "the covenant of redemption" whereby the Father showed His love for His Son by promising Him a redeemed people who would love, serve, and glorify Him forever (cf. John 6:37, 40; 17:23-24, 26). However, to complete the picture we must add that the Son showed His love for the Father by becoming the Lamb who was slain before the foundation of the world (1 Pet 1:19-20) and that the entire plan of redemption was an eternal promise made to sinful humanity as a demonstration of God's love for us. Our salvation is no afterthought with God. He planned it down to the last detail a long time ago. Our security and confidence in the Lord rest not only in His witness; they also rest on His word.

We Have His Word (Titus 1:3)

The eternal promise of eternal life entered time and space at "just the right time" (NLT). The HCSB says "in His own time"; the NIV says "at his appointed season"; Peterson in *The Message* paraphrases: "When the time was ripe, he went public with his truth." Now the "chain reaction" of God's wonderful plan adds another crucial link.

The eternal promise of eternal life from the God who cannot lie stepped into history as the Word of God made known through preaching, which message had been entrusted to Paul (and now us) by the commandment of God our Savior (cf. Titus 2:10; 3:4).

Amazingly, God has placed His eternal plan of salvation in the hands of people like you and me. We as heralds of the gospel are recipients of a divine trust, a sacred treasure. The message we preach is not our word; it is His Word. This is our commitment. This is His commandment. This is our calling. We preach His Word and no other word. We preach His gospel and not another gospel. Certainly some may preach the gospel better, but no one will preach a better gospel.

We Are Separated unto the Lord
TITUS 1:4

Paul now introduces us to the recipient of this letter, a man named Titus. Titus is mentioned 13 times in the New Testament (2 Cor 2:13; 7:6, 13, 14; 8:6, 16, 23; 12:18 [2 times]; Gal 2:1, 3; 2 Tim 4:10). He was a Greek, a non-Jewish convert who became something of a "test case" for the gospel and the fact that one does not need to become a Jew, evidenced by circumcision, to be saved. Titus had a special relationship to the troubled church at Corinth, and his work there and here on the difficult island of Crete revealed Paul's confidence in him. Playfully, we can say he was Paul's "hit man," his "Green Beret," his "spiritual Navy SEAL," who could go into the hard places and set things in order, get things fixed, make things right.

Paul again provides a word of encouragement concerning our security in Christ and the fountain of blessings from which we drink as we draw strength for service.

We Share a Common Faith

Titus was a "true son in our common faith." Paul used this same expression "true son" for Timothy in 1 Timothy 1:2. It suggests that Paul was their spiritual father, having led both to faith in Christ. The phrase "common faith" may refer to the same saving faith both Paul and Titus had experienced. More likely it refers to "the faith," the body of Christian truth, "that was delivered to the saints once for all" (Jude 3).

Titus was to preach the same message Paul preached. It is the faith that was to be taught in the first century, and it remains the faith that is to be taught in the twenty-first century. Like Titus we share in this common faith and have been entrusted to proclaim it faithfully. While methods may change, the message always remains the same. The "sound teaching" (v. 9) necessary to build a vibrant, dynamic, and genuine New Testament church is rooted and grounded in this common faith. There is no room for wavering or compromise on this.

We Are in God's Family

Many beautiful metaphors and images describe the relationship of God to His people. We are His temple, a building, a body, His bride. We are also family, and that was Paul's focus as he brought his greeting to an end.

When we receive Jesus as Savior we also receive God as Father. As "God our Savior" in verse 3, the Lord (deity) Jesus (humanity) Christ (God's anointed) is "our Savior" in verse 4. The title **Savior** appears 12 times in the New Testament, six of those times in Titus. The question of who is Savior must have been an issue on the island of Crete. Three times it is applied to God (1:3; 2:10; 3:4), and three times it is applied to Jesus (1:4; 2:13; 3:6). The equality of essence as God and yet their distinction in person is plainly and clearly revealed.

Because we are family, we are loved by our Father and our Savior. Flowing from that love are the three Christian blessings of grace, mercy, and peace. "Grace" is unmerited favor; it is what gets us into the family. "Mercy" is unlimited compassion; we could say it is what keeps us in the family. "Peace" is unsurpassing wholeness; it is what we enjoy once we're in the family. All of this and more is ours because we share a common faith and we are a part of God's family.

Conclusion

Grace inspires godliness. Salvation inspires service. Those who understand that God's love for them and His desire for their salvation originates in eternity past and continues through eternity future will be compelled to love Him and serve Him. They will do so not out of obligation but out of gratitude, "gospel gratitude." A man who is captured by the love of his wife will return that love not because he has to but because he wants to. A person captured by the love of Jesus will love Him in return, not because he has to but because he wants to. He saved you that you might serve Him. He saved you that you might enjoy Him.

Reflect and Discuss

1. What is your purpose in life? What is God's grand purpose for His church? How does your purpose contribute to God's purpose?
2. What is the relationship between servanthood and apostleship? Is it possible to be called and sent out without being a slave of God in Christ? Why? How is this, in turn, related to sanctification?
3. How does theology sometimes interfere with missions? Should it? How should theology sometimes empower and propel missions?

4. Does the balance of ministry in your church favor seeking the salvation of the lost or growth in godliness of believers? Is this the way it should be?

5. What passages of the Bible provide you the most assurance for "the hope of eternal life"?

6. Do some Christians have a greater gift for communicating the gospel? Do some have a greater or lesser responsibility to do so? How can those with less of a gift fulfill their obligation?

7. Do you know of anyone who has a special ability to go into difficult situations in church communities and make things right? What gifts are employed in those situations?

8. In two or three sentences, what is the "common faith" shared by Paul, Titus, and us?

9. What is your favorite analogy for the people of God—His temple, His body, His bride, or His family? Why?

Qualifications of a Godly Leader

TITUS 1:5-9

Main Idea: Qualified leaders of the church must be men who exemplify godliness in every area of their lives—their commitments, conduct, character, and convictions.

I. **He Must Be a Man with Godly Commitments (1:5-6).**
   A. Be faithful to the church (1:5).
   B. Be faithful to others (1:6).
   C. Be faithful to your wife (1:6).
   D. Be faithful to your children (1:6).
II. **He Must Be a Man of Godly Conduct (1:7).**
   A. Understand the need of a good reputation.
   B. Understand the nature of your calling.
   C. Understand the necessity of a balanced life.
III. **He Must Be a Man of Godly Character (1:8).**
   A. Pursue the right priorities.
   B. Possess the right perspective.
   C. Produce the right pattern.
   D. Promote the right passion.
IV. **He Must Be a Man with Godly Convictions (1:9).**
   A. Be devoted to the truth.
   B. Be diligent to teach.

Leadership is crucial to the success of any organization. The church is no exception. Everything rises or falls on leadership, and no corporation, no organization, no body of believers in the Lord Jesus Christ will rise above its leadership.

Leadership is influence. If no one is following you, then you are not leading. Today, as always, there is a tremendous need for good, godly leadership in the church. We need men who, by their integrity of life, maturity in Christ, competency in theology, and authenticity in ministry, gain the allegiance of a congregation that knows the love and soul of their shepherd. They trust him (a trust that must be earned not demanded) to provide and protect, feed and lead, teach and tend to their spiritual needs.

As we plant churches across North America and around the world and as we seek to revive dying churches and reenergize plateaued ones, the great need of the hour is biblical, godly shepherds who find their job description laid out in Scripture and not some marketing guide or CEO manual. Contrary to what some leadership experts say, we are shepherds; we are not ranchers, managers, or corporate heads out to raise money, build buildings, draw crowds, and measure up to the world's criteria for success.

God believes leadership of the local church is so important that He addresses the issue in detail four times in the New Testament: Acts 20:28-38; 1 Timothy 3:1-7; Titus 1:5-9; and 1 Peter 5:1-4. Emphasis in each list falls on a leader's personal character and theological competency. God is primarily interested in *who you are* and then *what you do*. He well understands that the latter will flow from the former. Ultimately, pastors are to be examples to the church of how the gospel produces godliness. What, then, is God looking for in those who will lead His people here on earth? In his letter to Titus, Paul addressed four essential characteristics.

He Must Be a Man with Godly Commitments
TITUS 1:5-6

Apparently Paul had ministered briefly on the island of Crete. On his trip to Rome to appear before Caesar, he made a brief stop that is recorded in Acts 27:7-21, but his words here indicate a time of ministry not noted elsewhere in Scripture.

The details regarding when and by whom Crete was evangelized are not clear. However, we do know, according to Acts 2:11, that Cretans were present in Jerusalem on Pentecost. Perhaps some were converted and returned home to spread the good news about Jesus. The work, however, proceeded slowly on this 146-mile-long island in the Mediterranean.

Being situated in the location known as the mythical birthplace of Zeus; famous for the legendary Minotaur, a half-bull and half-human monster; and deeply immersed in worship of the emperor as universal savior, these fledgling congregations needed serious attention, and they needed it quickly. Titus was the man for the job and, from his job description and from God's expectations for His leaders, we learn what a man with godly commitments looks like.

Be Faithful to the Church (Titus 1:5)

Paul gives two reasons why he left Titus in Crete. First, "to set right what was left undone," that is to set in order or straighten out the situation, like an orthodontist straightens crooked teeth. Second, Titus was left in Crete "to appoint elders in every town" as he had been commanded or "directed." Faithfulness to the church means being the right man for the job and knowing what the job is: Fix and repair what is broken. Put men who measure up to God's standard and expectations in positions of leadership. The health of the church demands qualified leadership.

There are two and only two offices in the church: elders and deacons. Elder, overseer, and pastor are used interchangeably in Scripture to refer to the same office. The term *elder* is the more common and almost always appears in the plural in the New Testament when addressing the leaders of the church. However, no specific number is ever dictated, and the emphasis in Scripture always falls on their character, not on a specific number. Concerning the latter I believe Scripture, by its silence, grants a degree of flexibility within a congregational form of government.

Being faithful to the church means we will mend what is broken, straighten what is crooked, and start at the top by making sure good, godly leaders are put in place to lead "God's flock" (1 Pet 5:2).

Be Faithful to Others (Titus 1:6)

The first and overarching qualification given is that an overseer must be "one who is blameless," which means above reproach. It speaks of one who is not liable to accusation or question as to his personal character and integrity. From this hallmark flows all other character qualities. It is so important that Paul repeats it in verse 7. This is a life worth copying, an example worth following. It is a model and a pattern of a man of God no one can accuse, charge, or question with any degree of credibility.

Be Faithful to Your Wife (Titus 1:6)

The next characteristic given is "the husband of one wife," which literally translates "a one-woman man." That an elder is not a polygamist is a given. Most likely Paul is not disqualifying the widower or those never married. What of the divorced? Here the issue becomes somewhat murky.

Personally I do not disconnect "blameless" and "one-woman man." Hence any man guilty of adultery is disqualified for life from leadership. My understanding of this verse is that any divorcee should not pastor. However, I exercise Christian grace and give room for Christian conscience at this point.

Bottom line: this is a man who is in love with, committed to, and devoted to only one woman, and that woman is his wife. John McArthur says, "An elder must have an unsullied, lifelong reputation for devotion to his spouse and to sexual purity" (MacArthur, *Titus*, 28). A lustful man who flirts with women other than his wife also would disqualify himself for leadership in God's church. Addiction to pornography tragically would disqualify him as well.

Be Faithful to Your Children (Titus 1:6)

Closely associated with being faithful to your wife is being faithful to your children. The qualification of "having faithful children" addresses the importance of family leadership. Indeed the family is the proving ground for leadership in the church. First Timothy 3:5 states this clearly: "If anyone does not know how to manage his own household, how will he take care of God's church?"

Now, there is a debate surrounding this qualification. Must a leader have (1) faithful, well-behaved, obedient children or (2) children who are believers? That they are the former is without question. That they are the latter is the expectation. Chapell says this applies to children while they are in the home and, "We are not necessarily looking at the beliefs and actions of one child but at the character of the family as a whole . . . , our assessment is to be based on observations of children's conduct and convictions made over time, not on isolated statements or actions" (Hughes and Chapell, *1 and 2 Timothy and Titus*, 297).

While under our watch care, however long that is, our children cannot be characterized by "wildness or rebellion." A godly leader, a godly dad, will do whatever is necessary in terms of time and attention to nurture his children in the training and instruction of the Lord (Deut 6:4-9; Eph 6:4).

He Must Be a Man of Godly Conduct
TITUS 1:7

Pastors are to be overseers of the local church. We are "God's managers," whose function is to give direction and oversight over the church of God. It is easy to see that the term "overseer" is interchangeable with "elder" (v. 5). As overseers, what is the essence of the godly conduct we must exhibit?

Understand the Need of a Good Reputation

The characteristic of being "blameless" or above reproach is repeated for emphasis and because it is foundational. Note the wording: "An overseer . . . *must* be blameless" (emphasis added). It is essential not optional. It relates to our life inside and outside the church, in our communities and neighborhoods, at restaurants and the dry cleaners, where we shop and buy gas. The specifics of what a blameless life looks like are spelled out in the following verses.

Understand the Nature of Your Calling

We are given a description of our calling as "God's administrator" or a steward of God. It refers to a household manager responsible to and accountable to God. Ultimately we please Him, serve Him, and obey Him. Any man who does not understand this station in the ministry is not fit to minister. When things get tough, he will quit; when times are hard, he will break and run. No, God's administrator gets his marching orders from King Jesus, and he looks to Him for approval and applause!

Understand the Necessity of a Balanced Life

In rapid-fire succession Paul then lists 11 character qualities of the man of God growing out of his blameless life as a God-called steward. The first five listed in verse 7 are negative. The following six in verse 8 are positive.

He must not be "arrogant" or self-centered and self-interested. This describes someone who is a proud self-pleaser with no regard for God's will or the needs of others.

He must not be "hot-tempered." This describes someone who is easily provoked, one with a short fuse, prone to fits of rage and anger. The opposite of an angry and quarrelling spirit is a gentle spirit that reflects "the gentleness and graciousness of Christ" (2 Cor 10:1).

Also, he must not be "addicted to wine" or a "drunkard." This refers to someone who is given to drink causing him to lose his mental sharpness and sound judgment. Addressing the enormous danger and damage of the consumption of alcohol in our day, MacArthur writes,

> Most elders in modern cultures have no justifiable reason for drinking any alcoholic beverages and putting themselves in the way of temptation. They also have a responsibility, even more than other believers, to avoid exercising a Christian liberty that might "somehow become a stumbling block to the weak" and cause a fellow believer to be "ruined, the brother for whose sake Christ died" (1 Cor 8:9, 11). (MacArthur, *Titus*, 37)

Closely associated with the previous characteristics, he must not be "a bully." An elder cannot be a fist fighter, given to acts of violence, a brawler, verbally or physically abusive, or hurtful. As overseers we are to build up the church not beat it down.

The last negative characteristic is "not greedy for money." The overseer must not use the ministry as a money-making business. Money is not our motive. As 1 Peter 5:2 says, we minister "not for the money but eagerly." In 1 Timothy 6:10, Paul also warns, "For the love of money is a root of all kinds of evil, and by craving it, some have wandered away from the faith and pierced themselves with many pains."

He Must Be a Man of Godly Character
TITUS 1:8

Paul then notes six positive and desirable character qualities that describe the man of God and that counterbalance the five negatives in the previous verse. These six characteristics fill out what it means to be "blameless."

Pursue the Right Priorities

The first two positive character qualities are "hospitable" and "loving what is good." "Hospitable" means a "lover of strangers." We are ones who open our hearts and homes to others. In the first-century world, hospitality "was a very practical expression of love, not a source of entertainment" (Towner, *1–2 Timothy and Titus*, 227). We help those in need, whether friend or stranger, believer or unbeliever. Race, social status, even lifestyle does not prevent us from loving and helping others. Here the beauty and credibility of the gospel are put on display for all to see.

The phrase "loving what is good" describes a virtue lover, one who has a passion for that which is good—good as defined and described by God (cf. Phil 4:8). That which by its nature is good and that which is good for others shape our priorities and our lives.

Possess the Right Perspective

Having a right perspective is characterized as being "sensible." He must be self-controlled, sober minded, under mental and emotional control. This is a man who has an accurate and balanced view of life. Both in his judgments and in his actions, he acts with wisdom and common sense. He sees life from God's perspective and acts accordingly. He is focused with the right priorities in view. This virtue is so crucial to the health of the church that Paul mentioned it five times in the first two chapters (1:7; 2:2, 5, 6, 12). Titus 2:11-12 is a good reminder that this kind of character is cultivated by God's grace, for it is the grace of God that instructs or trains us "to live in a sensible, righteous, and godly way in the present age."

Produce the Right Pattern

Flowing from the right priorities and a right perspective is a pattern of life characterized as "righteous" and "holy." An elder must be someone a church can follow in the way he treats others and in the way he lives before others. To be "righteous" means being just, fair, equitable, and honest in how you deal with others. Credibility in ministry can stand or fall right here because the just man will reflect the character of God Himself! The word "holy" is not the usual word for holiness, though it has the same basic meaning. It carries the idea of pure and unpolluted. This is the man committed to godliness and Christlikeness. He pursues a life untainted by moral pollution or stain. His life is a reflection of the Christ who has redeemed him and lives within him.

Promote the Right Passion

Finally, an overseer must be "self-controlled." This means having control over oneself and being in control of one's strength. We should have complete self-mastery over our passions and impulses, bringing the will under the control of a God we love and trust. Peterson says it is the man who has "a good grip on himself" (1:8 *The Message*). We monitor ourselves day in and day out, submitting our lives to the x-ray vision and CAT-scan detail of God's perfect Word. We are like the man who looks daily into the reflecting mirror of Scripture but does not forget "what kind of man he was" (Jas 1:24). This kind of self-control is only possible for the person who is mastered by the Word of God and led by the Spirit of God.

He Must Be a Man with Godly Convictions
TITUS 1:9

Paul then moves from the elder's personal qualifications to his ministerial and doctrinal qualifications. False teaching will inevitably lead to false living. Wrong belief will inevitably lead to a wrong life. Paul believed we must have definite convictions both about truth and about the teaching of that truth. Again, there is no room, not one inch, for compromise.

Be Devoted to the Truth

This conviction is described as "holding to the faithful message as taught." It is possible to have the faithful (true, genuine) message but lose it or hold it haphazardly. It is possible to hold fast to what is *not* the true and faithful message because we leave what we were taught for something we think is better. Being devoted to the truth, "holding fast the faithful word" (NASB), means respecting the Bible as the inspired and inerrant Word of God. It means affirming the Bible's priority, authority, and sufficiency for what we believe and how we will live. It means the minister of God places himself gladly and willingly, and in full submission, under the Word. He is a Word man, a Word minister, a Word-constrained and captivated slave. He will preach this Word and only this Word. He would never think of standing before a congregation and doing anything less than proclaiming the Word of God. He will honor *what* God has said, and he will honor *how* God has said it. Bottom line: he will be an expositor of Holy Scripture.

Be Diligent to Teach

The aim of a pastor holding fast to the Word of God is "so that he will be able both to encourage with sound teaching and to refute those who contradict it." Sound teaching may be the heart of Titus. The phrase occurs four times in the New Testament, *all* in the pastorals, with two of those in Titus. Literally it is "healthy teaching." Again, if there is healthy teaching, then there can be sick, weak, even deadly teaching. With sound doctrine, healthy teaching, we "exhort" and "encourage." Faced with false, weak, sickly teaching that "contradicts" by compromise, opposition, or neglect, we "refute" with sound doctrine.

The faithful elder is both a teacher and a defender, a preacher and a physician. Constantly and consistently he takes up the task to comfort and confront, admonish and attack. To confront and expose false teaching will not make us popular. To expose the false teachings, half gospels, and deceptive messages of a "prosperity theology," "open theism," or old-fashioned liberalism now dressed up as a new or generous orthodoxy will not win us the applause of men. Lest we think this too harsh, we must recall what Paul says in Romans 16:17, "Watch out for those who cause dissensions and obstacles contrary to the doctrine you have learned. Avoid them."

No, ours is a biblically balanced and theologically balanced agenda. **We encourage**. These are our positive theological affirmations. **We refute**. These are our negative but necessary, apologetical, and polemical refutations. We understand the danger of swallowing theological poison, especially when it is sugarcoated! Our godly convictions are not for sale. They are not candidates for compromise. However, to take on such an assignment, our lives and our message better match up. Colossians 1:28 is a great summary of this balanced approach: "We proclaim Him, warning and teaching everyone with all wisdom, so that we may present everyone mature in Christ."

Conclusion

In his classic *The Reformed Pastor*, Richard Baxter wisely warns, "Take heed to yourselves, lest your example contradict your doctrine, . . . lest you unsay with your lives what you say with your tongues; and be the greatest hinderers of the success of your own labors" (*Reformed Pastor*, 63, 67–68). The faithful pastor must have no part in such a contradiction. For the glory of God and the good of His people, his life will match his belief; what he believes will connect with how he lives. Then he will be a leader worth trusting. Then he will be a leader worth following.

Reflect and Discuss

1. How are church leaders like CEOs? Considering the nature of a church and God's definition of success, how are church leaders different from CEOs?

2. Which leaders in your church are comparable to biblical elders, and which to deacons? Should anything in your church structure be changed to make it more biblical?

3. Why is faithfulness in marriage so important for a church elder? What is the connection between sexual purity and suitability for leadership in secular organizations?

4. Do you know a man who seems to be leadership material, but his children are rebellious? How is he attempting to deal with them? Are the challenges he faces in his family different from what he would encounter in a church? How so?

5. What is the difference between being blameless and being perfect?

6. If an elder is ultimately accountable to God, how does he also serve people? How do people benefit if their elder is obedient to God? How is a leader's accountability to God evaluated and enforced?

7. Should an elder be permitted to drink wine with meals? Beer with friends? Why? Are elders held to a different standard than the rest of the church? Why?

8. What is the difference between viewing ministry as a profession and as a calling?

9. How are the good characteristics in Titus 1:8 related to having the "mind of Christ" (1 Cor 2:16)?

10. Do you know elders who love the Word but are not good at teaching it? Do you know any who are talented teachers but who do not know the Word well? Which is more beneficial? Which is more dangerous?

11. What might a church become if the elders fail to encourage? What if they fail to refute?

The Ministry of Confrontation

TITUS 1:10-16

Main Idea: For the church to be sound in the faith, its leaders must confront false teaching and false teachers.

I. **We Must Confront Those Who Are Divisive (1:10-11).**
    A. They are destitute in how they talk (1:10).
    B. They are dangerous in what they think (1:10-11).
    C. They are dishonest in why they teach (1:11).
II. **We Must Confront Those Who Are Deceived (1:12-14).**
    A. Who they are is clear (1:12-13).
    B. What they believe must be confronted (1:13-14).
III. **We Must Confront Those Who Are Defiled (1:15-16).**
    A. They lack purity (the inside) (1:15).
    B. They lie in their profession (the outside) (1:16).

Do you think of yourself as a spiritual "she bear" who is called by God to protect her cubs, a "spiritual physician" who must diagnose doctrinal cancer and remove it from the body to ensure its health and life, a "spiritual detective" who through careful investigation must detect spiritual evidence of a spiritual crime already in progress?

The Bible is filled with concern about false teaching and its danger to the people of God. Limiting our survey to the New Testament, we find strong words and warnings from Jesus, Paul, Peter, John, and Jude.

Jesus

Beware of false prophets who come to you in sheep's clothing but inwardly are ravaging wolves. (Matt 7:15)

For false messiahs and false prophets will rise up and will perform signs and wonders to lead astray, if possible, the elect. And you must watch! I have told you everything in advance. (Mark 13:22-23)

Paul

I know that after my departure savage wolves will come in among you, not sparing the flock. And men will rise up from your own number with deviant doctrines to lure the disciples into following them. (Acts 20:29-30)

For I am jealous over you with a godly jealousy, because I have promised you in marriage to one husband—to present a pure virgin to Christ. But I fear that, as the serpent deceived Eve by his cunning, your minds may be seduced from a complete and pure devotion to Christ. For if a person comes and preaches another Jesus, whom we did not preach, or you receive a different spirit, which you had not received, or a different gospel, which you had not accepted, you put up with it splendidly! (2 Cor 11:2-4)

Now the Spirit explicitly says that in later times some will depart from the faith, paying attention to deceitful spirits and the teachings of demons, through the hypocrisy of liars whose consciences are seared. They forbid marriage and demand abstinence from foods that God created to be received with gratitude by those who believe and know the truth. (1 Tim 4:1-3)

But know this: Difficult times will come in the last days. For people will be lovers of self, lovers of money, boastful, proud, blasphemers, disobedient to parents, ungrateful, unholy, unloving, irreconcilable, slanderers, without self-control, brutal, without love for what is good, traitors, reckless, conceited, lovers of pleasure rather than lovers of God, holding to the form of godliness but denying its power. Avoid these people!

For among them are those who worm their way into households and capture idle women burdened down with sins, led along by a variety of passions, always learning and never able to come to a knowledge of the truth. Just as Jannes and Jambres resisted Moses, so these also resist the truth, men who are corrupt in mind, worthless in regard to the faith. But they will not make further progress, for their lack of understanding will be clear to all, as theirs was also. (2 Tim 3:1-9)

Peter

*But there were also false prophets among the people, just as there will
be false teachers among you. They will secretly bring in destructive
heresies, even denying the Master who bought them, and will bring swift
destruction on themselves. Many will follow their unrestrained ways,
and the way of truth will be blasphemed because of them. They will
exploit you in their greed with deceptive words. Their condemnation,
pronounced long ago, is not idle, and their destruction does not sleep.*
(2 Pet 2:1-3)

John

*Children, it is the last hour. And as you have heard, "Antichrist is
coming," even now many antichrists have come. We know from this
that it is the last hour. They went out from us, but they did not belong
to us; for if they had belonged to us, they would have remained with
us. However, they went out so that it might be made clear that none of
them belongs to us.*

*But you have an anointing from the Holy One, and all of you
have knowledge. I have not written to you because you don't know
the truth, but because you do know it, and because no lie comes from
the truth. Who is the liar, if not the one who denies that Jesus is the
Messiah? This one is the antichrist: the one who denies the Father
and the Son. No one who denies the Son can have the Father; he who
confesses the Son has the Father as well.* (1 John 2:18-23)

*Dear friends, do not believe every spirit, but test the spirits to determine
if they are from God, because many false prophets have gone out into
the world.*

*This is how you know the Spirit of God: Every spirit who confesses
that Jesus Christ has come in the flesh is from God. But every spirit
who does not confess Jesus is not from God. This is the spirit of the
antichrist; you have heard that he is coming, and he is already in the
world now.* (1 John 4:1-3)

*Many deceivers have gone out into the world; they do not confess
the coming of Jesus Christ in the flesh. This is the deceiver and the
antichrist.* (2 John 7)

Jude

> *Dear friends, although I was eager to write you about the salvation we share, I found it necessary to write and exhort you to contend for the faith that was delivered to the saints once for all. For some men, who were designated for this judgment long ago, have come in by stealth; they are ungodly, turning the grace of our God into promiscuity and denying Jesus Christ, our only Master and Lord.* (Jude 3-4)

> *But you, dear friends, remember what was predicted by the apostles of our Lord Jesus Christ; they told you, "In the end time there will be scoffers walking according to their own ungodly desires." These people create divisions and are unbelievers, not having the Spirit.* (Jude 17-19)

God has called us as ministers of the gospel of Jesus Christ to a ministry of reconciliation. He has also called us to a ministry of rebuke. He has called us to a ministry of comfort. He has also called us to a ministry of confrontation. Here in Titus 1:10-16 the focus is on rebuke and confrontation. In close connection to his discussion of the faithful minister who should be set free to serve our Savior (1:1-9), Paul now addresses those who need to be stopped in their tracks and whose mouths need to be muzzled. He describes them as **divisive, deceived**, and **defiled**, and he teaches that we cannot ignore them; we must confront them.

We Must Confront Those Who Are Divisive
TITUS 1:10-11

Titus 1:10-16 is intimately connected with verses 5-9, which is demonstrated by the word "for" that begins verse 10. We are to **exhort** ("encourage" HSCB) and **refute,** for there are many who "overthrow whole households" ("disrupting entire families," *Message*). Here we see the importance of appointing qualified pastors who are godly in character and sound in doctrine. These false teachers no doubt are personable and persuasive, attractive, and ambitious. What they teach has just enough truth to deceive the immature, and it comes with enough cleverness to fool the gullible. However, if we conduct a closer and more careful analysis, we find just beneath the surface the malignant disease of their deadly doctrine. What does a true and genuine inspection reveal?

They Are Destitute in How They Talk (Titus 1:10)

There were "many," not a few, false teachers at Crete, who had apparently risen to some degree of prominence in the churches. Notice how they are described. They are "rebellious people, full of empty talk and deception, especially those from Judaism" (v. 10). "Rebellious" speaks of their **attitude**. "Empty talk" addresses their **actions**. These men were a law unto themselves, claiming a direct pipeline to God. They are not and would not be held accountable to anyone, a tell-tale sign of all false teachers. This rebellious, egocentric spirit produces what Paul calls **empty talk** or useless words. They are "cotton candy preachers"—a lot of show but no substance.

They Are Dangerous in What They Think (Titus 1:10-11)

One of the most dangerous characteristics of false teachers is that they are deceivers of themselves and especially of others. They are spiritual seducers, disguising their personal ambition and theological agenda in the trappings of religious piety and prosperity.

In the situation at Crete, the peddlers of "theological pornography" were Judaizers who offered a *Jesus plus* theology, which is always a *minus Jesus* theology. Add to Christ and you subtract Christ. This is the spiritual mathematics of these masters of deception. Corrupted in their own thinking, they corrupt the thinking of others and "overthrow whole households." Like a fast-spreading cancer they do not infect one but many. This is how effective they can be. Propagators of a "man-centered message" and a "what-I-can-do gospel," they deflect our focus from Christ and His adoration to ourselves and our accomplishments. The beauty and greatness of Jesus is at best ignored and at worst denied. This is why "it is necessary to silence them" (v. 11). They are ruining the unity of the church, its witness in the community, and ultimately the name of "our great God and Savior, Jesus Christ" (2:13).

They Are Dishonest in Why They Teach (Titus 1:11)

Paul pulled no punches as he went on the offensive in the ministry of confrontation. These men must be muzzled, stopped, shut up. Confront them with the truth of the gospel. That is our primary weapon. Confront them with the real results of their activity: they ruin whole households. Confront them with their motive for ministry: dishonest gain. These types of persons are nothing less than ministerial mercenaries! They are hired guns, ministers motivated by money. False teachers love money, crave money, and talk about money. As 1 Timothy 6:4-5 says, they "imagine that godliness is a way to material gain." This is the theology of a prosperity pastor in Atlanta, Georgia, who says that "you're a fool for Christ so you might as well be a rich fool."[21]

Of course we ourselves must be careful not to be seduced more subtly by this mind-set. We must ever be on guard against this "entitlement mentality" that expects, solicits, and even manipulates the favor of others. Unfortunately, this happens all too often. In the ministry of confrontation, we must confront the divisive, all the while examining our own hearts lest we develop these same false motives.

We Must Confront Those Who Are Deceived
TITUS 1:12-14

Paul's words are strong and to the point. They are also strategic and difficult to refute. The heart of confrontation is seen here: "Rebuke them sharply, that they may be sound in the faith" (v. 13). The spiritual danger is acute, and so he must be direct in his exposé of these religious charlatans, these spiritual imposters.

Who They Are Is Clear (Titus 1:12-13)

A careful study of any teacher will bring to light his true colors. We simply have to take the time, listen carefully, and weigh what we hear on the scales of God's perfect Word. This alone and this always must be our standard of measurement. Paul calls to the witness stand one of Crete's heroes from the past, one of their own prophets, the sixth-century poet, priest, and prophet Epimenides. His words were not soft or sugarcoated. They were cutting and condemning.

"Cretans are always liars, evil beasts, lazy gluttons." Eugene Peterson's paraphrase says they "are liars from the womb, barking dogs, lazy bellies." The inhabitants of Crete were so characterized by lying that "to Cretanize" meant to lie. In our modern context we might say "ministerially speaking!" You cannot believe or trust such teachers. They lie to themselves, and they will lie to you. As the text says, "Cretans are always liars." The phrase "evil beasts" refers to people who live on the sensual plane, controlled by their appetites and passions, their lust and desires. As evil beasts they tear apart

---

[21] Creflo Dollar, quoted in John Blake, "The Riches of God," *Atlanta Journal/ Constitution*, August 23, 1997.

and rip to shreds without thought, reason, or concern for the welfare of others. They are an idol to themselves. Cretans are also described as "lazy gluttons." They were self-indulgent, overfed, without self-discipline or control. They feed and feast at the expense of others.

To these words, coming from one of their own, Paul simply adds, "This testimony is true." In reading this, do not miss Paul's application—it was not to every Cretan but to these false prophets propagating spiritual perversion both in what they taught and in how they lived. To such false teachers we are called to respond.

What They Believe Must Be Confronted (Titus 1:13-14)

Paul's solution to this situation is to the point, but it was also pastoral. There is a wonderful balance in how we engage in the ministry of confrontation. We are to "rebuke them sharply." Addressing the church that had been lax and hesitant to deal with this crisis, Paul is firm in his instructions. As a surgeon cuts away diseased and infectious tissue that threatens the health of the body, we must cut away this toxic teaching.

What is our goal in performing this spiritual surgery? It is pastoral. It is redemptive. It is so that those who are self-deceived and deceiving others may be "sound in the faith." We cut to cure. We operate to liberate those trapped in the quicksand of spiritual bondage and malnutrition. We confront, but we confront in love. We love them enough to point out their error and with the hope of their recovery to spiritual health and vitality.

Paul readily saw the gangrene of "Jewish myths" (fables) and "commands of men" (man-made rules) that turn from the truth. Religious speculations that go either *beyond* or *against* Scripture and rules and regulations that add works to grace are man centered rather than Christ centered, are humanistic rather than Christocentric. Paul says we must confront and denounce them for the lies they are.

Those who taught these Jewish myths and man-made rules were appropriately described as those "who reject the truth." Rather than holding firm "the faithful message as taught" (v. 9), they turn away from the truth. Once they knew it, but now they deny it. Once they lived it, now they leave it. This only makes them all the more dangerous.

We Must Confront Those Who Are Defiled
TITUS 1:15-16

Again we are reminded: belief and behavior go together. **Sound doctrine** and **good works** are twin companions. False teaching contaminates. It defiles whatever it touches. Just as a single drop of ink can defile and render undrinkable a pure glass of water, false teaching, even a drop, can pervert and destroy the pure gospel of grace and mercy of Jesus Christ. Why must we confront the defiled?

They Lack Purity (Titus 1:15)

"To the pure, everything is pure" is something of a proverb, a pithy saying, a maxim. It is a test of moral character and echoes the words of Jesus in Mark 7:15-23:

> *Nothing that goes into a person from outside can defile him, but the things that come out of a person are what defile him. . . . Don't you realize that nothing going into a man from the outside can defile him? For it doesn't go into his heart but into the stomach and is eliminated. . . . What comes out of a person—that defiles him. For from within, out of people's hearts, come evil thoughts, sexual immoralities, thefts, murders, adulteries, greed, evil actions, deceit, promiscuity, stinginess, blasphemy, pride, and foolishness. All these evil things come from within and defile a person.*

Philip Towner rightly concludes, "Purity that counts comes only through faith in Christ" (*1–2 Timothy and Titus*, 232).

In contrast to the pure, "to those who are defiled and unbelieving nothing is pure; in fact, both their mind [how they think] and conscience [their moral judgment] are defiled" (v. 15). Their whole inner self is corrupted. It is no wonder they "reject the truth." Intellectually and morally they are defiled; every aspect of who they are is infected with the disease of sin. Here is a concise description of what we called the doctrine of **total depravity**.

John MacArthur notes, "When a person is pure in heart and mind, his perspectives on all things are pure, and that inner purity produces outer purity" (*Titus*, 65). Tragically, the opposite is also true. When a person is corrupt and impure in heart and mind, his perspectives on all things are corrupt and impure, and that inner impurity produces outer impurity.

They Lie in Their Profession (Titus 1:16)

The mind and the conscience are connected to a vital organ in the body: the tongue. How we think will give way to how we speak. Lie to ourselves, and we will lie to others. Lie to ourselves, and we will lie about God.

These false prophets profess to know God, but with their works they deny Him. Trusting in their own works, their own wisdom, their own righteousness, they by their lives deny the God they profess to know. By their man-centered, humanistic message that focuses on what they can do, they make an idol of themselves. In the process they deny the truth of Scripture, question the sinfulness and inability of man to save himself, cheapen the cross, slight the Holy Spirit, and construct their own false system of salvation.

Bringing to light and exposing the real underlying belief system of such persons, Paul concluded with a ringing trio of condemnation and judgment. They were "detestable," a term that reflects God's attitude toward idolatry. They were "disobedient," rebellious, insubordinate—their way and agenda took precedence over God's. They were "disqualified," unfit, worthless, rejected for any good work. They were fakes, counterfeits, not the real and genuine article after all. Put to the test, they failed.

Conclusion

Charles Spurgeon gives a fitting conclusion to the ultimate aim of the ministry of confrontation. He writes,

> [P]rovided we are obliged to come to the conclusion that our minds are not pure, we need not end there, for there are means by which they may be made so! Glory be to God, if my mind and conscience are defiled, they need not always be so. There is cleansing. I cannot effect it for myself, nor can any outward forms do it. . . . But God has set forth Christ to be a Savior—and He shall save His people from their sins—from their sinfulness, too, and whoever believes in Christ Jesus, that is, trusts in Him, there is already in him the beginning of purity! God the Holy Spirit will give him more and more

of the likeness of Christ, for he that believes shall be saved from sin, from indwelling sin, from all sin, from the power as well as from the guilt of it! Faith will cleanse him, applying to him the precious blood and the water which flows from the side of Christ! Faith will, by the Holy Spirit's power, become a cleansing as well as a saving Grace! God grant it to us, and may we all be among the pure, unto whom all things shall be pure. ("A Searching Test," in *Metropolitan Tabernacle*, 62:351–52)

The ministry of confrontation is not easy, but it is essential. When the integrity of the gospel is at stake, we cannot run and hide. We must stand and fight. Armed with truth, motivated by love, and clothed with a pure life, we can engage the enemy and rescue the captive, observing both the exhortation and the warning in Jude: "Save others by snatching them from the fire; have mercy on others but with fear, hating even the garment defiled by the flesh" (Jude 23). Truth matters. Truth is important. Jesus said, "You will know the truth, and the truth will set you free" (John 8:32).

Reflect and Discuss

1. Do you have the ministry of confrontation? How do you use it? Do you enjoy it? How could this ministry be misused or abused?

2. What is the connection between confrontation and reconciliation? Have you known a person who could do both? What kinds of words, actions, steps, and measures are used in each case?

3. Have you heard a preacher on radio, TV, or the Internet who was rebellious or deceptive? What did this preacher say or do that showed he was a fraud?

4. Why is adding anything to the gospel of Jesus Christ in effect actually removing Christ from the gospel?

5. How might confronting a heretical elder disturb or upset a church? What can be done to help a church recover from such conflict?

6. What is purity? What does a pure person (v. 15) look like? How can a person achieve purity?

7. What is the relationship between Paul's call to confront false teachers (v. 13) and Jesus' command not to judge (Matt 7:1)?

Pursuing Godliness:
The Roles of Men and Women in the Church

TITUS 2:1-8

Main Idea: The gospel calls those within the church to pursue God's assignment of godliness, whether young or old, male or female.

I. **Pursue God's Assignment as an Older Man (2:1-2).**
   - A. Be a teacher (2:1).
   - B. Be levelheaded (2:2).
   - C. Be reverent (2:2).
   - D. Be self-controlled (2:2).
   - E. Be sound in the faith (2:20).
   - F. Be loving (2:2).
   - G. Be patient (2:2).

II. **Pursue God's Assignment as an Older Woman (2:3).**
   - A. Be reverent.
   - B. Be truthful.
   - C. Be levelheaded.
   - D. Be a teacher.

III. **Pursue God's Assignment as a Younger Woman (2:4-5).**
   - A. Love your husband (2:4).
   - B. Love your children (2:4).
   - C. Be self-controlled (2:5).
   - D. Be pure (2:5).
   - E. Be a homemaker (2:5).
   - F. Be good (2:5).
   - G. Be subject to your husband (2:5).

IV. **Pursue God's Assignment as a Younger Man (2:6-8).**
   - A. Be levelheaded (2:6).
   - B. Be a good example (2:7).
   - C. Be sound in doctrine (2:7).
   - D. Be sound in speech (2:8).

We live in a culture that is drowning in gender confusion. The lines have become blurred, and we are groping about trying to understand what it means for a man to be a man and a woman to be a woman, what it means for a man to be masculine and a woman to be feminine. A presidential candidate a few years back referred to himself as "metrosexual," a word that refers to a heterosexual male who is in touch with his feminine side. The candidate then went on to say, "I've heard the term, but I don't know what it means."[22] It is perfectly clear that the cultural engineers that dominate the media, our educational system—from the preschools to the university—and other strategic places of influence want to neutralize, if not eliminate, the gender distinctions and differences God has hardwired into human beings (Gen 1:26-27). This is the consistent drumbeat heard again and again, and unfortunately the church has not been immune to the cadence.

Practicing homosexuals are now ordained as bishops. Divorced ministers continue in places of service as if nothing significant occurred when their marriage covenant was broken. Women (married, divorced, single, heterosexual, and lesbian) now flock to seminaries and fill pulpits across the land declaring their liberation from the oppressive writings of the Bible. Even within evangelical fellowships women aspire to teaching positions that place them over men in Sunday schools, Bible studies, and local church worship services. The church is being shaped by secular culture more than by sacred Scripture. Never has the church needed more desperately to hear the words of Titus 2:1-8. This is a text that makes God's plan, God's assignments, God's roles for men and women in the church plain and clear. In this passage of Scripture, Paul outlined God's expectations for each of the four major groups in the church in terms of **gender** and **age**. He defined godly living that is "consistent with sound doctrine." Though the word itself does not appear, the driving concept in these verses can be summed up in one important word: **discipleship**. Older men need to disciple younger men, and older women need to disciple younger women. The gospel is to produce godliness in the lives of those within the church, whether old or young, male or female.[23]

---

[22] *Newsweek*, November 19, 2003, 23.

[23] In that context, and for teaching purposes, verses 1-8 can be viewed as something of a semantic chiasm, an A-B-B´-A´ structure (older *men*—older *women*—younger *women*—younger *men*).

Pursue God's Assignment as an Older Man
TITUS 2:1-2

Paul begins this section of Scripture by considering Titus in particular and older men in general and contrasting them with the false teachers who were harassing the church at Crete (1:10-15). These troublemakers were insubordinate, mouthy, and deceptive. They were liars, lazy, and motivated by money. They listened to the words of men, of popular culture, more than to the Word of God. They were infected with a defiled mind and a contaminated conscience, professing to know God but by their actions denying Him. They were "detestable, disobedient, and disqualified for any good work." Paul challenges Titus (v. 1) and the older, mature men (v. 2) to pursue a different path, a path that was "consistent with sound teaching." This is the path of gospel living that pleases God and provides a pattern for others to follow. He quickly defines seven essential characteristics of godliness for older men.

Be a Teacher (Titus 2:1)

Godly men are called by God to teach, recognizing that their teaching can take different and varied forms. "But you" is emphatic in the original language, denoting the sharp contrast between the false teachers and Titus. Titus was charged to "say the things that are consistent with sound teaching." The verb "say" is a present imperative (cf. 2:15), a word of command, here encouraging Titus to teach or instruct. Pastors are to teach things that are proper, in accord, fitting with sound doctrine. We must be true to the gospel of Jesus Christ and true to the Word of God both in belief and in behavior. The following verses provide the foundation that will ensure that we do not fail in this crucial task.

Be Levelheaded (Titus 2:2)

The more mature men in the church are admonished to be self-controlled, sober, temperate, or "level headed" (cf. 1 Tim 3:2, 11). This man is wise in his decision-making and careful when making judgments. He is clear on what really matters and decisive in making godly choices. He rightly uses his God-given talents and gifts, his time, his money, and his energy. He is a man with right and godly priorities, and he has as his motto for life one simple dictum: "All that matters in life is pleasing God."

Be Reverent (Titus 2:2)

Second, he is to be "worthy of respect." This man goes after that which is noble and morally valuable and worthy. It is a character trait that God expects of the deacon (1 Tim 3:8) and his wife (1 Tim 3:11).[24] This is the man who, while not being a prude or a Pharisee, takes no delight in inappropriate, off-color humor, vulgarity, or anything else that is suspect, questionable, or clearly out of bounds. He himself is worthy of honor and respect, particularly by younger men, because of the purity and integrity of his life.

Be Self-Controlled (Titus 2:2)

This is probably the key idea of this passage. Some form of the word appears to each of the four key groups of the church Paul addressed, though this is not readily apparent in our English translations (see vv. 2, 4-6): in verse 2 the older men are called to be "sensible"; in verse 4 the older women are called to "encourage" (or train) the younger women; in verse 5 the younger women are called to be "self-controlled," and in verse 6 the younger men are also called to be "self-controlled." This person has his passions under control and is self-disciplined. He is not careless or foolish with his words or in his behavior. John MacArthur summarizes well this quality of life, saying that such men "should have the discernment, discretion, and judgment that comes from walking with God for many years. They control their physical passions and they reject worldly standards and resist worldly attractions" (*Titus*, 74). They refuse to be conformed to this world but are transformed daily by a renewed mind bathed in Scripture (Rom 12:2).

Be Sound in the Faith (Titus 2:2)

Paul, in the last three terms in this verse, brings to our consideration the Christian triad of "faith, love, and endurance" (the natural outgrowth of hope). Mature godly men are to be sound or healthy in their confidence and trust in the Lord. This kind of personal faith is rooted in a daily walk with God as Father and an immersion of one's life in the Scriptures. This man not only knows *what* he believes and *why* he believes it; he

---

[24] First Timothy 3:11 may refer to a deaconess or a female assistant to a deacon. Such an assistant would naturally be his wife.

knows in *whom* he believes. This is the man who says of his God, "Even when I cannot trace His hand, I can always trust His heart."[25]

Be Loving (Titus 2:2)

Jesus said in John 13:35 to His disciples on the night He was betrayed, "By this all people will know that you are My disciples, if you have love for one another." Love is mentioned in a general sense here. We are to love God supremely, fellow believers genuinely, and lost humanity fervently. This kind of love, beautifully portrayed in 1 Corinthians 13:4-8, is to be the standard we strive to obtain day in and day out.

Be Patient (Titus 2:2)

The Christian, of all people, because of the hope that is within him, should be patient and steadfast; he should exhibit "endurance." Because we know how it will all come out in the end, we can endure testing, work through hardship, accept disappointment, and not give up under pressure and adversity. The mature, godly man does not lose heart, throw in the towel, or drop out of the race. Rather, he runs the race with endurance, fixing his eyes on Jesus, the author and finisher of faith (Heb 12:1-2).

My granddaddy Gallaway was a Titus 2:1-2 kind of man. A Georgia dirt farmer raised by a harsh stepmother, he had only a fifth-grade education. Even so, he was without question one of the godliest men I have ever known. Not well educated, afflicted with severe arthritis in his legs, and done wrong on more than one occasion because of his trusting nature, he never lost faith in his Lord, and he never questioned the plans and workings of God in his life. He lived simply on a day-by-day basis trusting in the Lord. He set an example any mother or father could have pointed to and said to their son, "I hope you grow up someday to be like Charley Gallaway in the way you love and serve the Lord." This is God's assignment for older men.

---

[25] This sentiment comes from a sermon by John MacDuff, "The Promised Land," 1859, and received popular attention in the song "Trust His Heart" on the album *Timeless* by Babbie Mason, 2005.

Pursue God's Assignment as an Older Woman
TITUS 2:3

Older women are now likewise charged with pursuing God's assignment of godliness in their personal lives as well as in their discipleship or mentoring of younger women. Again, much wisdom is presented for our careful consideration.

Several years ago Elisabeth Elliot wrote an article entitled "Where Are the WOTTs?" (*Pulpit Helps,* May 1997). She was moved to write the article after speaking to a group of pastors' wives and discovering that 80 percent of them were working outside the home. The question Elisabeth asked is simple and to the point: "Where are the godly older women who are to teach young mothers how to manage their children and homes? Where are the WOTTs, the Women of Titus Two?" Well, those women are described here in verse 3, and Paul provided them with a fourfold job description in terms of their own character that gave them the basis for their assignment of mentoring or discipling younger women as described in verses 4-5.

Be Reverent

"In the same way" connects verse 3 to verse 2. These "older women" have a task parallel to that of the older men. The first character trait they should pursue is reverence, a word that literally means "temple fitting" or appropriate behavior in a temple. The basic meaning is that this woman should live in such a way as is befitting a godly person. Her life and "behavior" are marked by holiness, reflecting the character of the Lord she loves and lives for.

Be Truthful

Godly women speak the truth; they are "not slanderers," making false and unfounded accusations. This Greek word is *diabolos,* the word from which we get our English word "devil." It is used to refer to our arch-enemy 34 times in the New Testament. A mature woman in Christ is not devilish in her speech, picking up gossip and spreading it abroad. This woman has a control, a governor, on her tongue. She knows that the saying "Sticks and stones may break my bones, but names (or words) will never hurt me" is not true. When she speaks, she speaks the truth, and she speaks it in love (Eph 4:15).

Be Levelheaded

This daughter of God is "not addicted to much wine," to much alcohol. The original language is strong, admonishing her not to become enslaved to too much wine so that it owns, dominates, and controls her. Mounce points out, "Alcoholism must have been a severe problem since it is an issue in the appointment of church leaders in every list (1 Tim 3:3, 8; Titus 1:7; cf. 1 Tim 5:23). While this is true in almost every culture (cf. 1 Cor 11:21) . . . it was especially true in Crete [where they viewed] heavy drinking as a virtue" (*Pastoral Epistles,* 410). It is of course certain and undebatable that if one never takes the first drink one will never have to worry about drunkenness or alcoholism and all the misery that follows in the footsteps of drink. Wisdom and witness would make this a wise course of action. Bottom line: a godly woman controls both her tongue and her appetite—of course, the same applies to godly men!

Be a Teacher

Like their godly counterpart, the older men, these mature disciples of Christ are to be adept at teaching. Indeed, "They are to teach what is good." This is a unique word in all of Greek literature and may have been coined by Paul himself. The focus, in light of what follows in verses 4-5, is the informal, one-on-one or small-group instruction that these mature women pass on to their younger spiritual sisters. Issues of marriage, family, and child rearing are set alongside basic matters of spiritual life in Christ. This mentoring of the younger by the more mature is a biblical pattern we have too often neglected to our great hurt and harm. Younger women desperately need the role modeling, teaching, discipling, insight, and practical wisdom that these older ladies can provide. Being more experienced in life and in the Lord, they can pass on a godly legacy that will hopefully reproduce itself for generations. A godly home will orbit around a godly wife and mother.

Pursue God's Assignment as a Younger Woman
TITUS 2:4-5

Cultural pressure and expectations have robbed many women of the blessings and joys of homemaking and motherhood. The Feminist Movement made promises on which it could not deliver. The fallout has been mammoth and disastrous, and we are still in the midst of the whirlwind. It is obvious from this text that a feminist agenda and the resulting confusion and rejection of God-ordained roles is not restricted to the late twentieth and early twenty-first centuries. The first century suffered from this malady as well, and so Paul confronted it head on. He laid down God's assignment for the older woman as it related to the younger: "Teach what is good." What good teaching did Paul have in mind? He answers that question in verses 4-5.

Love Your Husband (Titus 2:4)

Older women were to "encourage," "admonish" (NKJV), or "train" (ESV), to counsel and advise the younger women "to love their husbands." Interestingly, this is the only time in the Bible where a woman is encouraged to love her husband, the man in her life. Husbands of course receive multiple and detailed instruction in this regard (Eph 5:25-33; Col 3:19). Paul was concerned that a woman's first commitment under the lordship of Jesus Christ was to her husband and her marriage. The way a couple loves each other will model for the children the way they should love their future spouses. The fact is, we do not so much "fall in love" as we "learn to love." What a great thing it is for daughters to learn how to love their future husbands by watching their mother love their dad!

Love Your Children (Titus 2:4)

Few things are more natural for a mother than loving her children. However, a young mother must move beyond her natural innate affection to a specific lifestyle and plan of action that will cultivate in her children godly character and affection. Proverbs 29:15 says, "A rod of correction imparts wisdom, but a youth left to himself is a disgrace to his mother." The most important way a mother can love her children is to love them to a saving knowledge of Jesus Christ as their personal Savior and Lord. As she loves them physically, emotionally, educationally, morally, socially, and spiritually, she always has her eye on their need for Christ. In word and deed, she gently and with sensitivity puts before them the love of God and the work of Christ. She speaks to her child with grace and wisdom sharing with him or her the grace, mercy, and claims of Jesus Christ. Her greatest joy and most awesome heritage is godly children devoted to Jesus and His plan and purpose for their lives.

Be Self-Controlled (Titus 2:5)

Young women should also be sensible or "self-controlled." Paul again challenges a particular group in the church to exercise common sense and good judgment. The best way to learn this is to see it up close and personal in the life of another. Young women will best learn to exercise balance and wisdom in their lives as they observe it in the lives of older, more mature women.

Be Pure (Titus 2:5)

God calls a young woman to be "pure." Her moral life is above reproach, and she is by life and reputation a one-man kind of woman. She is faithful to her marriage vows and sexually gives herself to only one man, her husband. The man in her life trusts her and is confident in her. The God she serves sees His own character reflected in her life as it radiates forth from a heart surrendered to Jesus.

Be a Homemaker (Titus 2:5)

This lady is to be a good homemaker, "busy at home" (NIV). Her home is her primary base of operation and the main focus of her attention. Proverbs 31:10-31 teaches us that a diligent homemaker may be involved in a wide range of activities and interests. She is not lazy or a busybody, nor is she distracted by outside pursuits and responsibilities that eat up her precious time and attention. This woman is not seduced by the sirens of modernity who tell her she is wasting her time and talent as a homemaker and that it is the career woman who has purpose and is truly satisfied. The recent trend in women leaving the workplace and returning home has become too noticeable to be ignored. It is a reflection of what God planted in the heart of a wife and mother when He made her a female in His image. The blessings and joy she will discover as a wife, mother, and homemaker can never be matched by a career that in the end cannot make good on its promises. Being a homemaker is not an institutionalized form of bondage and slavery. It is the greatest context for a woman to experience liberation and liberty as she is set free by the plan of God to be the woman God created and saved her to be.

Be Good (Titus 2:5)

The word "kind" (or good) may modify "homemakers" or stand alone. A young woman should be kind. Simply said, she is to be like Jesus. She is to be gentle and considerate, gracious and merciful, even to those who may not treat her the same way. She is a "good woman" as the Bible defines good.

Be Subject to Your Husband (Titus 2:5)

In keeping with what is said consistently throughout the New Testament (Eph 5:21-24; Col 3:18; 1 Pet 3:1-5), wives were encouraged to be "submissive to their husbands, so that God's message will not be slandered." *Submission* means to yield in one's will to the leadership and direction of another. It is more of an attitude than an action, though one's attitude will certainly determine one's actions. Contrary to popular misconceptions, there is no inferiority in submissiveness. We see this plainly in the Trinity where Father, Son, and Holy Spirit are all equally God, and yet for the purpose of redemption, the Son submits in His assignment to the Father. Note also that a wife submits to her own husband, not every man. This charge is specific. Indeed, unless a husband asks his wife to do something unbiblical, illegal, immoral, or unethical, she is to follow his leadership. By doing this she will honor God and His Word, and she will reach, in a more effective manner, the heart of her husband.

Pursue God's Assignment as a Younger Man
TITUS 2:6-8

Paul then addresses the fourth group, younger men. The implication is that they would be instructed in the way they should live by Titus and other older men who would provide the encouragement and the example they needed. Younger men need strong, healthy role models provided by older men. In an article in the *South China Post,* Dr. Peter Karl writes,

> What a real man needs is another man to talk to and reinforce his maleness and help him be a better husband. . . . Without such a friend, men risk reverting to a mother-child relationship with a spouse. . . . Men become helpless and insecure and increasingly revert to the classic overgrown kid who expects to be mothered. . . . Men have few positive role models. (*South China Post,* April 23, 2000)

Paul recognizes the need younger men have for godly mentoring, and so he instructs them in a pattern of discipleship that would promote godly character, conviction, and commitment.

Be Levelheaded (Titus 2:6)

"Encourage" is a present imperative, giving it the force of a command that is continually to be set before the younger men. Like the others they are encouraged to be sensible, "self-controlled in everything." This means they are in control of their lives, thoughts, and passions. Proverbs 4:23 reminds us, "Guard your heart above all else, for it is the source of life." The self-controlled man actively engages the battle for the mind, knowing that he must control and discipline his thought life if he is to win the battles of the Christian life.

Be a Good Example (Titus 2:7)

Addressing Titus once again as he also speaks to the younger men, Paul tells him, "Make yourself an example of good works." The Greek word for "example" gives us our English word "type." Titus was to be a type or mold "into which others can be impressed and therefore bear a likeness to him" (Mounce, *Pastoral Epistles*, 413). The great preacher from Antioch, John Chrysostom, said, "Let the luster of your life be a common school of instruction, a pattern of virtue to all." Young men should be on the lookout for godly men they can emulate, men they can pattern their life after.

Be Sound in Doctrine (Titus 2:7)

Young men must not be fooled into following false doctrine. They must exhibit "integrity and dignity in [their] teaching." The focus falls here more on "how" one teaches than "what" one teaches. Both are essential of course, but purity in motive and authenticity in manner is what Paul was after. A life of moral integrity must accompany the teaching ministry. Content and character, *logos* and *ethos* go together and must complement each other if the truth is to be taught without compromise and corruption.

Be Sound in Speech (Titus 2:8)

Integrity in doctrine comes from a pure vessel that pours forth "sound" or healthy speech. Paul charged Titus in this way: "Your message is to be sound beyond reproach, so that the opponent will be ashamed, having nothing bad to say about us." The pure word from a pure vessel is not subject to legitimate condemnation or criticism. In fact, those who criticize such faithful and holy teachers will eventually shame themselves because their accusations are without merit or substance. Hughes and Chapell say, "There should be a multiplication of silencers as the godly influence of Titus spreads among the young men and helps to heal the embattled church" (*1 and 2 Timothy and Titus*, 332). The gospel in our own day has been subjected to a great deal of ridicule. Far too often the cause of offense has not been the message but the messenger. If persons refuse to come to Christ, let it be the message they say no to, not the messenger who, because of a shameful life, clouds and even hides the purity of the Word of salvation.

Conclusion

The implications of the gospel are for every person and every area of life. In this passage this is demonstrated by the application of "sound teaching" to both men and women, calling them to lives of godliness and discipleship. When we carefully consider the whole of biblical revelation and its implications concerning the issue of the role of men and women in the church and the work of the Lord, several important conclusions need to be affirmed and applauded.

First, both man and woman are created in God's image, equal before Him as persons and distinct in their manhood and womanhood.

Second, differences in masculine and feminine roles both in the home and in the church are ordained by God as part of His good plan for His good creation. This is intended for God's glory and our good.

Third, the fall in Genesis 3 introduced distortions into the relationship between men and women with tragic consequences. As it relates to the church, sin leads men toward a worldly love of power on the one hand or to the abdication of spiritual responsibility on the other. With respect to women, sin inclines them either to resist the parameters established by God for their assignments or to neglect the use of their gifts in appropriate and God-honoring ministries.

Fourth, redemption through the perfect atonement of the Lord Jesus Christ aims at removing the distortions introduced by the curse and the fall.

Fifth, in the Lord's church, redemption in Christ gives men and women equal rights and an equal share in the blessings of salvation. These rights and blessings are in perfect accord with the leadership and teaching assignments within the church given only to men. The role of the pastor-teacher is an office restricted to men.

Sixth, the God-given desire to serve the Lord that resonates both in men and in women should never be used to set aside the clear biblical pattern for ministry established by God in His Word. Seventh, billions of persons live without the knowledge of the saving Gospel of Jesus Christ. Countless other lost people live within those cultures that have heard the gospel. There are the heartbreak and miseries of sickness, malnutrition, homelessness, illiteracy, aging, drug and alcohol addictions, crime, incarceration, depression, and loneliness. Given this urgent need, no man or woman, boy or girl, having a God-given passion to make God's amazing grace known in word and deed, ever has to live without a vital and fulfilling ministry for the glory of God and the good of others in this fallen world.

Every child of God is called to proclaim the gospel to the lost. Every child of God is called to minister the Word. Every child of God is called to help the hurting. Every child of God at some time needs a mentor and is called to be a mentor. For the honor of Jesus and the sake of human souls, let us all be about the business of doing what God created us and saved us to do: His work, His way, and always for the praise of His Name.[26] This is God's assignment for both men and women in the church.

Reflect and Discuss

1. How do some denominations justify the changes in their policies regarding women in ministry? ordination of homosexuals? How do other denominations support their resistance to that kind of decision?
2. Does a man naturally become more levelheaded with age? Do you know any older men who are not levelheaded? Any younger men who are? How can a man cultivate this virtue?
3. How would you describe "self-control" for a Christian? Why is this such a crucial virtue?
4. Why can faith, love, and endurance (or hope) be used to gauge the spiritual health of a person? Which is currently flourishing in your life? Which needs attention?

---

[26] Concluding remarks summarized from portions of *The Danvers Statement* from the Council of Biblical Manhood and Womanhood (CBMW).

5. Why do many pastors' wives work outside the home? Is there an advantage or disadvantage to pastor's wives being mentors to the younger women in a church? Can "older women" who are not wives of elders function as mentors?

6. Where do today's young women learn how to think and behave? How would it be different if there were godly "older women" serving as mentors?

7. Which elements of a mother mentoring her daughter often come naturally? Which elements generally must be intentional? How have you seen this worked out in your family?

8. What did the feminist movement promise? What did it deliver? What aspects of society today can be attributed to the feminist movement? Weigh them against the Bible.

9. How does the proper implementation of submission keep the gospel from being slandered? How does an improper understanding of submission provoke slander from outsiders?

10. What do older men as mentors provide for young men that is different from what younger men would provide? From what women would provide? How can older men profit from continued relationships with peers? With men who are even older?

Servant Evangelism:
A Biblical Perspective on Slavery

TITUS 2:9-10

Main Idea: The gospel produces godly service that provides an opportunity for gospel proclamation.

I. **Be Productive for Your Superior (2:9).**
II. **Be Pleasing in Your Spirit (2:9).**
III. **Be Polite in Your Speech (2:9).**
IV. **Be Principled in Your Service (2:10).**
V. **Be Public in Your Sincerity (2:10).**
VI. **Be Praiseworthy for Your Savior (2:10).**

Few things reveal the depth and breadth of the total depravity of mankind like the institution of slavery. Treating those made in the image of God as a commodity to be bought and sold, this barbaric social structure reared its ugly head almost from the beginning of human history and has continued its cruel exploitation and abuse right on to the present. Ripping children from parents as if they were nothing more than a litter of puppies, separating husbands and wives because it was economically prosperous with no regard for the heartache and devastation it inflicted, the institution is a blight on the human race and demonstrates just how wicked the human heart can be.

In the first century one out of three persons in Rome and one in five elsewhere was a slave. A person could become a slave as a result of capture in war, default on a debt, inability to support and "voluntarily" selling oneself, being sold as a child by destitute parents, birth to slave parents, conviction of a crime, or kidnapping and piracy. Unlike the slavery that arose in the Americas in the 1600s, slavery in the ancient world was racially indiscriminate, cutting across racial, social, and national lines. As with many other pieces of property, slaves had no rights (Brooks, "Slave/Servant," 1286). And yet the state of slaves varied in the ancient world. Some were forced to work in the fields and mines in gangs, while others were highly skilled workers and trusted administrators. It has been noted that frequently slaves were better off than free laborers (Elwell, "Slavery," 1112). Still, if a slave attacked his master, every slave in the household was killed, and until the time of Christian emperors, the penalty for rebellion was crucifixion (Elwell, "Slavery").

One would have thought that with the spread of Christianity, slavery would have met its demise. Unfortunately that was not the case. Justinian (AD 527–565) sought to abolish slavery, but the numbers again grew, and after the collapse of the Roman Empire, it merged into serfdom. The Crusades boosted slave trade, and in Venice, Christian slaves were actually sold to Muslims (Elwell, "Slavery"). But what about the modern era and the enslavement of some 24 million Africans, many of whom were sent here to America and found themselves in servitude to Christian masters? Any honest history must note that the enslavement of Africans by Africans was common and had been so for hundreds of years. Still, the pattern changed radically from the fifteenth century onward, and the crimes humanity visited on fellow humanity were shameful beyond imagination. Persons were kidnapped, families destroyed, and unbridled cruelty was rampant. And what of Christians? What about Baptists? What were we doing as a nation?

While many of the nation's founding fathers were in fact abolitionists, the movement failed to take root in the new country.[27] By the late

---

[27] The following is taken from Anderson, "Slavery and the Founders."

When America was founded, there were about half a million slaves. Approximately one third of the founders had slaves (George Washington and Thomas Jefferson being the most notable). Most of the slaves lived in the five southern colonies.

Benjamin Rush and Benjamin Franklin (both signers of the Declaration of Independence) founded the Pennsylvania Society for Promoting the Abolition of Slavery in 1774. Franklin saw slavery as "an atrocious debasement of human nature," and Rush went on to head a national abolition movement.

John Jay was the president of a similar society in New York and said, "To contend for our own liberty, and to deny that blessing to others, involves an inconsistency not be excused."

John Adams opposed slavery because it was a "foul contagion in the human character" and "an evil of colossal magnitude." His son, John Quincy Adams, so crusaded against slavery that he was known as "the hell-hound of abolition."

It's important to note that when these anti-slavery societies were founded, they were clearly an act of civil disobedience. In 1774, for example, Pennsylvania passed a law to end slavery. But King George vetoed that law and other laws passed by the colonies. The King was pro-slavery, and Great Britain (at the time) practiced slavery. As long as the colonies were part of the British Empire, they would also be required to condone slavery.

1700s and early 1800s you find Baptists in the South arguing, "What God sanctioned in the Old Testament, and permitted in the New, cannot be sin." Baptists like Fuller, Dagg, Boyce, and Broadus tragically came down on the wrong side of this issue. And it is simply impossible to deny that slavery played an important role in the formation of the Southern Baptist Convention in 1845, even if the northern Baptists forced the issue and basically shoved Baptists in the South into starting a new convention.

Thankfully, one must also acknowledge that Christians led the way in bringing to an end this horrible institution. Men like William Wilberforce, Granville Sharp, John Wesley, and Charles Finney led the charge. Quakers and Moravians, Methodists, and some Baptists voiced their opposition against great odds and were heard by God. Slavery was outlawed in 1807 in Britain and throughout its empire in 1827. Congress brought "slave trade" to a close in 1808, but the end of slavery in the United States would not come until 1865. Still, and do not miss the point: *only where there was a Christian impulse did slavery come to an end.* To this day slavery continues its reign of terror in many parts of the world where the glorious gospel of Jesus Christ has not yet taken hold. Where the gospel has found fertile soil, the institution of slavery has vanished into the midnight darkness.

Now I want to raise a question, answer that question, and clarify an issue needing clarification. What does the Bible say about slavery? What words of guidance and instruction do we find? In summarizing the biblical teaching, I believe the following to be an accurate description:

1. The Bible **regulates** but does not ordain or **require** slavery (Exod 21; Lev 25; Deut 15; Eph 6:5-9; Col 3:22–4:1; 1 Tim 6:1-2; Titus 2:9-10; 1 Pet 2:18-25). Slavery is not a divine institution. Note the absence of an Old Testament grounding in Ephesians 6:5-9!
2. Paul taught that if you can gain your freedom, then go for it (1 Cor 7:21-24), but do not let it consume you.

---

human nature itself, violating it's [sic] most sacred rights of life and liberty in the persons of a distant people who never offended him, captivating and carrying them into slavery in another hemisphere or to incur miserable death in their transportation thither." Unfortunately, this paragraph was dropped from the final draft because it was offensive to the delegates from Georgia and South Carolina.

3. Through a wise and strategic extension of the gospel, the New Testament sows the seed for the unmasking of slavery for the sin that it is and for its eventual destruction.

4. Scripture never advocates bloodshed or rebellion in confronting and overturning evil structures of society and culture. Rather, it attacks with the beauty of the gospel, the grace of God, and the ethic of love.

5. Paul turned the tables on the institution of slavery, placing it in eternal perspective! From the perspective of eternity, the slave is master of his master for the Master! The earthly master who does not know Christ in a real sense finds his eternal destiny in the hands of his slave who actually is the free man. It is the slave who knows Christ, it is the slave who possesses the gospel treasure that saves. From the gospel perspective it is the unbelieving master who is in the position of disadvantage.

Just as in verses 1-8, the gospel should produce godliness in the life of a believer as a testimony to the unbelieving world. For those who are under authority, the gospel produces godly service that provides an opportunity for gospel proclamation. Thus Paul put into action a strategy of servant evangelism whereby everyone in a position of service, everyone under authority, sees before them a fertile and open field for evangelism. Here is their mission field; here is their place of ministry. Now the question becomes, What will they see? How will they serve the One over them, regardless of the social, governmental, business, family, or religious context? Moving to our text, Paul lays before us six powerful principles that will shut the mouth of the evil one.

Be Productive for Your Superior
TITUS 2:9

"Slaves are to be submissive to their masters." How can we do this? Why should we do this? Colossians 3:24 provides the answer: "You serve the Lord Christ." Ultimately we are serving Jesus. Our motivation in serving others is wonderfully raised to a whole new plane. We want to serve this man, help this man, honor this man, because to do so is to honor our Lord.

Are there exceptions to this wide sweeping call to obedience? Yes, there are four: when it is unbiblical, illegal, unethical, or immoral.

Outside of these, our goal is to submit to him and serve him, all the while seeing the true Master, the Lord Jesus, who stands behind him.

Be Pleasing in Your Spirit
TITUS 2:9

The text commands the servant "to be submissive . . . in everything, and to be well-pleasing." This addresses both the **scope** and the **spirit** of my service. The **scope** is in everything. Now there is a small debate. Does "in everything" go with "be submissive to their masters" or with "well-pleasing"? Neither rendering greatly changes our understanding or the meaning of the text, but I understand it to refer to "well-pleasing" as it is in the NKJV: "to be well pleasing in all things." Growing out of an attitude of submissiveness that seeks to be productive for one's master, a servant strives in everything to be well-pleasing in **spirit**, in attitude. A Christian servant wants to please his master, delights in pleasing his superior. Ephesians 6:6-7 says, "Do God's will from your heart. Serve with a good attitude, as to the Lord and not to men."

Both in **action** and in **attitude**, the servant of Christ puts on display for all to see the grace of God that brings salvation for all people (Titus 2:11), "so that they may adorn the teaching of God our Savior in everything" (v. 10). We serve others gladly not begrudgingly, joyfully not resentfully. Only by means of the filling of the Spirit (Eph 5:18) and the mind of Christ (Phil 2:5) can servants of Christ serve others in this way.

Be Polite in Speech
TITUS 2:9

The kind of submission called for here is demonstrated by "not talking back," literally, "speaking against." Servants of Christ do not back-talk or mouth off. They are not argumentative, contentious, or disagreeable. They do not gripe about their boss behind his back and compromise their testimony as a follower of Jesus Christ.

Words are powerful weapons. In a matter of seconds, a testimony built over a lifetime can be destroyed by a few careless words. The wisdom of Proverbs is crucial at this point:

A worthless person, a wicked man goes around speaking dishonestly. (Prov 6:12)

The one who guards his mouth protects his life; the one who opens his lips invites his own ruin. (Prov 13:3)

*A worthless man digs up evil, and his speech is like a scorching fire.
   A contrary man spreads conflict, and a gossip separates close friends.* (Prov 16:27-28)

A fool's lips lead to strife, and his mouth provokes a beating. (Prov 18:6)

A fool's mouth is his devastation, and his lips are a trap for his life. (Prov 18:7)

Life and death are in the power of the tongue, and those who love it will eat its fruit. (Prov 18:21)

*Without wood, fire goes out; without a gossip, conflict dies down.
   As charcoal for embers and wood for fire, so is a quarrelsome man for kindling strife.* (Prov 26:20-21)

I said, "I will guard my ways so that I may not sin with my tongue; I will guard my mouth with a muzzle as long as the wicked are in my presence." (Ps 39:1)

A person's speech is one of the clearest indications of what is in a person's heart. The servant of Christ will be polite in speech, especially when talking to and about his boss. This is the practical application of the gospel to the details of life, even our speech.

Be Principled in Your Service
TITUS 2:10

In addition to "not talking back," slaves are not to be found "stealing" or "pilfering" (NKJV). The servant of Christ is not a thief! Rather he is a man you can trust when you are not around. He is honest, dependable, a man of integrity. He does not take what belongs to another while justifying in his mind that he has earned it and that he deserves it.

This servant will go the extra mile in maintaining his financial accountability. There will be no inflated expense accounts, falsified time sheets, or unauthorized use of his employer's resources. From a paper clip to a corporate jet, he will conduct himself with absolute honesty and integrity. After all, he serves Christ, and he would never think of stealing from Jesus.

Be Public in Your Sincerity
TITUS 2:10

In contrast to "not talking back or stealing," the servant of Christ is to demonstrate "utter faithfulness." The conjunction "but" denotes a strong adversative, an emphatic rejection of what goes before it: "Not stealing *but* showing faithfulness." The word "demonstrating" means to show forth. The idea is that our faithfulness and fidelity to our masters is evident and visible to all. Our trustworthiness, reliability, and dependability are continually on display. No one needs to be looking over our shoulder. We are known for our loyalty and integrity. Others may cheat the boss but not us. Others may betray the boss but not us. Others may become embittered at their boss, especially if they serve a tyrant or bully. But not us. As servants of Christ, in stark and remarkable contrast, we will put on public display the gospel's transforming power that enables us to bless rather than curse, to serve rather than steal.

Be Praiseworthy of Your Savior
TITUS 2:10

Being a faithful, honest, gracious, kind, and submissive servant has a noble end: to "adorn the teaching of God our Savior in everything." This kind of servant makes beautiful and attractive the teaching of God our Savior, and he does this in everything and in every way. Though he is a slave or servant, the one under authority makes gorgeous the things of God by his productive, pleasing, polite, principled, public service. It is indeed a praiseworthy service as it puts on display the character of God shining forth from one of His children. Hayne Griffin is right on target when he says,

> The effect of individual Christian behavior on unbelievers should not be underestimated. Inevitably, unbelievers judge the gospel message by the lives of those who embrace it. As we live and identify ourselves as Christians, we can make the gospel message attractive and credible by our godly attitudes

and behavior. However, if we are perceived as unloving and hypocritical, we provide unbelievers with good reason to be skeptical about the power of the gospel. Paul's exhortations, both to these Cretan groups and to Christians of every age, should alert us to the tremendous importance of being in reality what we profess in word. (Lea and Griffin, *1, 2 Timothy, Titus,* 308)

In commenting on this verse, Spurgeon writes,

The life of the Christian, even if he is a servant, is to be an ornament of Christianity. Christ does not look for the ornament of His religion to the riches or the talents of His followers, but to their *holy lives,* "that they may adorn the doctrine of God our Savior in all things." ("Adorning the Gospel," in *Metropolitan Tabernacle,* 41:275)

This is godliness that is worthy of the praise of our Savior.

Conclusion

Why does Paul provide this charge to those who are under the authority of another? I think the answer is easily given. Without the mind of Christ, the filling of the Spirit, and a spiritual perspective on now and eternity, we will be,

- rebellious not submissive
- irritable not pleasant
- ugly not polite
- thieves not honest
- unfaithful not faithful
- an embarrassment not a blessing

to a Savior we say we adore.

When you are in the position of disadvantage, when you are the servant rather than the master, then you will discover if your faith is real and your profession genuine. It will not be by accident that you are in this position. A sovereign God put you there so that, by your life, those who see you will also see the beauty of your Lord, the beauty of Jesus as you serve others just as you would Jesus.

Reflect and Discuss

1. How did Baptists and other Christians come to be on the wrong side of the issue of slavery? Are there any other issues—past or present—where most Christians have failed to discern God's will?

2. How is being an employee similar to being a slave? How is it different?

3. How does being pleasing in our service demonstrate the grace of God?

4. What is more serious, "talking back" or "stealing"? How many aspects of workplace integrity can you list?

5. How does being a good servant adorn the gospel? How have you seen this demonstrated in a secular workplace?

6. How is the responsibility of a servant (employee) to live with integrity different from that of a master (employer)? How is it the same? Which is easier to fulfill?

The Amazing Grace of God

TITUS 2:11-15

Main Idea: The grace of God is the foundation for godly living.

I. **God's Grace Teaches Us How We Should Live (2:11-12).**
   A. God's grace has come to us (2:11).
   B. God's grace must change us (2:12).
II. **God's Grace Teaches Us Where We Should Look (2:13).**
   A. We know what to look for: His coming.
   B. We know whom to look for: our Savior.
III. **God's Grace Teaches Us Who Is Lord (2:14).**
   A. Jesus paid for us.
   B. Jesus purifies us.
   C. Jesus possesses us.
   D. Jesus prepares us.
IV. **God's Grace Teaches Us What We Should Learn (2:15).**
   A. Learn doctrine.
   B. Learn duty.
   C. Learn discernment.
   D. Learn dedication.

No doctrine of Scripture is more precious to mankind than the doctrine of salvation. And no word is more crucial to the doctrine of salvation than the word **grace**. That the sovereign God of creation would reach down from heaven and rescue undeserving sinners from the bondage and slavery of sin, from spiritual death and eternal separation from God in a place called hell, can only be described in one word: **grace**.

Salvation is a wonderful doctrine of the Bible. It is a badly misunderstood doctrine as well, especially as it relates to our understanding of the work of Christ and how it applies to sinners. It is not popular in our day to claim that Jesus is the only way to God. Modern culture and theologies see this as too narrow and restrictive, intolerant, unloving, and unworthy of the God we imagine God to be.

Three theological ideas dominate the contemporary religious scene when it comes to the issue of salvation. First, **universalism**, and the related term **pluralism**, teaches that there are many ways—or even an unlimited number of ways—to God. This is the idea that all roads lead to God, and therefore everyone will eventually be saved and make it to heaven. This is a popular position among more liberal theologians as well as among those who embrace New Age ideologies. This view is well represented by theologian John Hick, who says,

> Most New Testament scholars today do not believe that Jesus, the historical individual, claimed to be God incarnate. The old exclusivist view that only Christians are saved has been abandoned by the majority of Christian theologians and church leaders. There is, in fact, a basic moral outlook which is universal, and I suggest that the concrete reality of salvation consists in embodying this in our lives in a spiritual transformation whose natural expression is unrestricted love and compassion. The basic moral teaching of the religions remains the same. It constitutes the universal ideal. What are called the conflicting truth-claims of the religions do not in fact conflict, because they are claims about different human awarenesses of the divine. We are living today in a time of transition which amounts to a move to a new paradigm of Christian thought. ("Only True Religion?" 3–11)

Second, **inclusivism** affirms that Jesus is the only Savior but that it is possible to be saved by Jesus even though you may never have personally trusted Him for salvation. Inclusivism teaches that salvation can be received through a positive response to God's revelation in nature and conscience (called general revelation) or possibly even through other world religions. Although other religions have an imperfect understanding of the one true God, the truth that they do possess is seen to be adequate to save a person. It is said that we may be able to recognize these "anonymous Christians" (a phrase coined by the Roman Catholic theologian Karl Rahner) by the good deeds they do. Hence, belief in a works salvation often accompanies this position. Clark Pinnock and John Sanders are representative of this perspective. Pinnock writes:

> According to Acts 4:12, then, Jesus has done a unique work for the human race, the good news of which needs to be preached to the whole world. But this uniqueness does not entail exclusivity. . . . The Son through whom all things were made is constantly at work in the world. The Spirit of God broods over

the whole creation and over history. We should not think of God as absent from the world except where the name of Jesus of Nazareth is pronounced. Although for many evangelicals the finality of Christ spells exclusivism, I believe our high Christology can also create space for openness and generosity to the world's peoples. We do not need to think of the church as the ark of salvation, leaving everyone else in hell. . . . I have always been impressed by the view put forward at the Second Vatican Council to the effect that the person who dies having sincerely sought after God, but not having learned about Jesus, will not be automatically condemned in the judgment but will be given the opportunity to plead the blood of Christ. ("Acts 4:12," 112–14)

Sanders is even more clear in how he believes someone can get to heaven without personally trusting Christ:

The Father reaches out to the unevangelized through both the Son and the Spirit via general revelation, conscience and human culture. God does not leave himself without witness to any people. Salvation for the unevangelized is made possible only by the redemptive work of Jesus, but God applies that work even to those who are ignorant of the atonement. God does this if people respond in trusting faith to the revelation they have. ("Inclusivism," 36)

Third, **exclusivism** is the teaching that has been held by the majority of the church for most of its history. It is the orthodox, evangelical position, teaching that salvation comes only through a personal faith commitment to Jesus Christ as Savior and Lord. This does not exclude those who never reach an age of moral responsibility and accountability, such as infants and small children, or those who are incapable of moral discernment, such as mentally handicapped people. Evangelicals have overwhelmingly held the view that these individuals are the objects of God's saving grace and mercy.[28] But exclusivism does affirm the absolute uniqueness and finality of God's revelation in Jesus. He alone is the one and only Savior, as taught in John 14:6; Acts 4:12; and 1 Timothy 2:5.

---

[28] See Akin and Mohler, "Why We Believe that Infants Who Die Go to Heaven." Another great treatment of this issue is MacArthur, *Safe in the Arms of God.*

Only in Him can one be saved. God would not have sent His only Son to die on a cross if He could have saved us by some other means. The cross of Christ is God's great testimony that Jesus is the exclusive way to the Father. The preaching of the gospel is how this great testimony is made known for salvation throughout the world (Rom 10:9-17).

As we think about the doctrine of salvation, several important texts in the Word of God address various facets of our salvation. In John 3 Jesus teaches us about spiritual birth. Romans 3 teaches us about justification by faith in Christ. In 2 Corinthians 5 we learn about reconciliation with God. Galatians 3 teaches us about deliverance from the curse of the law. Hebrews 7–10 tells us about Jesus our great high priest and His perfect sacrifice for sin. In 1 John 2:2 and 4:10 we see His propitiatory work of atonement. In Titus 2:11-15 we learn about the grace of God that brings salvation to all men!

In Titus 2:11-15, Paul highlights the **grace** of God and the **glory** of God. What he discusses concerning these two realities can also be summed up in one word: Jesus. So, what does God want us to know and embrace when it comes to the "glory of the One and Only Son . . . , full of grace and truth" (John 1:14)?

God's Grace Teaches Us How to Live
TITUS 2:11-12

The conjunction "for" ties the weighty sentence of verses 11-14 to the practical instruction of verses 1-10. It shows us that God's commands are rooted in His grace. Here then is the doctrinal foundation for the practical instruction. In this instance belief follows behavior, and yet, in a real sense, belief and behavior continue to be woven together in a beautiful tapestry of biblical teaching in the text before us. From this we are assured that what God demands of us is possible because of what He first has done for us and in us.

God's Grace Has Come to Us (Titus 2:11)

The "grace of God" refers to His unmerited favor, His goodness and kindness, His compassion and mercy demonstrated toward undeserving sinners. This grace of God "has appeared with salvation" or "brings salvation" (NKJV), the deliverance and rescue from sin and its judgment. The crucial point is clear: no grace would mean no salvation. Mounce writes, "'Grace' is a one-word summary of God's saving act in Christ, given freely to sinners who believe (cf. 1 Tim 1:2)" (Mounce, *Pastoral Epistles*, 422).

Salvation by the grace of God "has appeared . . . for all people." That is, He has made this salvation known in a way previously unknown, and He has made it known for all the world to see. The perfect atonement of Jesus Christ the eternal Son of God made all men savable. There is a universal and unlimited provision. Every sin of every person has its answer in Jesus. No nation, tongue, people, or person is excluded from His saving work. Those who perish in the horrors of hell must walk over a blood-stained cross that bears their name. By His nature our God is a saving God. His gracious gift of salvation has appeared for all. That includes you and that includes me. Hallelujah! What a Savior!

God's Grace Must Change Us (Titus 2:12)

There has been a dispute among certain evangelicals called the "Lordship Salvation" debate. In its most extreme those who oppose lordship salvation say the following:

1. Repentance is not necessary for salvation.
2. Faith is simply intellectual assent to a proposition.
3. The will is not involved in the act of conversion.
4. Good works may or may not follow faith, i.e., one should separate salvation from discipleship.
5. Apostasy of a saved person is possible via what is called "dead faith" (a bizarre understanding of James 2:14-26).

I would submit that Titus 2:12 deals a death blow and puts to an end once and for all "to any theology that separates salvation from the demands of obedience to the Lordship of Christ" (Mounce, *Pastoral Epistles*, 423). Without calling for **perfection**, Paul says that a new **direction** in a person's life is the outgrowth and expectation of God for those experiencing His salvation.

The grace of God, the goodness of God, the greatness of God, the glory of God instructs us **negatively** "to deny godlessness and worldly lusts" and **positively** "to live in a sensible [toward ourselves], righteous [toward others], and godly way [toward God]." We are called to live this way "in the present age," right now, today. Jerry Bridges summarizes this well:

Self-control ["sensible"] expresses the self-restraint we need to practice toward the good and legitimate things of life, as well as the outright denial of things clearly sinful. Upright or righteous conduct refers to just and right actions toward other people, doing to them what we would have them do to us (Matt 7:12). Godliness is having a regard for God's glory and God's will in every aspect of our lives, doing everything out of reverence and love for Him. (*Discipline of Grace*, 88)

And remember: it is grace, God's amazing grace, that teaches us to live this way. I cannot do it in my power, my strength, my genius, my ability. No, His grace breaks the power of cancelled sin! It not only saves, it also transforms. God's grace teaches us how to live.

God's Grace Teaches Us Where We Should Look
TITUS 2:13

Living in this present age (v. 12) is a constant reminder that there is an age to come. This earth is not my home, and this world is not my final destination. With father Abraham we are "looking forward to the city that has foundations, whose architect and builder is God" (Heb 11:10), and we look for Jesus "who rescues us from the coming wrath" (1 Thess 1:10).

We Know What to Look For: His Coming

While we live in this present age, we are called to "wait." Waiting or looking speaks of an eager and confident expectation. And what are we looking for? It is the "blessed hope" and the "appearing of the glory of our great God and Savior, Jesus Christ." Thus we have a twofold appearing in this passage of Scripture. There is the appearance of **God's grace** (v. 11) and **God's glory** (v. 13). Both appearances speak of the same person: Jesus. The **grace** that has appeared speaks of His first coming. The **glory** that will appear speaks of His second coming. With a constant gaze and the experience of grace, our eyes are fixed heavenward with one and only one hope: His coming.

We Know Whom to Look For: Our Savior

We don't look for **anyone** coming from heaven but **someone** coming from heaven. It is not Gabriel or Michael or any of the rest of the angelic host. No, they simply will not do. They are inadequate for what we hope for and what we need. We look and long for the one who is "our great God and Savior, Jesus Christ." Here is a clear and magnificent statement of the deity of the Son. It joins other wonderful direct declarations of this truth like John 20:28; Romans 9:5; Hebrews 1:8; 2 Peter 1:1; and 1 John 5:20.

He is our "great God" not our greater God, for after Him no one is great! He is our great God, the object of our worship, Creator and Savior, forgiver of sins, final Judge, the One to whom we pray, the One in whom all the fullness of deity dwells in bodily form (Col 2:9). He is my "Savior," my deliverer, my Redeemer, my rescuer; He is Jesus the Christ, God's Messiah, God's anointed, the One who came in fulfillment of Old Testament promises and the One who is coming again. God's grace teaches us where we should look and to whom we should look as we wait.

God's Grace Teaches Us Who Is Lord
TITUS 2:14

The doctrine of salvation can appropriately be discussed in three tenses: past, present, and future.

- Past: we are delivered from sin's penalty → justification.
- Present: we are delivered from sin's power → sanctification.
- Future: we will be delivered from sin's presence → glorification.

In these verses Paul addresses all three: sin's penalty in verses 11 and 14; sin's power in verses 12 and 14; and sin's presence in verse 13. All of this finds its efficiency in the perfect atoning work of Christ, a work that is put on marvelous display here in verse 14. Consider this fourfold portrait.

Jesus Paid for Us

Jesus "gave Himself for us." This refers to the vicarious and substitutionary nature of Christ's death. The purpose given for His death is "to redeem us from all lawlessness." Here we see the costly and liberating work of redemption (cf. Matt 20:28; Acts 20:28; 1 Tim 2:6; 1 Pet 1:18-19). In the words of Ellis J. Crum,

> He paid a debt He did not owe,
> I owed a debt I could not pay!

This is the way Jesus described the reason for His coming: "For even the Son of Man did not come to be served, but to serve, and to give His life—a ransom for many" (Mark 10:45). The apostle Paul spells it out clearly in 2 Corinthians 5:21: "He made the One who did not know sin to be sin for us, so that we might become the righteousness of God in Him." Jesus paid for us.

Jesus Purifies Us

He purchased us to purify or "cleanse" us! His grace takes us out of the pigpen; it does not help us enjoy the pigpen. Sin makes us guilty and dirty. Grace makes us innocent and clean. This is the promise of the new covenant: "I will also sprinkle clean water on you, and you will be clean. I will cleanse you from all your impurities and all your idols" (Ezek 36:25). Jesus cleanses and purifies us by virtue of His vicarious and substitutionary death.

Jesus Possesses Us

He **purchased** us, to **purify** us, to **possess** us, literally "for Himself a people for His own a possession." Drawing from the imagery of Exodus 19:5, Peter makes this same point:

> *But you are a chosen race, a royal priesthood, a holy nation, a people for His possession, so that you may proclaim the praise of the One who called you out of darkness into His marvelous light. Once you were not a people, but now you are God's people; you had not received mercy, but now you have received mercy.* (1 Pet 2:9-10)

What security is ours! Once we were Satan's, now we are the Son's. Once we were sin's, now we are the Savior's. Once we were foreigners, now we are family. Now I belong to Jesus:

> Jesus my Lord will love me forever,
> From Him no power of evil can sever.
> He gave His life to ransom my soul,
> Now I belong to Him.
> Now I belong to Jesus.
> Jesus belongs to me.
> Not for the years of time alone,
> But for eternity.[29]

---

[29] Norman J. Clayton, Wordspring Music, 1938.

Jesus Prepares Us

As those who are His, we have a holy passion: "eager to do good works." Unlike the Cretans who were disqualified or unfit for any good work (1:16), we have a consuming desire to honor our great God and Savior for His glorious work of redemption. Our works are the natural response to His work. Zeal for Him becomes our daily desire, having been prepared by Him for this kind of life. Grace teaches us who is Lord. Grace empowers us to serve Him as Lord.

God's Grace Teaches Us What We Should Learn
TITUS 2:15

Verse 15 concludes chapter 2 and opens the door for chapter 3. John MacArthur says verse 15 "is one of the clearest and strongest statements in Scripture about the spiritual authority of men whom God calls to minister His Word and shepherd His people" (*Titus*, 125). Beginning with the verb "speak" or "say," Paul follows up in rapid-fire succession with three more imperatives of command: "encourage . . . rebuke . . . let no one disregard." The man of God could speak in this way "with all authority" because of His authority: the great God and Savior Jesus Christ. From what Titus was to teach we can see what we should learn.

Learn Doctrine

The command given is continually to "say" or "speak" these things. "These things" certainly refers to 2:11-14, but it is likely that it refers to the entire letter, a letter filled with "sound teaching" (1:9; 2:1). Believers must know what they believe about the person and work of Jesus Christ, salvation, the church, and the future.

Learn Duty

Four of the fourteen imperatives in Titus are in this verse. "Encourage" addresses our duty before God and men. Paul encourages; he comes alongside to challenge us in the way we should live as we look for "the blessed hope" (2:13).

Learn Discernment

If "encourage" speaks to us about the way we should go, "rebuke" (1:13) admonishes us concerning the way we should not go. "Encourage" has as its primary audience the faithful. "Rebuke" has as its primary audience the unfaithful. When we confront and correct, we do so with all authority. We do not compromise or kowtow. We do not dialogue or debate. Discerning both the error and the danger in our midst, we shepherd our sheep, we protect our sheep, with a firm and steady hand.

Learn Dedication

Speaking the truth will not always be popular, but it will always be necessary. It will require courage, conviction, and "Christ-confidence." This will enable you to stand humbly tall, refusing to be intimidated by naysayers and opponents. You will not let anyone "disregard," despise, look down on you, for you are looking upward and heavenward for your orders from your great God and Savior.

Conclusion

This passage shows us that the grace of God is the foundation for godly living in the here and now. It is rooted in Christ's past work on the cross and the promise of His future return. Martin Luther summarized how we ought to live in light of this passage. He said, "I live as though Christ died yesterday, rose again today, and is coming again tomorrow."[30] Our present pursuit of godliness is sandwiched in between the death and resurrection of Christ and His second coming—the grace of His first coming and the glory of His return. Our hearts should well up with praise in response to the grace of God. It truly is amazing grace. Consider the words of this old hymn and respond in praise to our great God and Savior Jesus Christ:

> Wonderful grace of Jesus, Greater than all my sin;
> How shall my tongue describe it, Where shall my praise begin?
> Taking away my burden, Setting my spirit free,
> For the wonderful grace of Jesus reaches me.

---

[30] Source unknown. Sometimes attributed to Theodore Epp.

Wonderful grace of Jesus, Reaching the most defiled.
By its transforming power Making him God's dear child.
Purchasing peace and heaven For all eternity—
And the wonderful grace of Jesus reaches me.[31]

The amazing grace of God! I am so glad it reaches me! Aren't you glad it reaches you?

Reflect and Discuss

1. Which Bible passages might pluralists or universalists use to support their views?
2. Which Bible passages might seem to teach inclusivism?
3. How should we respond to the objection that exclusivism goes against the biblical emphasis on the love of God?
4. How would you explain that the grace of God in Christ is sufficient and available for all people, but not all people will be saved?
5. What is the connection between salvation and obedience? Does God's grace come with conditions? Is it possible to receive grace by faith without one's life changing?
6. Do non-Christians "wait for" something? How does "hope" add meaning to the everyday life of Christians?
7. How does the fact that you are God's "possession" encourage you? How does this idea emphasize God's part in your sanctification?
8. What do you think of when you hear the word *doctrine*? How would you label or define biblical doctrine in a way that might make it more attractive? Appealing?
9. In what way does learning doctrine and Christian conduct "encourage" a person (v. 15)? Can being rebuked also result in encouragement?
10. As you meditate on the grace of God in Jesus, what aspects stir your heart to worship Him?

---

[31] "Wonderful Grace of Jesus," words and music by Haldor Lillenas; public domain.

New Birth for a New Life

TITUS 3:1-8

Main Idea: We have been born again to live a new life of good works.

I. **We Must Be Ready for Good Works (3:1-3).**
   A. In the present we can help others (3:1-2).
      1. We submit obediently (3:1).
      2. We serve eagerly (3:1).
      3. We speak gently (3:2).
      4. We show humility (3:2).
   B. In the past we harmed others (3:3).
      1. Sin deceives.
      2. Sin disobeys.
      3. Sin dictates.
      4. Sin detests.
      5. Sin desires.
      6. Sin destroys.
II. **We Have Been Regenerated for Good Works (3:4-7).**
   A. God cares for us (3:4).
   B. God changes us (3:5).
   C. God has come for us (3:6).
   D. God comforts us (3:7).
III. **We Will Be Rewarded for Good Works (3:8).**
   A. We should affirm good works.
   B. We should be active in good works.

Nicodemus was a respected religious leader in the first century. He was both a Pharisee and a member of the Sanhedrin, the ruling counsel of the nation of Israel. He was devoutly religious, theologically well educated, and held in the highest esteem by those who knew him. He was, by any standard of measurement, a good man.

However, visiting the young itinerant rabbi from Galilee one evening after dark, he was shocked to hear he was not ready to enter the kingdom of God (John 3). What reason did Jesus give him? He had never been born from above; he had never been born again; he had never experienced the miracle of new birth, the work of the Spirit of God the Bible calls regeneration.

Millard Erickson defines regeneration as "the other [divine] side of conversion. It is completely God's doing. It is God's transformation of individual believers, his giving a new spiritual vitality and direction to their lives when they accept Christ . . . it involves something new, a whole reversal of the person's natural tendencies" (*Theology*, 955–57). In other words, it is new birth for a new life.

The word itself only occurs twice in the New Testament. One is Matthew 19:28, which refers to the cosmic regeneration in the eschaton. The other is here in the text before us in Titus 3:5. Paul was vitally interested in both the **nature** of the new birth and the **results** of the new birth. He was unalterably convinced that the new birth would be evident in a new life—a new life exploding in good works. Good works form a sandwich or *inclusio* for our text as they begin the discussion in verse 1 and conclude it in verse 8. Regeneration is the apex of the text appearing in the middle of the passage in verses 5-6. Thus the two are essentially related to each other as we consider the full dimension of our salvation. Paul divides his analysis of the relationship between regeneration and good works into three parts.

We Must Be Ready for Good Works
TITUS 3:1-3

God saved us in order that we would do good works. Ephesians 2:10 reminds us we were created in Christ Jesus for good works. Good works never save, but good works flow from those who are saved. The order is crucially important. Living in a culture that was hostile to the gospel and corrupted by moral sin at every turn, Paul admonishes those in Crete to live distinctively different lives. He does so by giving them and us principles to live by in verses 1-2, principles that stand in stark contrast to how we used to live as described in verse 3.

In the Present We Can Help Others (Titus 3:1-2)

"Remind them" calls to remembrance those things that they were previously taught. Flowing naturally out of the previous section (2:11-15), verses 1-2 show the application of the gospel to the believer's life in this world. Paul provides seven commands that fall roughly into four categories.

We submit obediently (3:1). We are "to be submissive to rulers and authorities, to obey." Jesus said in Matthew 22:21, "Therefore give back to Caesar the things that are Caesar's, and to God the things that are God's." Paul adds in Romans 13:1, "Everyone must submit to the governing authorities, for there is no authority except from God, and those that exist are instituted by God." Peter also says in 1 Peter 2:13-14, "Submit to every human authority because of the Lord, whether to the Emperor as the supreme authority or to governors as those sent out by him to punish those who do what is evil and to praise those who do what is good."

Christians are not anarchist or rebels. We do not subvert the government or disobey the government unless it brings us into direct conflict with the commands of God (Acts 5:29). And even then our disobedience is passive not active, and we willingly accept the consequences of our actions. This submission is evidence of submission to and trust in God.

We serve eagerly (3:1). We are to "be ready for every good work." The word "every" indicates the command is comprehensive. Complementing this command is Galatians 6:10: "Therefore, as we have opportunity, we must work for the good of all, especially for those who belong to the household of faith." Titus 2:14 reminds us that Christ has redeemed us to create a people for Himself who are "eager to do good works." We look to aid others, assist others, help others in any and every opportunity.

We speak gently (3:2). We are to "slander no one" and are to "avoid fighting." Again the scope is comprehensive. We malign or curse no one with our words, stirring up strife, ill will, and trouble. No, we are peaceable and gentle, uncontentious and forbearing, friendly and considerate.

We exercise sweet reasonableness out of a life of wisdom that refuses to hold a grudge and that also gives others the benefit of the doubt (cf. 1 Cor 13:4-8). The regenerate person refuses to cultivate and then exercise verbal or physical abuse. As far as it is possible, on our part, we seek to "live at peace with everyone" (Rom 12:18).

We show humility (3:2). We are "to be kind, always showing gentleness to all people." This is the exact opposite of the slandering and fighting Paul just warned against. In fact, the call to show "gentleness" or "humility" sums up well the prior six commands. It is a conscious placing of others ahead of ourselves. It is in attitude and action esteeming others better than ourselves (Phil 2:3). It is the essence of the mind of Christ (Phil 2:5).

Paul knew that one way to appreciate who we are now is to remember who we used to be, to draw a contrast between how we now cannot act with how we then had to act before we met Jesus Christ.

In the Past We Harmed Others (Titus 3:3)

Through the new birth we are a new creation (2 Cor 5:17). What a difference Jesus has made! Paul knew this was true for us. He knew it was true for him. He begins verse 3 with an emphatic "we." Exactly what has Jesus saved us from besides the fires of hell and eternal separation from God? In one word it is sin. But sin, like the mythological hydra, is a many-headed creature that attacked and subdued us from every conceivable direction. As we consider these truths, Charles Spurgeon reminds us: "Do not let me talk about these things this morning while you listen to me without feeling. I want you to be turning over the pages of your old life and joining with Paul and the rest of us in our sad confession of former pleasure in evil" ("The Maintenance of Good Works," in *Metropolitan Tabernacle*, 34:496). If we are to see clearly our need for the new birth, we must deeply know the nature of our own sin. Paul noted six ways in particular that sin enslaved and held us captive.

Sin deceives. We ourselves (all of us with no exceptions) were once "foolish" (we were senseless, ignorant, and without spiritual understanding) and "deceived" (we were led astray, misled, and guided by another in the wrong direction). In short, sin makes you stupid!

Sin disobeys. We were "disobedient." Our natural bent was to disobey and seek our own way: disobedient to God (cf. 1:16), authorities, parents—everyone and everything. We were self-centered, self-deceived, Satan-deceived rebels.

Sin dictates. We were "enslaved by various passions and pleasures." Professing to be liberated and free, we were in actuality in bondage and slavery to a cruel and never-satisfied taskmaster: ourselves. Lust and pleasure controlled us. We flirted with both beauties only to discover no matter how much we gave them, they were never satisfied, it was never, never enough. What fools we truly were to give ourselves to two mistresses who promised so much but gave so little of any real value.

Sin detests. We were "living in malice." We lived with "an evil attitude of mind which manifest itself in ill-will and desire to injure" (Hiebert, *Titus and Philemon*, 88). This describes one with a vicious character who desires to bring good to no one.

Sin desires. We lived in "envy," an unquenchable desire to possess what we do not have. John MacArthur with great insight notes, "Envy is a sin that carries its own reward: it guarantees its own frustration and disappointment. By definition, the envious person cannot be satisfied with what he has and will always crave for more" (*Titus,* 149). Sexual sin illustrates this perfectly, wanting more until it goes "all the way," only to find even this is not enough.

Sin destroys. We were "hateful" and were continually "detesting" or hating one another. "Hateful" was our nature and attitude, a natural outgrowth of envy. "Detesting" was our character and action. In contrast to living a life of love that characterizes the disciples of Jesus (John 13:35), we lived a life of hate that gave evidence we were disciples of the Devil.

This is a picture of who we were but not of who we are. The gospel changed everything! We are now a new creation and are ever ready for good works. But how? How is this possible?

We Have Been Regenerated for Good Works
TITUS 3:4-7

After showing who we once were, Paul then reveals what has been done for us. At one time in our lives we were dead, doomed, and depraved, "But God," says Ephesians 2:4. At one time in our lives, we were a spiritual corpse, controlled by our sin nature, Satan, and the world, condemned with no hope, no future, "But when the kindness of God our Savior and His love . . . appeared," says Titus 3:4. Praise God for these revivals in the Bible. What does this one in Titus teach us? Four precious truths.

God Cares for Us (Titus 3:4)

Paul begins with the basic and beautiful truth that God loves us. In fact both His goodness and His love have made an appearance. This is the third appearing in Titus! We see the grace of God in 2:11, the glory of God in 2:13, and now the goodness of God in 3:4. This goodness, this love and kindness, has its source in God our Savior. The theme of Christ as our "Savior" appears here for the fifth time of six occurrences in Titus. "The kindness of God and His love" have as their object mankind—sinners in need of a Savior.

God Changes Us (Titus 3:5)

Here is the greatest verse in the Bible on the doctrine of regeneration, the new birth experienced by those who repent of their sin and put their trust completely and exclusively in Jesus Christ. Paul begins by first telling how regeneration did not happen, countering the false thinking that has plagued humanity for all of our existence. His words could not be clearer: "He saved us—not by works of righteousness that we had done." Salvation is not earned. Regeneration is not something you can work up. You were dead, spiritually—without a heartbeat, no pulse, nothing. Any good you had done was "like filthy rags" in the eyes of a holy God (Isa 64:6 NKJV). On your best day you had nothing to give God, and if you have never realized that, then you have never been saved. No, we cannot work our way into heaven.

"But," Titus 3:4-5 says, "he saved us . . . according to His mercy." He delivered us from sin and its slavery, rescued us from death, hell, and the grave. Why? Kindness, love, mercy. What? Saved us. How? Washing of regeneration and renewing of the Holy Spirit.

Regeneration consists negatively of removal of filth and positively of a renewing, both brought about by the Holy Spirit. Regeneration washes us, makes us clean through the new birth. The imagery of washing has nothing to do with baptism, for it is the Holy Spirit who is washing us, not externally but internally. The picture looks back to Ezekiel 36:25-27, where the prophet writes:

> *I will also sprinkle clean water on you, and you will be clean. I will cleanse you from all your impurities and from all your idols. I will give you a new heart and put a new spirit within you; I will remove your heart of stone and give you a heart of flesh. I will place My Spirit within you and cause you to follow My statutes and carefully observe My ordinances.*

This picture is also seen in Ephesians 5:26, where it portrays our being cleansed by the washing of water by the Word. Thus the Spirit and the Word work in tandem to make us brand-new in Jesus Christ. Indeed that is exactly where Paul looks next.

God Has Come for Us (Titus 3:6)

God is generous when He gives us His Spirit. Verse 6 says, "He poured out this Spirit on us abundantly through Jesus Christ our Savior." Paul is probably referring back to Pentecost and the coming of the Spirit in Acts 2. However, what God did then for the believers gathered in the upper room, He now does for every believer in and through regeneration. His Spirit comes to be with us and in us abundantly.

God Comforts Us (Titus 3:7)

To be "justified" means to be declared righteous. By virtue of the imputed righteousness of Christ, we stand before God just as if we had never sinned and just as if we had always obeyed God perfectly. We are not made justified; we are declared justified. And how did we receive this legal acquittal, this forensic standing of righteousness before God? Paul here adds a fourth motive as to why our great God saved us.

His goodness or kindness moved Him to save us (v. 4). His love moved Him to save us (v. 4). His mercy moved Him to save us (v. 5). His grace moved Him to save us (v. 7).

Having saved us, regenerated us, renewed us, and justified us, He now comforts us with a word about our future. We are "heirs with the hope of eternal life." This is a reality now, though it is not yet our full possession. There is no question that this inheritance will be received. As a work of our triune God, the Father (v. 4-5), the Son (v. 6), and the Holy Spirit (v. 5), it is a signed, sealed, and settled issue.

We Will Be Rewarded for Good Works
TITUS 3:8

Five times in the Pastoral Epistles, we find the phrase, "This saying is trustworthy" (1 Tim 1:15; 3:1; 4:9; 2 Tim 2:11; Titus 3:8). It usually serves to emphasize the importance of the words that are to follow. Here the phrase points back to verses 4-7. Further, the faithful saying may be something of a creedal statement, a hymn, catechetical guidance, or liturgical material. Because of the importance of the words, they should be repeated, memorized, or even sung. They should also have daily and personal application in our lives, and that is exactly what we see in the closing verse of this section.

We Should Affirm Good Works

This "trustworthy" saying and the words that make it up should be affirmed and affirmed constantly. Paul spells this out specifically: "I want you to insist on these things. . . . These are good and profitable for everyone." These are words of truth, of divine origin, and we do a good work to teach them repeatedly (cf. Deut 6:7-9). A blessing for all is certain to occur.

We Should Be Active in Good Works

Those who have been regenerated and renewed by the Holy Spirit are now described simply as "those who have believed God." And, because they have believed and do believe, they should "be careful to devote themselves to good works" (cf. 1:16; 2:7, 14; 3:1, 8, 14). You see, the new birth will result in a new life. Death is replaced by life. The flesh is captive to the Spirit. Evil works are overcome by good works. Such works are more assuredly good and profitable for everyone, saved and unsaved, the latter seeing the beauty of our new life and being drawn to the Christ who changed us, the Christ who can change them too! This is indeed a great reward for those of us who have been regenerated by the gospel of King Jesus.

Conclusion

In an article entitled "Scholars, Interfaith Families Grapple over What Passport Needed for Heaven," Amy Green discusses the perennial question, Who goes to heaven? (*Sun Herald*, May 8, 2005). Discussing the problem John 14:6 presents and the more liberal view of Roman Catholicism since Vatican II, she reports of a Presbyterian pastor in Memphis, Tennessee, who says in a sermon that John 14:6 is "a club with which we beat others over the head." The pastor goes on to say,

> "What I encourage people to do is look at the broader themes of the Bible, and what we see is a God who loved the world, a God whose intention is that all creation be made whole and healed. A lot of people kind of had a gut feeling that their God was a more loving God and a bigger God than they had imagined . . . and were yearning to have their large and loving view of God validated. And I think that's what happened."
>
> The sermon affirmed what Heather Pearson Chauhan had believed all along. Chauhan, 31, an obstetrician/gynecologist, grew up a Christian and then married a Hindu man she met in medical school. Her husband converted to Christianity after they wed, and now the couple plans to raise their 4-month-old son a Christian.

"To define religion or Christianity as this narrow path I think is not a global perspective," she says. "Everyone gets to God a different way."

Not so, says the Word of God. Only those who have been regenerated by the power of God, been renewed by the Spirit, been justified by grace, and believed in Jesus and Jesus alone will go to heaven. Yes, we all need a new birth for a new life today and forever. This new life overflows into a life of good works that testify to the goodness of our God and His love for all people in Jesus Christ. This is the power of the gospel. This is the new birth for a new life.

Reflect and Discuss

1. Why did Jesus rebuke Nicodemus for not knowing about being born again (John 3:10)? What does the Old Testament teach about regeneration?

2. What was Paul's relationship to the Roman government? What was that government's view of Christianity? How does this background affect our understanding of Paul's command to "be submissive to rulers and authorities" (v. 1)?

3. How can Christians be holy and serve all people without coming off as being "holier than thou" or as thinking of themselves as superior?

4. Which best describes your life before you were saved: foolish, deceived, enslaved, malicious, envious, or hateful? Did you feel unloved (Hos 1:6), alienated (Hos 1:9), blind (Matt 23:26), lost (Luke 19:10), rebellious (1 Tim 1:9), hopeless (Eph 2:12), or dead (Eph 2:1)?

5. When you consider your former way of life, does it make you sad, angry, or depressed? Does taking time to remember your past help you to better appreciate the difference Jesus has made in your life?

6. What did you have to do to receive regeneration? Why are people tempted to take some credit for what God has accomplished?

7. What attributes of God moved Him to save you? What virtue in you moved God to save you?

8. What blessings of eternal life do we already enjoy? What blessings of eternal life are we assured to obtain in the future?

9. What have you done to deserve the blessing promised to you in Christ? How does this motivate you to good works, including telling everyone about God's grace?

10. How would you respond to someone who says that the exclusivity of evangelical Christianity diminishes the love of God?

Church Discipline: A Missing Essential in the Life of the Contemporary Church

TITUS 3:9-15

Main Idea: We must practice church discipline in submission to the Word of God.

I. Avoid the Foolish (3:9).
  A. They are unwise.
  B. They are unprofitable.

II. Reject the Divisive (3:10-11).
  A. They must be disciplined.
  B. They can be dangerous.
  C. They are destructive.

III. Follow the Leader (3:12-13).
  A. Listen to their advice.
  B. Lend your assistance.

IV. Maintain Good Works (3:14).
  A. Good works must not be neglected.
  B. Good works must meet needs.

V. Enlist the Faithful (3:15).
  A. Express the love we share.
  B. Pray for the grace we need.

The New Testament has a great deal to say about church discipline. Jesus addresses it in Matthew 18:15-20, and Paul does so repeatedly in texts like Romans 16:17-18; 1 Corinthians 5:1-13; 2 Corinthians 2:5-11; 13:1-3; Galatians 6:1-2; 2 Thessalonians 3:6-12; and here in Titus 3:9-15. This fact alone makes it all the more remarkable that no aspect of church life in our day is more neglected than this one. Indeed, the contemporary church's disregard for this clear teaching of Holy Scripture is perhaps its greatest visible act of disobedience to our Lord. This rebellion is not without significant consequences. John L. Dagg rightly notes, "When discipline leaves a church, Christ goes with it" (*Church Order*, 274).

For Baptists this is striking when you consider that we have historically viewed church discipline as an essential mark, "the third mark," of the church, right alongside the Word rightly preached and the ordinances properly administered. Al Mohler notes that a disciplined church as an essential mark of the church goes back at least to the Belgic Confession of 1561 ("Church Discipline," fn. 2, 26–27). One can also find the roots of this missing jewel of church life in the earliest Anabaptist confession, *The Schleitheim Confession of 1527* and its Article 2 on "the Ban" (Akin, "Expositional Analysis").

And yet, none of Southern Baptists' most recent confessions—*The Baptist Faith and Message* 1925, 1963, and 2000—has a statement on this biblical teaching! Greg Wills notes that church discipline began to wane in Southern Baptist life in the 1870s and rapidly decreased thereafter, and "by the 1930's it was quite rare—most reported exclusions were merely the cleaning of church rolls of names of members long inactive and forgotten" ("Southern Baptist," 9–10). Of course today we seldom do even this. Even those who have expired and left this world for the world to come find it difficult, if not impossible, to have their names removed from the church roll!

How did we get here? How did we get to a place where the "people of the book" exercise such a blatant act of disobedience to a clear command of Christ and a crucial component of church life? Certainly there have been abuses of the practice, though even the memory of this is so far removed from our own day that I seriously doubt one of us can point to a single example. No, we have been seduced in a far more insidious fashion. This subtle slide away from biblical faithfulness can be seen in both practical and spiritual aspects. The effects spread throughout the whole church, but the problem finds its origin at the top, with the leadership, with the pastors.

First, we have lost our theological nerve, the courage to confront as well as comfort, to admonish as well as exhort. Out of fear of offending, we have slunk away into the false security of silence.

Second, we have been overcome by moral compromise. Our churches look and act so much like the world we would hardly know where to begin if we did restore church discipline.

Third, we are simply and sadly biblically illiterate. Lay this deficiency at the feet of preachers who have jettisoned an expository model of preaching and thereby allowed us to avoid and neglect the hard doctrines of Scripture like church discipline.

Fourth, practical expediency and, I might add, personal ambition have played all-too-important roles. A bigger membership means greater bragging rights. It affords a more attractive platform to make the move to a larger and more influential pulpit or denominational post. I wish I did not believe that there was any merit to this particular observation. However, too many conversations with too many ministers make the case unavoidable.

Where then do we turn for an answer, a solution, a cure to this critical condition in which we find Christ's church? Surely the answer must be found in returning to God's Word, which gives us the model that provides a way out and the way forward. While Titus 3:9-15 is not a text deemed as one of the major Scriptures on church discipline, it does provide a foundation for a general treatment of this issue as well as specific counsel for particular situations that demand the practice of this necessary and lost treasure of the church. Here Paul provides five principles by which the body of Christ is to conduct the practice of church discipline.

Avoid the Foolish
TITUS 3:9

These are Paul's final words to his son in the ministry, Titus. Like the consistent beating of a drum, Paul repeatedly challenges those at Crete to maintain sound doctrine and good works. It is essential that a church protects and values its doctrinal and moral integrity. Those who would cause compromise in either area must be confronted and, if unrepentant, avoided. To do so is loving. Not to do so is to mistake sentimentality for love. Victor Masters understood this well: "Sentimentality is an enemy of church discipline. Sentimentality is the love of man divorced from love of truth. . . . It cloaks a big lot of hypocrisy and moral decay" (Wills, "Southern Baptist," 9–10).

Paul once more warns against the false teachers at Crete, particularly their "unprofitable and worthless" deeds. In 3:1-8, Paul charges Titus to "insist" that God's people be devoted to good works since they are good and profitable for everyone. In verse 9, Paul now draws a contrast. He says, "But avoid foolish debates, genealogies, quarrels, and disputes about the law." In other words, insist on good works but avoid what is foolish. The word "avoid" could be translated "shun." It is a present imperative, a word of command, calling for constant and consistent vigilance. Why must we avoid, shun, turn away from the kind of people who fit this description? Two reasons are given: "They are unprofitable and worthless."

They Are Unwise

Paul describes these troublemakers first as those who engage in "foolish debates, genealogies, quarrels, and disputes about the law." He says these things are "worthless." They are unwise and not worth your time. In his context the troublemakers were Judiazers who added both to the words of Scripture and to the work of our Savior. They debated theological minutiae, created fanciful allegories and mythologies based on biblical genealogies, and added works to the doctrine of salvation by grace alone through faith alone in Christ alone. Thinking of themselves as the theological elite, spiritual know-it-alls, they tore up and would continue to tear up "whole households" (1:11) if left unchecked. These kinds of persons are not to be debated but denounced and dismissed. Dealing with aberrant theology is not the time for dialogue; it is the time for action—action that is quick and swift. But there is a second reason we must avoid the foolish.

They Are Unprofitable

Going beyond Scripture, adding to the work of Christ, advocating a "Jesus plus" and a "faith plus" and a "Word plus" theological agenda, these false teachers are "unprofitable." Nothing good comes from their attitude or their teachings. Avoiding them has as its goal bringing to light their error and their sin. It is redemptive and restorative. It is essential and not optional. The risks are too great. We must avoid the foolish.

Reject the Divisive
TITUS 3:10-11

Refusing to enter into unnecessary theological wranglings does not mean doing nothing. As the stakes rise, so must the response. Paul here, in essence, summarizes the teachings of Jesus on church discipline found in Matthew 18:15-20. Note carefully the sin we confront: it is public, habitual, serious, and lacking repentance. We are not called to be spiritual garbage inspectors or theological peeping Toms. When we become aware of a sinning brother or sister, we go to them first individually, second with witnesses, and finally with the whole fellowship being involved if there is no repentance. If at any point the evidence of genuine repentance comes forth, the process of discipline stops, and the ministry of restoration begins. (Let me add that restoration to fellowship does not entail restoration to leadership. God's standard for the latter is higher than His standard for the former.)

The ministry of church discipline is mandatory if we are to be faithful to our head, who is Christ. We do it for the sake of the body and for the sake of the sinning brother. Dietrich Bonhoeffer saw the crucial nature of this when he wrote: "Nothing can be more cruel than that leniency which abandons others to sin. Nothing can be more compassionate than that severe reprimand which calls another Christian in one's community back from the path of sin" (*Life Together,* 105). Paul makes three helpful observations concerning the divisive.

They Must Be Disciplined (Titus 3:10)

"Reject" is another present imperative. The NIV translates it as "warn." The Greek word for "divisive" gives us our English word "heretic." However, its first-century meaning referred to "a person who is quarrelsome and stirs up factions through erroneous opinions, a man who is determined to go his own way and so forms parties and factions" (Hiebert, *Titus and Philemon,* 75). This is the man who, as John MacArthur says, "is a law unto himself and has no concern for spiritual truth or unity" (*Titus,* 164). Paul's instructions are clear: Warn him once; warn him twice. If there is no repentance, then he must be rejected.

Dealing with such an individual in this manner has pastoral benefits. It will keep the issue on the level of principle and not personality. Personality battles result when we delay in taking action and are perceived to be showing favoritism. This is always a lose-lose scenario and must be avoided. We must move quickly in the initial stage when the sin is discovered. We may extend the "grace of patience" as we seek the repentance of the one living in sin. However, we must be clear, above board, and timely. We cannot go once and then walk away as if all is forgiven if there is no change. Vigilance and steadfastness are required, all the while keeping Galatians 6:1-2 before our mind's eye: "Brothers, if someone is caught in any wrongdoing, you who are spiritual should restore such a person with a gentle spirit, watching out for yourselves so you also won't be tempted. Carry one another's burdens; in this way you will fulfill the law of Christ."

They Can Be Dangerous (Titus 3:11)

Why must habitual, public, serious, unrepentant sinners be disciplined? Because they are dangerous. Paul says such a person is "perverted and sins." "Perverted" or "warped" is in the perfect tense and means twisted, turned inside out. "Sins" is in the present tense. Here is a man living life upside down and inside out. This is his settled state, heart, and mind. It is his continuous habit of life. God forbid that we who love this person would stand by and do nothing!

They Are Destructive (Titus 3:11)

Sin is destructive. It damages and destroys. What it can do to a community of believers is serious. What it does to the sinner enslaved by its addiction is tragic. "Self-condemned" is an interesting word. Though I am well aware of the etymological fallacy, this is one instance when an etymological investigation proves insightful and fruitful. When the Greek word *autokatakritos* is broken down into its parts it means "to judge down on oneself," hence to be "self-condemned." In action and attitude the sinner is without excuse, passing judgment on himself. Oh, he may not see it, for he is warped, twisted, self-deceived. He may even attempt to use Scripture to justify his sin. Often he will claim the leading of the Spirit and sometimes even the providence of God. There are times when he may even say, "My head tells me this is wrong, but my heart tells me it was never more right."

With grief, humility, self-examination, and a broken heart, we must confront him and, if necessary, shun and reject him. Following Paul's directive in 1 Corinthians 5:1-13, we must turn him over to Satan with a hope and prayer that the discipline of the heavenly Father (Heb 12:5-13) will bring him to brokenness and repentance and that he will give evidence he is indeed God's child after all. We have our duty. God has His.

Follow the Leader
TITUS 3:12-13

Verses 12-15 are Paul's final words to Titus. However, their close proximity to verses 9-11, as well as the instructions we find in them, should give us pause. Do the words we find here amplify Paul's teaching on church discipline while at the same providing a farewell message? I think they do, and the counsel we discover is pastorally helpful in guiding us through the delicate and difficult waters of church discipline.

Good, godly leadership is absolutely a must if a church is to carry out the ministry of loving confrontation. Such leadership must be in place and evident to the congregation. This leadership will be visible among the elders as well as to the laity. Church discipline is no place for a lone ranger. Going solo in this arena is suicidal. It is also unbiblical. Following the leader means there is a leader. It means establishing credibility and earning trust. When you have that, you can act decisively and courageously. How does God want a church to respond to its leadership?

Listen to Their Advice (Titus 3:12)

In the midst of great challenge and controversy, Paul stepped forward and made important decisions—decisions that affected numerous lives but decisions that would ensure the necessary ministries of the church would continue.

Paul would relieve Titus of his responsibilities on Crete by sending Artemas (of whom we know nothing) or Tychicus (of whom we know quite a bit). Haynes Griffin informs us that Tychicus was "Paul's traveling companion (Acts 20:4), a 'dear brother and faithful servant in the Lord' (cf. Eph 6:21; Col 4:7), and his personal representative to churches (2 Tim 4:12)" (Lea and Griffin, *1, 2, Timothy and Titus*, 331). Both men were capable of fulfilling Paul's instructions in 3:10-11, or he would not be sending them. This would free Titus to come to Nicopolis on the western coast of Achaia or the southern province of Greece (MacArthur, *Titus*, 167). Paul would be going there for the winter to rest, strategize, and spend time with Titus. Because Paul would be sending godly, spiritual reinforcements who could handle any troublemakers if more should arise, Titus could set aside this work and move ahead to a new ministry, a ministry that would soon take him to Dalmatia (2 Tim 4:9).

Lend Your Assistance (Titus 3:13)

Church discipline should not be the primary focal point of the church's ministry. It should not require the neglect of other vital activities because of its necessity and practice. In fact I believe Paul envisioned it as a natural component of the fabric of what the church is and does, a painful but essential aspect of Christian discipleship.

Paul instructs Titus on the principles of church discipline while at the same time giving attention to other ministries needing to be carried out. In all of this Paul needed the help of others, and others gladly lent their aid to their trusted leader. He asked the church at Crete to "diligently help Zenas the lawyer and Apollos on their journey."

"Zenas the lawyer" is the only Christian lawyer noted in all of the New Testament, probably a Roman jurist; and Apollos is the eloquent Alexandrian who came on the stage in Acts 18–19 and was highly revered in Corinth (cf. 1 Cor 1:11-12). They were apparently with Titus on Crete or on their way to the island. If present, they had no doubt lent their assistance to him in the ministry of church discipline described in 3:10-11. Now their services were needed elsewhere, the discipline matters at Crete being under control. Titus should send them on quickly, making sure "they will lack nothing."

In all of this we see church discipline as a natural dimension of the multifaceted ministries of church life. It is not preeminent, but neither should it be an anomaly!

Maintain Good Works
TITUS 3:14

"Good works" is a reoccurring theme throughout this short letter. The phrase occurs six times in a letter that is only 46 verses, driving home the point that though we are not saved by faith plus works, we are saved by a faith that does work (Eph 2:8-10; Titus 3:5). The presence and practice of these good works provide the context for the healthy practice of church discipline. Further, one of those good works we are to be doing is church discipline. What does Paul say here about good works?

Good Works Must Not Be Neglected

Paul once more reminds Titus of the importance of maintaining good works. He says, "Our people must also learn to devote themselves to good works." "Learn" is another present imperative and is related to our word for discipleship. "Devote" or maintain speaks of a consistent pattern or lifestyle of good works. "Good works," including the good works of 3:9-10, are to be our habit of life. They are the norm and not the exception, for to neglect them is to function in a substandard way, below the bar God has set for the church. Tony Evans is on target when he notes, "A church that does not practice church discipline of its members is not functioning properly as a church, just as a family that does not discipline is not a fully functioning family" (*God's Glorious Church*, 222).

Good Works Must Meet Needs

Good works are a good thing. God foreordained that we would do them as a display of His work of art, which we are becoming (Eph 2:10). Good works serve a positive agenda: "for cases of urgent need." Good works have a negative function as well: "that they will not be unfruitful," "live unproductive lives" (NIV), "end up with nothing to show for our lives" (*The Message*).

The good work of church discipline will meet the need and bear the fruit of the glory of God, love for the sinner, restoration of the wayward, purity of the church, protection of the fellowship, and witness to the world. It is a good work of duty. It is a good work of necessity. Avoiding the ever-present sins of legalism and judgmentalism, we testify to God, one another, and the world that holiness and purity matter. We proclaim through biblical discipline that love cares and confronts. It can be tender, but sometimes it also must be tough. What it cannot do is stand by and do nothing when one of the family is ensnared by sin. We do not discipline the world and have no intention of doing so. To them we proclaim the gospel of Jesus Christ. We practice the ministry of loving confrontation to ourselves. As the revivalist Charles Finney wrote, "If you see your neighbor sin, and you pass by and neglect to reprove him, it is as cruel as if you should see his house on fire, and pass by and not warn him" (*Lectures*, 45). Good works indeed meet urgent needs.

Enlist the Faithful
TITUS 3:15

This final verse is a farewell statement from friends to friends. It is all encompassing. The word "all" is used twice, at the beginning and the end of the verse. And yet, subtly and just beneath the surface, we find two words of wisdom for the life and ministry of confrontation: love and grace. Those whose lives are characterized by these twin towers of the Christian life are the persons qualified for the hard task and difficult assignment of church discipline. Paul addresses these Christian companions by means of a greeting and a prayer.

Express the Love We Share

All who were with Paul expressed their greeting and love for Titus. Like Paul, they knew the challenges he was facing, and they wanted him to know they cared, they stood with him, and they were on his side. This could only encourage him in the tough task he was facing. As those of the same faith, they were one with him in the battle.

Pray for the Grace We Need

Bitterness is an ever-present enemy to those in the ministry. This is especially the case when we are called to the ministry of confrontation and discipline. Paul's final words were not merely his customary practice; they surely provided great comfort to Titus: "Grace be with all of you." Only God's grace will give us balance, self-control, wisdom, and endurance. By God's grace and for God's glory, we will be equipped and enabled to stand and serve, even when the odds are against us and the battle seems all for nothing. It never is hopeless, though, as long as the battle we fight is the Lord's! His amazing grace is what we need when the fire is hot or the water is deep. Such is often our lot in the ministry of confrontation. At such times only His grace will sustain us. Amazingly, we shall discover, it is all we need.

Conclusion

So, why do we practice church discipline? My friend Mark Dever provides five reasons: It is for the good of the person disciplined, for the good of other Christians as they see the danger of sin, for the health of the church as a whole, for the corporate witness of the church, and for the glory of God, as we reflect His holiness (*9 Marks*, 166). Ultimately, we must practice church discipline in submission to the word of God.

One might ask, "How do we begin to implement church discipline?" Let me be pastoral and practical in my response. First, we must teach the people in our church what the Bible says about church discipline. Second, we must begin to implement church discipline lovingly, wisely, gently, and slowly. Premature action is a certain formula for disaster. Third, we also must apply church discipline to areas like absentee membership as well as the specifics we find in the various lists of Scripture. We will do this not to cause hurt but to bring about healing within the body of Christ.

Bryan Chapell is correct when he writes:

> [T]here is a difference between needing to divide and loving to divide. A divisive person loves to fight. The differences are usually observable. A person who loves the peace and purity of the church may be forced into division, but it is not his

character. He enters arguments regrettably and infrequently. When forced to argue, he remains fair, truthful, and loving in his responses. He grieves to have to disagree with a brother. Those who are divisive by nature lust for the fray, incite its onset, and delight in being able to conquer another person. For them victory means everything. So in an argument they twist words, call names, threaten, manipulate procedures, and attempt to extend the debate as long as possible and along as many fronts as possible. Divisive persons frequent the debates of the church. As a result the same voices and personalities tend to appear over and over again, even though the issues change. (Hughes and Chapell, *1 & 2 Timothy and Titus*, 364)

In the final analysis church discipline is a painful but necessary extension of Christian discipleship. We do it not because it is pleasant but because we must. We do it because overlooking sin is not gracious but dangerous. Confronting sin is not optional but essential. Dealing with sin is not judgmental but remedial. Correcting sin is not carnal but spiritual. Thomas Oden says, "Only those who take sin seriously take forgiveness seriously" (*Corrective Love*, 47). Our Lord did both, and so must we, as we lovingly and faithfully follow the divine directions for church discipline.

Reflect and Discuss

1. Have you ever seen church discipline practiced? Was it biblical? What issues seem to make church discipline impractical in the church today?
2. How do you determine if a debate or dispute is "foolish"? What are some examples you have encountered in church?
3. How would you apply Paul's command to "avoid" or "reject" someone in your church whom you determined is foolish or divisive?
4. How is Paul's exhortation to discern and reject foolish and divisive persons compatible with Jesus' commandment not to judge (Luke 6:37)?
5. How does confronting a divisive person benefit that person? How does it benefit the church?
6. How might it affect a leader if he comes to enjoy administering church discipline? How might it affect how it is received by the

offender and perceived by the congregation? What should a leader do if he finds himself enjoying it? Avoiding it?

7. Is it the loving thing not to confront a sinning brother or sister? Why?

8. What gave Paul the authority to assign leaders to the churches?

9. What might Zenas and Apollos have been doing in Crete (v. 13)? What principle can we draw from Titus 3:13 that still applies in the church today?

10. In what way does church discipline address an "urgent need" (v. 14)? How can it help a church avoid being "unfruitful"?

11. Why is grace especially needed in the administration of church discipline? Who needs more grace: the leader or the offender?

12. What aspects of church discipline could be implemented in your church immediately? What aspects would take time to implement? How would you begin?

WORKS CITED

Akin, Daniel L. "An Expositional Analysis of the Schleitheim Confession," *Criswell Theological Review* 2.2 (1988): 345–70.

Akin, Daniel L., and R. Albert Mohler Jr. "Why We Believe that Infants Who Die Go to Heaven," available online at http://www.danielakin.com/wp-content/uploads/2004/08/why-we-believe-children-who-die-go-to-heaven.pdf, accessed May 30, 2013.

Anderson, Kerby. "Slavery and the Founders," http://www.probe.org/site/c.fdKEIMNsEoG/b.4220987/k.BC60/Slavery_in_America.htm, accessed July 14, 2003.

Anselm of Canterbury. "Why God Became Man." In *A Scholastic Miscellany: Anselm to Ockham.* Ed. and trans. Eugene R. Fairweather. Library of Christian Classics 10. Philadelphia: Westminster, 1956.

Baldwin, Ethel May, and David V. Benson. *Henrietta Mears and How She Did It.* Glendale, CA: Regal Books, 1966.

Bauer, Walter, F. W. Danker, W. F. Arndt, and F. W. Gingrich. *A Greek-English Lexicon of the New Testament and Other Early Christian Literature.* 3rd ed. Rev. and ed. F. W. Danker. Chicago: University of Chicago Press, 2000. Abbreviated as BDAG.

Baxter, Richard. *The Reformed Pastor.* Edinburgh: Banner of Truth, 1979.

Begg, Alistair. "Steady as You Go." Reformation21. http://www.reformation21.org/articles/steady-as-you-go.php, accessed February 12, 2012.

Bonar, Andrew A., ed. *Memoirs of McCheyne Including His Letters and Messages.* Chicago: Moody, 1978.

Bonhoeffer, Dietrich. *Life Together—Prayer Book of the Bible.* In vol. 5 of *Bonhoeffer Works*, ed. Geffrey B. Kelly. Minneapolis: Fortress, 1996.

Bridges, Jerry. *The Discipline of Grace: God's Role and Our Role in the Pursuit of Holiness.* Colorado Springs: NavPress, 2006.

Brooks, James A. "Slave/Servant." In *Holman Illustrated Bible Dictionary.* Ed. Chad Brand, Charles Draper, and Archie England. Nashville: B&H, 2003.

Bruce, F. F. *The Book of the Acts.* The New International Commentary on the New Testament. Grand Rapids: Wm. B. Eerdmans, 1968.

Calvin, John. *Commentaries on the Epistles to Timothy, Titus, and Philemon.* Vol. 21. Grand Rapids: Baker, 1984.

Carson, D. A., and Douglas J. Moo. *An Introduction to the New Testament.* 2nd ed. Grand Rapids: Zondervan, 2005.

Chrysostom, John. "Homilies on the Epistles of St. Paul the Apostle to Timothy, Titus, and Philemon." In *Chrysostom: On the Priesthood, Ascetic Treatises, Select Homilies and Letters, Homilies on the Statues,* vol. 9 of Nicene and Post-Nicene Fathers. Series 1. Ed. Philip Schaff. 1886–1889. 14 vols. Repr., Peabody: Hendrickson, 1994.

Dagg, John L. *A Treatise on Church Order.* Charleston: The Southern Baptist Publication Society, 1858.

Dallimore, Arnold A. *George Whitefield: The Life and Times of the Great Evangelist of the Eighteenth-Century Revival, Vol. I.* Grand Rapids: Banner of Truth, 1970.

Dennis, Jon M. "Multiplying Men and Deploying Gospel Ministers." In *Preach the Word: Essays on Expository Preaching: In Honor of R. Kent Hughes.* Ed. Leland Ryken and Todd A. Wilson, 220–34. Wheaton: Crossway Books, 2007.

Dennis, Lane T., Wayne Grudem, J. I. Packer, et al., eds. *ESV Study Bible.* Wheaton: Crossway, 2008.

Dever, Mark. *The Church: The Gospel Made Visible.* Nashville: B&H Academic, 2012.

————. *The Message of the Old Testament: Promises Made.* Wheaton: Crossway, 2006.

————. *9 Marks of a Healthy Church,* expanded ed. Wheaton: Crossway, 2004.

Di Gangi, Mariano, ed. *A Golden Treasury of Puritan Devotion: Selections from the Writings of Thirteen Puritan Divines.* Phillipsburgh, NJ: P & R, 1999.

Douglass, Frederick. *Narrative of the Life of Frederick Douglass.* Mineola, NY: Dover, 1995.

Elliot, Elisabeth. *Shadow of the Almighty: The Life and Testament of Jim Elliot.* New York: Harper & Brothers, 1958.

————. "Where Are the WOTTs?" *Pulpit Helps* (May 1997): 10.

Elwell, Walter A. "Slavery." In *Evangelical Dictionary of Theology*. Grand Rapids: Baker, 1996.

Erickson, Millard. *Christian Theology*. Grand Rapids: Baker, 1998.

Evans, Tony. *God's Glorious Church*. Chicago: Moody, 2003.

Fee, Gordon. *1 and 2 Timothy, Titus*. New International Biblical Commentary on the New Testament. Peabody: Hendrickson, 1988.

Finney, Charles. *Lectures to Professing Christians*. New York & London: Garland, 1985.

Gordon, James M. *Evangelical Spirituality*. Eugene, OR: Wipf & Stock, 2000.

Green, Amy. "Who Goes to Heaven." *The Sun Herald*, May 8, 2005.

Greidanus, Sidney. *Preaching Christ from the Old Testament: A Contemporary Hermeneutical Method*. Grand Rapids: Eerdmans, 1999.

Grudem, Wayne. *Systematic Theology*. Grand Rapids: Zondervan, 1994.

Guthrie, Donald. *Pastoral Epistles*. 2nd ed. Grand Rapids: InterVarsity, 1990.

Harris, Murray J. *Slave of Christ: A New Testament Metaphor for Total Devotion to Christ*. Downers Grove: InterVarsity, 1999.

Hester, Dennis J. *The Vance Havner Quote Book*. Grand Rapids: Baker, 1986.

Hick, John. "Is Christianity the Only True Religion?" *World Faiths Encounter* 28 (March 2001): 3–11.

Hiebert, D. Edmond. *Titus and Philemon*. Chicago: Moody, 1985.

Hughes, R. Kent, and Bryan Chapell. *1 and 2 Timothy and Titus: To Guard the Deposit*. Wheaton: Crossway Books, 2000.

Hunt, Susan. *Spiritual Mothering: The Titus 2 Model for Women Mentoring Women*. Wheaton: Crossway, 1992.

Jensen, Phillip D., and Paul Grimmond. *The Archer and the Arrow*. Kingsford NSW, Australia: Matthias Media, 2010.

Jones, David W., and Russell S. Woodbridge. *Health, Wealth & Happiness: Has the Prosperity Gospel Overshadowed the Gospel of Christ?* Grand Rapids: Kregel, 2011.

Karl, Peter. *South China Post* (April 23, 2000).

Knight, George W., III. *The Pastoral Epistles*. The New International Greek Testament Commentary. Grand Rapids: Paternoster, 1992.

Krejcer, Richard J. "Statistics on Pastors." http://www.intothy word.org/apps/articles/?articleid=36562, accessed March 18, 2013.

Lea, Thomas D., and Hayne P. Griffin. *1, 2 Timothy, Titus*. New American Commentary. Nashville: B&H, 1992.

Lloyd-Jones, D. Martyn. *Preaching and Preachers.* Grand Rapids: Zondervan, 1972.

Luther, Martin. *Galatians.* The Crossway Classic Commentaries. Ed. Alister McGrath and J. I. Packer. Wheaton: Good News, 1998.

Luther, Martin, Henry Jacobs, and Adolph Spaeth. *Works of Martin Luther, with Introduction and Notes.* Vol. 2. Philadelphia: A. J. Holman, 1915.

MacArthur, John, Jr. *Safe in the Arms of God: Truth from Heaven About the Death of a Child.* Nashville: Thomas Nelson, 2003.

———. *2 Timothy.* Chicago: Moody, 1995.

———. *Titus.* Chicago: Moody, 1996.

Metaxas, Eric. *Bonhoeffer: Pastor, Martyr, Prophet, Spy.* Nashville: Thomas Nelson, 2011.

Mohler, R. Albert. "Church Discipline: The Missing Mark." *Southern Baptist Journal of Theology* 4.4 (Winter 2000).

Mounce, William D. *Pastoral Epistles.* Word Biblical Commentary. Nashville: Nelson, 2000.

Muggeridge, Malcolm. *Homemade,* July 1990.

Oden, Thomas C. *Corrective Love: The Power of Communion Discipline.* St. Louis: Concordia, 1995.

Packer, J. I. *God's Words: Studies of Key Bible Themes.* Grand Rapids: Baker, 1998.

Perkins, William. *The Art of Prophesying* with *The Calling of the Ministry.* Carlisle, PA: The Banner of Truth Trust, 1996.

Pinnock, Clark. "Acts 4:12—No Other Name Under Heaven." In *Through No Fault of Their Own.* Ed. William V. Crockett and James G. Sigountos. Grand Rapids: Baker, 1991.

Piper, John. "Charles Spurgeon: Preaching through Adversity." Desiring God. http://www.desiringgod.org/resource-library/biographies/charles -spurgeon-preaching-through-adversity, accessed February 28, 2012.

———. "Manhood, Womanhood, and the Freedom to Minister." Sermon from 1 Timothy 2:8-15, Bethlehem Baptist Church, June 18, 1989. For full transcript, go to www.desiringgod.org/resource-library/sermons/manhood-womanhood-and-the-freedom-to-minis-ter, accessed May 30, 2013.

———. *The Roots of Endurance: Invincible Perseverance in the Lives of John Newton, Charles Simeon, and William Wilberforce.* Wheaton: Crossway Books, 2006.

———. "A Vision of Biblical Complementarity." In *Recovering Biblical Manhood and Womanhood.* 2nd ed. Ed. John Piper and Wayne Grudem. Wheaton: Crossway, 2006.

Random Facts. http://facts.randomhistory.com/human-trafficking -facts.html, accessed March 15, 2013.

Roberts, Alexander, James Donaldson, and A. Cleveland Coxe. *The Ante-Nicene Fathers, Vol. VIII : Translations of the Writings of the Fathers Down to A.D. 325*. Oak Harbor: Logos Research Systems, 1997.

Ryken, Philip Graham. *1 Timothy*. Reformed Expository Commentary. Phillipsburg, NJ: P&R, 2007.

Sanders, John. "Inclusivism." In *What About Those Who Have Never Heard?* Ed. John Sanders. Downers Grove: InterVarsity, 1995.

Smith, Christian, and Melina Lundquist Denton. *Soul Searching: The Religious and Spiritual Lives of American Teenagers*. Reprint ed. New York: Oxford University Press, USA, 2009.

Spurgeon, Charles Haddon. *Grace*. New Kensington, PA: Whitaker House, 1997.

———. *The Metropolitan Tabernacle Pulpit*. Pasadena, TX: Pilgrim, 1981.

———. *Morning by Morning*. Peabody, MA: Hendrickson, 2006.

———. *The New Park Street Pulpit*, 6 vol., reprint ed. Pasadena, TX: Pilgrim, 1981.

———. *The Soulwinner*. New Kensington, PA: Whitaker House, 2001.

Stott, John. *The Message of 1 Timothy & Titus*. The Bible Speaks Today. Downers Grove: InterVarsity, 1996.

———. *The Message of 2 Timothy*. Downer's Grove, IL: IVP Academic, 1984.

Tomlin, Chris, Matt Redman, Jesse Reeves, and Jonas Myrin, "Our God (Is Greater)," *Passion: Awakening*. Brentwood, TN: Sparrow/sixsteps records, 2010.

Towner, Philip H. *1–2 Timothy and Titus*. IVP New Testament Commentary. Downers Grove: InterVarsity, 1994.

———. *The Letters to Timothy and Titus*. The New International Commentary on the New Testament. Grand Rapids: Eerdmans, 1994.

Ware, Bruce A. *Father, Son, and Holy Spirit: Relationships, Roles, and Relevance*. Wheaton: Crossway Books, 2005.

Warren, Rick. Pastors.com, March 2002. Cited in http://www.blazing grace.org/index.php?page=porn-statistics, accessed March 18, 2013.

Wills, Greg. "Southern Baptist and Church Discipline." *SBJT* 4.4 (Winter 2000): 4–14.

Yamauchi, E. M., "Gnosis, Gnosticism" in *Dictionary of Paul and His Letters*. Ed. Gerald F. Hawthorne, Ralph P. Martin, and Daniel G. Reid. Downers Grove: InterVarsity, 1993, 350–54.

SCRIPTURE INDEX